Nietzsche & the Political

Nietzsche's political thought has long been dismissed for its alleged naiveté and its antiliberal excesses. Yet, far from being of merely historical interest, his critique of late modernity in fact suggests a compelling alternative to the political models advanced by liberal, communitarian and postmodern theorists.

In *Nietzsche & the Political*, Daniel W. Conway takes Nietzsche seriously as a political thinker. Unlike other writers on the subject, Conway neither idolizes not demonizes. He carefully explores the consequences of Nietzsche's critique of modernity for his political thought from his earliest writings through to his mature work. Conway's clear and even-handed analysis is free from the obfuscatory jargon often associated with Nietzsche scholarship.

Nietzsche & the Political is a comprehensive introduction to Nietzsche's political thought. It also offers a thorough survey of Nietzsche's political legacy, including his influence on such seminal thinkers as Foucault and Habermas and his continuing importance to contemporary liberalism and feminist theory. It will be required reading for students of Nietzsche in philosophy, politics and sociology.

Daniel W. Conway is Associate Professor of Philosophy and Director of the Center for Ethics and Value Inquiry at Pennsylvania State University. He is the co-editor of *The Politics of Irony* and *Nietzsche und die antike Philosophie*.

Thinking the Political

General editors:
Keith Ansell-Pearson, *University of Warwick*
Simon Critchley, *University of Essex*

Recent decades have seen the emergence of a distinct and challenging body of work by a number of Continental thinkers that has fundamentally altered the way in which philosophical questions are conceived and discussed. This work poses a major challenge to anyone wishing to define the essentially contestable concept of 'the political' and to think anew the political import and application of philosophy. How does recent thinking on time, history, language, humanity, alterity, desire, sexuality, gender and culture open up the possibility of thinking the political anew? What are the implications of such thinking for our understanding of and relation to the leading ideologies of the modern world, such as liberalism, socialism and Marxism? What are the political responsibilities of philosophy in the face of the new world (dis)order?

This new series is designed to present the work of the major continental thinkers of our time, and the political debates their work has generated, to a wider audience in philosophy and in political, social and cultural theory. The aim is neither to dissolve the specificity of the 'philosophical' into the 'political' nor evade the challenge that 'the political' poses the 'philosophical'; rather, each volume in the series will try to show how it is only in the relation between the two that new possibilities of thought and politics can be activated.

Already published:
- Foucault and the Political *by Jon Simons*
- Derrida and the Political *by Richard Beardsworth*

Nietzsche & the Political

Daniel W. Conway

London and New York

First published 1997
by Routledge
11 New Fetter Lane, London EC4P 4EE

Simultaneously published in the USA and Canada
by Routledge
20 West 35th Street, New York, NY 10001

© 1997 Daniel W. Conway

Typeset in Sabon by
Florencetype Ltd, Stoodleigh, Devon

Printed and bound in Great Britain by
Clays Ltd, St Ives PLC

British Library Cataloguing in Publication Data
A catalogue record for this book is available from the British Library.

Library of Congress Cataloging in Publication Data
Conway, Daniel W.
      Nietzsche and the political/Daniel W. Conway.
         p.   cm.—(Thinking the political)
      Includes bibliographical references and index.
      ISBN 0–415–10068–2.   ISBN 0–415–10069–0 (pbk.)
      1. Nietzsche, Friedrich Wilhelm, 1844–1900—Contributions in
      political science.   I. Title.   II. Series.
JC233.N52C65   1996
320′.01–dc20   96–7867
                                                                          CIP

ISBN 0–415–10068–2 (hbk)
ISBN 0–415–10069–0 (pbk)

For Shannon

Contents

Acknowledgements   ix
List of abbreviations   xi

Introduction: voyage of the damned?   1

1   **Political Perfectionism**   6
    • The lawgiver 11   • The indeterminate animal 13
    • The use and abuse of Christian morality 18   • The
    Übermensch 20

2   **The Uses and Disadvantages of Morality for Life**   28
    • Nietzsche's defense of moral pluralism 28   • Nietzsche
    and Manu: moralities of breeding 34   • The *pathos* of
    distance 39

3   **Perfectionism in the Twilight of the Idols**   43
    • Nietzsche's critique of modernity 43   • The political
    microsphere 47   • Light amid the shadows: an attempt at
    aesthetic education 50   • Moral perfectionism 52   • Moral
    perfectionism and/as ethical egoism 56

4   **Regimens of Self-Overcoming: The Soul Turned Inside Out**   61
    • "*Thus* it *shall* be!" The philosopher as legislator 61
    • Self-overcoming 65   • Self-creation vs. self-discovery 70
    • Self-overcoming and self-experimentation 72   • The case
    of Nietzsche 75

5   **The Philosopher's *Versucherkunst***   78
    • An attempt at an invitation to temptation 78   • The

manifold genius: Philosopher, artist, and saint 81 • An
unintended experiment: Resentment as expendable affect 94

6 **Comedians of the Ascetic Ideal**   100
   • The ascetic ideal 100   • Harming the ascetic ideal 104
   • Hijacking the ascetic ideal 107   • Knowledge: a form
   of asceticism 111   • Therapies of survival: educating the
   body 113

7 **Nietzsche's Political Legacy**   119
   • The standard reading of Nietzsche 119   • Nietzsche and
   contemporary liberalism 123   • Nietzsche and feminism 130
   • Nietzsche and Foucault 138

   Notes   143
   Index   161

Acknowledgements

This book developed as a product of my friendship with Keith Ansell Pearson and David Owen, to whom I am deeply indebted for their encouragement and criticism. I am also grateful to Graham Parkes and Tracy Strong, both of whom read the entire manuscript and judiciously suggested salutary revisions. I am furthermore indebted to the many friends and colleagues who have discussed Nietzsche's political philosophy with me over the years, including Panos Alexakos, Babette Babich, Debra Bergoffen, Ann-Marie Bowery, Howard Caygill, William Connolly, Claudia Crawford, Simon Critchley, Brian Domino, Shannon Duval, Robert Gooding-Williams, Kathleen Higgins, Robert Irelan, Salim Kemal, Laurence Lampert, Duncan Large, Bernd Magnus, Alexander Nehamas, Kelly Oliver, Robert Pippin, Stanley Rosen, Richard Schacht, Alan Schrift, Charles Scott, Gary Shapiro, David Stern, John Seery, Robert Solomon, and Michael Zimmerman. The research for this book was made possible by a generous grant from the Research and Graduate Studies Office of the College of the Liberal Arts at The Pennsylvania State University; my special thanks to Dean Susan Welch and Associate Dean Raymond Lombra. Finally, I gratefully acknowledge permission to use portions of the following publications:

"*Das Weib an sich*: The Slave Revolt in Epistemology," in *Nietzsche: Feminism and Political Theory*, ed. Paul Patton (London: Routledge, 1993), pp. 110–129.

"Love's Labour's Lost: The Philosopher's *Versucherkunst*," in *Nietzsche, Philosophy and the Arts*, eds Daniel W. Conway and Salim Kemal (Cambridge: Cambridge University Press).

"Autonomy and Authenticity: How One Becomes What One Is," *St. John's Review*, vol. XLII, no. 2, May 1994, pp. 27–39.

"Comedians of the Ascetic Ideal: The Performance of Genealogy," in *The Politics of Irony: Essays in Self-Betrayal*, eds Daniel W. Conway and John E. Seery (New York: St. Martin's Press, 1992), pp. 73–95.

"Foucault, Michel," *The Encyclopedia of Philosophy, Supplement*, ed. David M. Borchert (Macmillan and Co.), pp. 201–202.

List of abbreviations

All references to Nietzsche's works appear in the body of the text; individual writings are identified by the abbreviations listed below.

AC   *The Antichrist(ian)*, trans. Walter Kaufmann, in *The Portable Nietzsche*, ed. and trans. Walter Kaufmann (New York: Viking Penguin, 1982).

BGE   *Beyond Good and Evil*, trans. Walter Kaufmann (New York: Random House, 1966).

BT   *The Birth of Tragedy*, trans. Walter Kaufmann (New York: Random House, 1967).

CW   *The Case of Wagner*, trans. Walter Kaufmann (New York: Random House, 1967).

D   *Daybreak*, trans. R.J. Hollingdale (Cambridge: Cambridge University Press, 1982).

EH   *Ecce Homo*, trans. Walter Kaufmann (New York: Random House/Vintage Books, 1989).

GM   *On the Genealogy of Morals*, trans. Walter Kaufmann and R.J. Hollingdale (New York: Random House/Vintage Books, 1989).

GS   *The Gay Science*, trans. Walter Kaufmann (New York: Random House, 1974).

H   *Human, All-Too-Human*, trans. R.J. Hollingdale (Cambridge: Cambridge University Press, 1986).

NCW   *Nietzsche Contra Wagner*, trans. Walter Kaufmann, in *The Portable Nietzsche*, ed. and trans. Walter Kaufmann (New York: Viking Penguin, 1982).

SE   *Schopenhauer as Educator*, trans. R.J. Hollingdale, in *Untimely Meditations*, trans. R.J. Hollingdale, intr. J.P. Stern (Cambridge: Cambridge University Press, 1983).

TI   *Twilight of the Idols*, trans. Walter Kaufmann, in *The Portable Nietzsche*, ed. and trans. Walter Kaufmann (New York: Viking Penguin, 1982).

WP   *The Will to Power*, trans. Walter Kaufmann and R. J. Hollingdale (New York: Random House, 1967).

Z   *Thus Spoke Zarathustra*, trans. Walter Kaufmann, in *The Portable Nietzsche*, ed. and trans. Walter Kaufmann (New York: Viking Penguin, 1982).

Rather than giving page references to any one particular edition, I have adopted a system that is widely used in Nietzsche scholarship and allows readers to identify the passages cited whatever edition they may be using:

1. All arabic numbers denote sections. For instance, GS 238 refers to section 238 of *The Gay Science*.
2. All roman numbers denote parts or standard subdivisions in those works of Nietzsche where section numbers start anew with each part or subdivision. Thus GM II:21 refers to the *Genealogy of Morals*, essay II, section 21; and TI VII:3 refers to *Twilight of the Idols*, essay VII, section 3.
3. Citations from the preface of a particular work are identified by "P", as in EH P:4—a reference to *Ecce Homo*, preface, section 4.

Occasionally I have thought it helpful to include parts of the original German text from the standard critical edition of Nietzsche's works (Friedrich Nietzsche, *Sämtliche Werke: Kritische Studienausgabe in 15 Bänden*, ed. G. Colli and M. Montinari, Berlin: de Gruyter/Deutscher Taschenbuch Verlag); these German passages appear in square brackets.

Introduction:
Voyage of the Damned?

> At long last the horizon appears free to us again, even if it should not
> be bright; at long last our ships may venture out again, venture out to
> face any danger; all the daring of the lover of knowledge is permitted
> again; the sea, *our* sea, lies open again; perhaps there has never yet been
> such an "open sea."
>
> —*The Gay Science*, 343

Nietzsche tends to cast modernity in a blindingly negative light, alternately describing it in terms of the onset of European nihilism, the
inexorable spread of decadence, the advent of the last will, the flaccid
reign of the last man, the twilight of the idols, and so forth. But the shipwreck of modernity also produces in him a cathartic, liberating effect,
granting him a measure of freedom from the superlative (albeit fading)
values of the age. The horizon of modernity may not be bright, but it is
at long last free, and Nietzsche hopes to exploit this freedom to impress
his signature onto the successor age to modernity.

Nietzsche's contributions to politics, and to political philosophy, are
notoriously difficult to reckon. He not only stands in defiant opposition to
the general political trends of modernity, but also refuses the "scientific"
methodologies preferred by his contemporaries. Deeply contemptuous of
the reluctant advocates, unwitting valets, and involuntary memoirists who
pose as original thinkers, he never undertakes to deliver a solemn, sonorous
treatise on politics. Understandably wary of philosophical system-building,
he conveys his political insights via lightning epigrams and apothegmatic
proclamations, generally ignoring the quaint Alexandrian custom of furnishing evidence, arguments, and justifications. While his contemporaries
celebrate the triumphs of the new *Reich* or frolic in the surging tide of
democratic reforms, he scours the premodern world for sober realists and
exemplars of political wisdom. He chooses as his interlocutors such

untimely figures as Homer, Manu, Thucydides, Socrates, Plato, Epicurus, Caesar, and St. Paul.

It is now a commonplace for scholars to attribute the difficulty of Nietzsche's political thinking to his writerly styles, experimental masks, pagan irreverence, antiquarian prejudices, arrested naiveté, resentment of modernity—even to the palpable dissatisfactions of his personal/sexual/ emotional/psychological life. These commonly cited idiosyncrasies collectively point, however, not so much to the difficulty of his political thinking, as to its inferiority. Nietzsche is commonly received as an incisive critic, or as an *agent provocateur*, but not as a political philosopher of the first rank. He is an erratic, iconoclastic genius, whose prurient excesses we might contemplate in hygienic detachment (perhaps as a naughty diversion from our more serious work in political philosophy), but in the end he is utterly harmless to the prevailing idols of modernity. Prematurely dismissive of the democratic reforms and liberal ideals that define the highest achievements and aspirations of the age, he has nothing constructive to say to us about political life in late modernity. An outrageous critic, to be sure, but undeniably second-rate, and perhaps downright naive.

The difficulty of Nietzsche's political thinking is attributable not to any personal or epistolary quirks, but to its unusually grandiose scope. He wishes to return to the very ground of politics itself, to excavate the site of politics, and to retrieve the founding question of politics. He consequently has no use for the small-minded pomposity that often passes in modernity for political thinking. He is quite content to leave the details of government, regulation, production and distribution to his fussy German contemporaries. Although his philosophy has spawned many of the revolutionary, antifoundational insights that continue to contour postmodern and post-structuralist thought, his political thinking remains unmistakably modern (or even premodern) in its orientation and design. In fact, his political philosophy bears a closer resemblance to the conservative republicanism of his predecessors than to the progressive liberalism of his contemporaries.[1]

While most representatives of modernity are content to confect self-congratulatory justifications for its misguided projects, Nietzsche is inclined to ask after modernity itself: does it warrant the future of humankind? What might be made of its modest successes and colossal follies? What, if anything, might follow in its turbulent wake? Unless we raise such basic, decisive questions, politics amounts to nothing more than busy work for the petty managers and bureaucrats whom modernity produces in such sterile abundance.

Unlike those prudent seafarers who seek shelter and anchorage, Nietzsche relishes the danger of voyages on the "open seas." No other critic of modernity has dared to venture so far from the *terra firma* of a (supposedly) foundational critical standpoint. No other seafarer has so boldly—and foolishly—renounced conventional routes and instruments of navigation:

> We sail right *over* morality, we crush, we destroy perhaps the remains of our own morality by daring to make our voyage there—but what matter are *we*! (BGE 23)

To pursue Nietzsche's critique of modernity is to set sail on uncharted seas. His odyssey transports him to various ports of call, none more exotic than the *terra incognita* of political legislation. Taking advantage of the palpable degeneration of modern political institutions, he dares to raise a calamitous, and previously unapproachable, question of political legislation: *what ought humankind to become?*

Although this might fairly be viewed as the founding question of politics, to which all political thinkers and legislators ought carefully to attend, Nietzsche insists that it is in fact rarely considered at all. This neglect is partially attributable to historical circumstances, for such questions can be raised only in the twilight of an age, when widespread failure and dissolution call into question the very meaning of human existence. That Nietzsche can raise the founding question of politics thus constitutes sufficient proof that previously satisfying justifications of human existence are no longer viable. This is no idle question, raised to satisfy an academic curiosity: as modernity stumbles toward exhaustion, the last will of humankind, "the will to nothingness," looms on the horizon.

The prospect of the "will to nothingness" points to another reason for the pandemic neglect of the founding question of politics. Raised only in those historical periods in which humankind no longer feels worthy of its past glories, this question presupposes neither an affirmation nor a confirmation of the future of the species. Indeed, Nietzsche does not assume in advance of his daring voyages that humankind necessarily ought to become anything at all. He retrieves the founding question of politics in order to call humankind itself, and its future, into question. In light of the pervasive decay of modernity, he asks, should humankind capitulate to its "will to nothingness"? Or should political legislators devise measures to ensure the survival of humankind? If so, at what future expense to the species as a whole? At stake here is nothing less than the justification of humankind itself, the warrant for its future as a viable, thriving species.

Of course, merely raising the founding question of politics implies neither one's willingness, nor one's capacity, to venture a definitive answer. Having raised the question, one might judge the extant responses to be adequate, or recoil in horror from the weight of the acquired responsibility, or defer the question to "others" (mortal or divine), or promptly shelve the question altogether. While Nietzsche is often criticized for failing to deliver a detailed articulation of "his" vision of the future of humankind, it is not clear that this is, or should be, his political task. Owing to the unique historical conditions under which this question becomes both intelligible and meaningful, those who would raise the question are in no position to answer it with any degree of specificity. Just as the crepuscular flight of the Owl of Minerva seals, for Hegel, the practical impotence of reason and understanding, so Nietzsche's attention to the *question* of modernity signals the irreversible decline of modernity itself. Indeed, since his own critical perspective is tinctured by the decadence that besets modernity, we should receive any specific answer he might venture to the founding question of politics with heightened suspicions.

Yet the inherent danger of raising—much less answering—the founding question of politics is nevertheless grave, for one thereby glimpses the shores of that undiscovered country that Nietzschean cartography locates "beyond good and evil." Once raised, this question cannot be returned to oblivion, and it must change us forever—even if we refuse to answer it. Nietzsche likens the advent of European nihilism to the arrival at one's door of an "uncanny" solicitor, who demands entry into one's home, claiming it to be his home as well (WP 1). Just as one may choose to ignore the entreaties of this persistent guest, so one may choose either to refuse the founding question of politics, or to pretend that this question has already received a final, definitive answer. Toward this end, Nietzsche helpfully catalogs the various tricks, therapies, and penances devised over the years to distract human beings from the founding question of politics. What one may *not* choose, however, is never to have heard this guest at one's door, never to have shunted off onto others the responsibility for determining the future of humankind.

While a serious consideration of the founding question of politics need not commit one to a perfidious eugenics project, or to illiberal social engineering, it *does* commit one to a potentially crippling dalliance with Nietzsche's "immoralism." As astute critics have nervously warned throughout the twentieth century, *nothing Nietzsche says* definitively rules out the illiberal political regimes with which his name has been linked. He neither discerns nor acknowledges any prima facie restrictions on the type of answer a lawgiver might formulate to the founding question of politics. According to Nietzsche, political lawgivers are bound in their deliberations by no moral considerations whatsoever—all of which have been cast adrift in the passage beyond good and evil—but only by a fidelity to their own respective visions of the future of humankind. The supposed priority of a liberal response to this question, a response that aims to secure the future of humankind by eliminating suffering and promoting individual freedom, is "merely" an accident of history, which attests more convincingly to the advance of decadence than to the political merits of liberalism itself.

Nietzsche proffers no assurance (and certainly no hope) that he will respect the liberal ideals of modernity, for he views the advent of the "will to nothingness" as a greater danger than the demise of liberalism. He aims simply to secure the future of the species, hoping to forestall the "suicidal nihilism" that threatens humankind. In light of the prevailing historical conditions of his political thinking, his account of his own "destiny" is perhaps fitting after all:

> I know my fate. One day my name will be associated with the memory of something tremendous—a crisis without equal on earth, the most profound collision of conscience, a decision that was conjured up *against* everything that had been believed, demanded, hallowed so far. I am no man, I am dynamite . . .
> It is only beginning with me that the earth knows *great politics*.
> (EH XIV:1)

1
Political Perfectionism

I hear with pleasure that our sun is swiftly moving toward the constellation of *Hercules*—and I hope that man on this earth will in this respect follow the sun's example? And we first of all, we good Europeans!
—*Beyond Good and Evil*, 243

Nietzsche's attempt to retrieve the founding question of politics reflects his conviction that it is the business of politics to legislate the conditions of the permanent enhancement of humankind (BGE 257). Humankind is best enhanced, he believes, not through the Whiggish reforms and liberal ideals favored by modernity, but through the cultivation of those rare individuals who body forth an expanded complement of human powers and perfections. He consequently recommends that social resources should be reserved and mobilized for the production of great human beings.

As we have seen, Nietzsche treats the founding question of politics as a philosophical question of ultimate justification or legitimation. He thus asks: in what incarnation, if any, might humankind justify its continued existence and warrant its unsecured future? It is important here to bear in mind the historical context of Nietzsche's critical enterprise. In a famous note from 1886, he confirms the advent of European nihilism. This means, he explains, that humankind itself lacks an aim or purpose that might redeem the suffering endemic to its very existence: "What does nihilism mean? *That the highest values devaluate themselves.* The aim is lacking; 'why?' finds no answer" (WP 2). A justification of human existence is furnished by any aim (or goal or purpose), whose pursuit promises to enable human beings to endure the suffering of their meaningless existence. In lieu of some such aim, human beings might be forced to find meaning for themselves in their own self-annihilation, in the will never to will again.

Here we should note that Nietzsche does not automatically assume either that he will arrive at some such justification, or that human existence should necessarily continue. The "highest values" ever attained by Western civilization have now "devaluated themselves." He must consequently begin anew, as it were, in the quest for a goal that might redeem humankind as a whole. Since he too is implicated in the besetting decadence of modernity, he is not optimally appointed to create new values and erect new ideals. For all of his celebrated love of life and *amor fati*, moreover, he is also deeply impressed by the thanatonic wisdom of Silenus, who counseled his captors to retreat immediately into the unquenchable stream of the Dionysian *Ur-eine*. Nietzsche consequently seeks to discover an aim or goal that might actually warrant the future of humankind, rather than merely prolong the miserable existence of a dying, misbegotten species. As he sees it, humankind needs an erotogenic goal to galvanize the will, a promise of the future that would renew our confidence in the continued development of the species.

Throughout his productive career, Nietzsche's political thinking centers around a simple, yet powerful, thesis: human existence is justified only by the presence of those exemplary individuals who re-define the horizons of human perfectibility. In perhaps his most (in)famous articulation of this thesis, he explains that

> We ought really to have no difficulty in seeing that, when a type [*Art*] has arrived at its limits and is about to go over to a higher type, the goal of its evolution lies not in the mass of its exemplars and their wellbeing, let alone in those exemplars who happen to come last in point of time, but rather in those apparently scattered and chance existences which favorable conditions have here and there produced . . . For the question is this: how can your life, the individual life, receive the highest value, the deepest significance? How can it be least squandered? Certainly only by living for the advantage of the rarest and most valuable exemplars [*du zum Vortheile der seltensten und werthvollsten Exemplare lebst*], and not for the advantage of the majority, that is to say those who, taken individually, are the least valuable exemplars. (SE 6)

While it might be tempting to dismiss this passage (written in 1874) as a youthful indiscretion, a perusal of Nietzsche's later writings reveals a persistent fascination with the central political role played by superlative human beings. In one of his last books he proclaims that

> The problem I thus pose is not what shall succeed mankind in the sequence of living beings (man is an *end*), but what type of man shall be *bred*, shall be *willed*, for being higher in value, worthier of life, more certain of a future. Even in the past this

higher type has appeared often—but as a fortunate accident, as
an exception, never as something *willed*. (AC 3)[1]

At the center of Nietzsche's political thinking thus stands his commitment
to the position known as *perfectionism*, which constitutes his general answer
to the founding question of politics.[2] He locates the sole justification of
human existence in the continued perfectibility of the species as a whole, as
evidenced by the pioneering accomplishments of its highest exemplars. In
Schopenhauer as Educator, for example, he argues that it is the primary task
of culture itself to oversee the production of great human beings:

> It is the fundamental idea of *culture*, insofar as it sets for each
> one of us but one task: *to promote the production of the philoso-*
> *pher, the artist, and the saint within us and without us and*
> *thereby to work at the perfecting of Nature.* (SE 5)

Translating this "fundamental idea" into more familiar political terms, he
insists that "humankind ought to seek out and create the favorable conditions under which those great redemptive men can come into existence" (SE
6). In order to correct for the profligacy of Nature, political legislation must
ensure the conditions of the emergence of true genius. In this (relatively)
early essay, Nietzsche advocates the precise social conditions—including
hardship, neglect, material disadvantage and institutional indifference—
under which both Schopenhauer and he emerged as philosophers.[3]

Since human existence derives enduring meaning only through the
exploits of its rarest and most exotic specimens, the task of politics is to
legislate the conditions under which such exemplars will most likely
emerge. This task is by no means simple, for, as Nietzsche indicates in
the passage cited above, exemplary human beings usually emerge only by
accident, as "lucky strikes" on the part of careless peoples and cultures.
The political lawgivers he envisions must consequently legislate against
the indifference of Nature itself:

> The accidental, the law of absurdity in the whole economy of
> humankind, manifests itself most horribly in its destructive effect
> on the higher men whose complicated conditions of life can only
> be calculated with great subtlety and difficulty. (BGE 62)

He thus describes the enormity of the task that awaits the "new philosophers," to whom he entrusts the future of humankind:

> To teach man the future of man as his *will*, as dependent on a
> human will, and to prepare great ventures and over-all attempts
> [*Gesammt-Versuche*] of discipline and cultivation by way of

putting an end to that gruesome dominion of nonsense and accident that has so far been called "history." (BGE 203)

With his "help," Nietzsche believes, the successor epoch to modernity
might suspend this cowardly reliance on chance and resolutely attend to
the "breeding" of exemplary human beings.

Nietzsche's childlike fascination with the heroic exploits of world-
historical figures is attributable to their respective contributions to the
enhancement of humankind as a whole. Thucydides, Caesar, Michelangelo, Napoleon, Goethe, Bizet, and so on—all represent irreversible
advancements on the part of humankind as a whole. In the prodigious
shadow cast by this higher humanity, the meaning and value of human
existence can never revert to the (anachronistic) standards revered in
bygone ages. Like those intrepid wards of Prometheus, whose plucky
accomplishments with the divine flame won from Zeus a stay of execution, this higher humanity confers a measure of dignity and grace onto
an otherwise undistinguished species. The dice-throwing gods may continue to laugh at the folly of their puny human playthings, but they are
sufficiently intrigued by these specimens of higher humanity to renew the
spectacle. Even Christianity, that great leveler of humankind and enemy
of perfectionism, recognizes the need to single out particular saints and
martyrs as exemplary specimens of faith, piety, and suffering.

A significant disadvantage of the term "perfectionism" is its misleading
connotation of a *final* perfection or completion of the species. While it is
true that great human beings continually exceed the achievements of their
predecessors, these transfigurative exploits are both chaotic and unpre-
dicted; they expand the horizon of human perfectibility along any number
of unanticipated planes and vectors. The enactment of previously unknown
human perfections is furthermore not immediately visible in its full relief;
centuries, even millennia, may pass before humankind as a whole acknowledges the unparalleled achievements of its highest exemplars. Any attempt
to identify in advance the *final* perfection of the human soul thus amounts
to nothing more than an exercise in idealism, which Nietzsche comes to
view in his post-Zarathustran writings as the philosophical antipode to his
own "realism" (EH II:10).

Based on his careful observations of human "nature" and history,
Nietzsche assumes that the species as a whole is both dynamic and
evolving. As far as he knows, humankind neither progresses inexorably
toward some preordained omega point, nor fulfills a cosmic destiny that
consigns the weak and infirm to a premature extinction. Through the
signal exploits of its highest representatives, humankind reaches ever
beyond itself, but it reaches for no pre-established goal or *telos*. Each
successive transfiguration further limns the unknown depths and reaches
of the human soul. Indeed, Nietzsche's perfectionism is at all intelligible

only in the event that the human soul is in fact predicated of sufficient plasticity to accommodate the completion and perfection he envisions.

The emergence of great human beings contributes to the enhancement of humankind both directly, by advancing the frontier of human perfectibility, and indirectly, by encouraging (some) others to flourish as well. The ethical life of any thriving community draws its sustenance and vitality from such individuals, and it cannot survive without them. Far from the mere ornaments to which they have been reduced in late modernity, superlative human beings are in fact responsible for the catalysis of culture itself. Nietzsche adamantly maintains that "only he who has attached his heart to some great man is by that act *consecrated to culture*" (SE 6). He later maintains, apparently with no hyperbole intended, that

> A people is a detour of Nature to get to six or seven great men.—
> Yes, and then to get around them. (BGE 126)

Superlative human beings contribute to an enhancement of the species as a whole, for they embody, and thus reveal, heretofore unknown perfections resident within the human soul. By continually expanding the complement of extant human perfections, these exemplars confer upon the species as a whole a quasi-divine status, an ephemeral intimation of immortality.

Great human beings accomplish the catalysis of culture not as a consciously articulated goal, but as an indirect and unintended by-product of their "private" pursuits of self-perfection. While they directly enhance the lives only of themselves and those select few who share their refined aesthetic sensibilities, they indirectly enhance the lives of all who are even minimally invested in the project of culture. Indeed, everyone who enters "the circle of culture" stands to benefit from the production of exemplary human types, for a justification of human existence would be impossible in their absence. Hence the central paradox of Nietzsche's perfectionism: the enhancement of humanity and the enrichment of ethical life are dependent upon the exploits of "immoral" exemplars who hold no conscious or intentional stake in the lives of those whom they succor and renew. In fact, he insists, these exotic specimens must be allowed (and indeed encouraged) to free themselves from the chains of conventional morality if they are to contribute to the permanent enhancement of humankind.

An exemplary human being thus embodies a concrete way of life, a set of situated practices that not only demonstrate the perfectibility of the human soul, but also remind (some) others of the powers and perfections resident within themselves. One such exemplar, Nietzsche suggests, is the (pre-Pauline) Jesus, who bodied forth a "deep instinct for how one must *live* . . . a new way of life, *not* a new faith" (AC 33). The redemptive and justificatory powers of these exemplary human beings are aptly expressed in the dexter king's unsolicited paeon to Zarathustra:

> Nothing more delightful grows on earth, O Zarathustra, than a lofty, strong will: that is the earth's most beautiful plant. A whole landscape is refreshed by one such tree . . . Your tree here, O Zarathustra, refreshes even the gloomy ones, the failures; your sight reassures and heals the heart even of the restless. (Z IV:11)

Even a decadent people or epoch stands to be renewed by the exploits of its representative exemplars. Reeling from the mediocrity and degeneration that make him "weary" of humankind as a whole, Nietzsche hopes to steal a tonic glimpse of "a man who justifies *humankind*, of a complementary and redeeming lucky strike on the part of humankind for the sake of which one may still *believe in humankind!*" (GM I:12) While these decadent "heroes" are not likely to be confused with the commanders and conquerors who populate vital epochs, they nevertheless serve to excite confidence in the future of humanity. One such "hero" is Aristophanes, whom Nietzsche describes as

> that transfiguring, complementary spirit for whose sake one *forgives* everything Hellenic for having existed, provided one has understood in its full profundity *all* that needs to be forgiven and transfigured here. (BGE 28)

The example of Aristophanes is pertinent not only because Nietzsche too must negotiate the shades and shadows of a twilight epoch, but also because Aristophanes, the irreverent scourge of our beloved Socrates, does not resemble the familiar heroes of Greek antiquity. If Nietzsche is to introduce his readers to the representative exemplars of late modernity, then he must somehow divert our attention from traditional models of heroism, which are no longer applicable. In a preliminary education of his readers' sensibilities, he thus prefers Aristophanes to a more commonly revered contemporary:

> Nothing . . . has caused me to meditate more on *Plato's* secrecy and sphinx nature than the happily preserved *petit fait* that under the pillow of his deathbed there was found no "Bible," nor anything Egyptian, Pythagorean, or Platonic—but a volume of Aristophanes. How could even Plato have endured life—a Greek life he repudiated—without an Aristophanes? (BGE 28)

The Lawgiver

The term "perfectionism" carries an indelibly negative connotation, but it accurately focuses our attention on the vital core of Nietzsche's political thinking. His commitment to perfectionism is perhaps best understood as the product of his attempt to accede to the perspective of the *lawgiver*, who aspires to attain (and perhaps to implement) a panoptic vision of the future of humankind.

The lawgiver plays a unique role within the economy of Nietzsche's political thinking. Lawgivers are typically *not* rulers, and they only rarely gain influence over actual rulers. That the lawgiver is typically ignored by modern rulers constitutes Nietzsche's general objection to modern politics, which succeeds largely in presenting the aimlessness and indolence of modernity as princely virtues. (Whether premodern rulers were more appreciative of the wisdom of the lawgiver, as Nietzsche occasionally suggests, remains to be demonstrated.) While actual rulers usually attend only to the local exigencies of personal or popular aggrandizement, the lawgiver attempts to legislate on behalf of humanity as a whole. Hence Nietzsche's attempt to retrieve the founding question of politics: what ought humankind to become?

While most rulers formulate and justify their legislations by appealing to the prosperity of a particular people or polity over a specific, short-term duration, the lawgiver appeals exclusively to the permanent enhancement of humankind as a whole. Legislating from an "immoral" perspective beyond good and evil, the lawgiver cannot be concerned with (or even acknowledge) the "rights" and "freedoms" of individual tribes and peoples, much less those of individual human beings; nothing less than the future determination of the species is at stake. When appealing to the hyperopic perspective of the lawgiver, Nietzsche consequently sounds monstrously cold and cruel, especially to his liberal audiences of the twentieth century. Such is the nature not of the man himself, but of the "immoral" perspective he adopts as a political thinker. He too cares, in his own way, about distributive justice, social welfare, moral education, and other hallmarks of modern political life, though he neither ascribes to these goals the highest political priority, nor thinks them a worthy challenge for his prodigious intellectual gifts. *Qua* lawgiver, no one can be concerned with the particular lives of individual human beings.

Critics often respond that the "immoral" standpoint of the lawgiver is simply the wrong perspective for political thinkers to adopt. It is often remarked, in fact, that Nietzsche attempts thereby to usurp divine authority, daring to consider a question that mere mortals are neither meant nor fit to raise. The charge of impiety is essentially valid, but it is most helpful in framing the historical context of his political thinking. So long as superlative values and metaphysical systems perdure, there is no need, and no opportunity, to raise the founding question of politics. In the absence of any supernatural or metaphysical source of meaning, however, humankind must create for itself sufficient reason for its continued, imperiled existence. Meaning of this magnitude, Nietzsche believes, derives only from the "heroic" exploits of the highest exemplars of the human species. No other means of securing meaning for human existence is currently feasible. When the gods falter or flee, mere mortals must step into the breach.

Although the secular, anthropocentric justification that Nietzsche promises will not be sufficient for those wretched souls who remain inured to the "metaphysical comforts" dispensed by Platonism and Christianity, it is the only mode of justification that it is possible to obtain in the shadow of the dead God. This is not to say, however, that the advent of nihilism marks the end of metaphysics and supernaturalism. Like his predecessor obituarist, the Madman (GS 125), Nietzsche realizes that his cognitive insight into the death of God carries no volitional charge. While he still hopes, fatuously, to occasion a miraculous transformation in his God-fearing readers, he also concedes that "given the way of men, there may still be caves for thousands of years in which [God's] shadow will be shown" (GS 108). Most human beings continue to prostrate themselves before the rotting corpse of the fallen god, either indifferent to, or enchanted by, its cadaverous stench. Even Nietzsche himself occasionally (if surreptitiously) pays his respects to the existentially challenged deity, appealing reverentially to "divine" truths and idols that he expressly disallows to others.

The Indeterminate Animal

The task of "great politics" is neither to destroy nor to transcend the all-too-human within us, but to bring the all-too-human to completion and perfection. But whence the need for the "perfection" of the species at all? Why is humankind in general, in any of its historical incarnations, dependent upon the redemptive exploits of its "highest" specimens? Why are the labors of "ordinary" human beings, however modest or clumsy they may be, insufficient to warrant the future of the species?

Nietzsche's earliest attempts to provide adequate answers to these questions pointed to the failure of Nature to preside over the timely production of exemplary human beings. Nature on its own is a "bad economist" (SE 7). If allowed to pursue the dilatory schedule to which it is accustomed, Nature would continue to produce great human beings, but always as unforeseen accidents, and never with the frequency and regularity that Nietzsche deems necessary for the healthy renewal of culture:

> Nature wants always to be of universal utility, but it does not know how to find the best and most suitable means and instruments for this end . . . Nature is just as extravagant in the domain of culture as it is in that of planting and sowing. It achieves its aims in a broad and ponderous manner: and in doing so it sacrifices much too much energy. (SE 7)

The goal of politics, on this early account, is to assist Nature in attaining more efficiently the ends at which it consistently, if heedlessly, aims. The lawgiver must consequently intervene to arrange for a more productive distribution of Nature's (dis)array of resources. In a moment of feckless serendipity that he will later disown, Nietzsche presents the perfection of Nature and the perfection of humankind as dovetailing harmoniously in the production of the exemplary human being (SE 5).

He thus conceived of his early perfectionism as a relatively unobtrusive campaign to assist Nature in its dawdling production of exemplary human beings, and so as a contribution to the perfection of Nature itself. He later changes his mind on this point, attempting in his post-Zarathustran period to correct for the anthropocentric bias of his early writings. Although his account of the precise relationship between *nomos* and *physis* remains tricky throughout his productive career, he now situates Nature beyond good and evil. Nature appears no longer as a "bad" economist, but as an indifferent one, exhibiting no discernible attunement either to human interests or to human designs (BGE 9).

Nietzsche's early "answer" furthermore begs the question of the *need* for redemptive human beings in the first place. If it is true that humankind requires *some* of these heroes for its continued survival and justification, then it certainly stands to reason that *more* of them might be desirable. But what, exactly, is involved in the process of "perfection" that these exemplary human beings must continue and guide? In what precise respects does humankind stand imperfect and incomplete?

As his critics often remark, Nietzsche does not present an adequately specific account of his vision of the eventual perfection of humankind. Yet he does provide a general sketch of the "completion" he has in mind. Here he draws from his speculative forays into philosophical anthropology, which assume ever greater importance in his post-Zarathustran writings. Vowing to proffer strictly naturalistic explanations for allegedly supernatural phenomena, he attributes the incompleteness of humankind not to some "original sin" or fall from "grace," but to its desperate reliance on consciousness as an organ of internal regulation. Unlike all "natural" animals (including their pre-moral, hominid ancestors), human beings have forcibly renounced the pre-reflective guidance afforded them by their unconscious drives and impulses. In a pioneering insight that Freud would later borrow, Nietzsche traces the discontents of humanity to

> the serious illness that man was bound to contract under the stress of the most fundamental change he ever experienced—that change which occurred when he found himself finally enclosed within the walls of society and of peace. The situation that faced sea animals when they were compelled to become land animals

> or perish was the same as that which faced these semi-animals,
> well adapted to the wilderness, to war, to prowling, to adven-
> ture: suddenly all their instincts were disvalued and "suspended."
> . . . [T]hey were reduced to thinking, inferring, reckoning, co-
> ordinating cause and effect, these unfortunate creatures; they
> were reduced to their "consciousness," their weakest and most
> fallible organ! (GM II:16)

This violent transition to the peace and tranquillity of civil society left
the human animal incomplete and indeterminate. Having refused Nature's
original determination of its destiny, the human species must forge a
destiny of its own, with unreliable consciousness as its only guide:

> [M]an is more sick, uncertain, changeable, indeterminate [*unfest-
> gestellter*] than any other animal, there is no doubt of that; he
> is the *sick* animal . . . [H]ow should such a courageous and
> richly endowed animal not also be the most imperiled, the most
> chronically and profoundly sick of all sick animals? (GM III:13)

Nietzsche consequently defines man as the "*indeterminate animal* [*nicht
festgestellte Thier*]" (BGE 62), for only the human animal actively participates (though not always voluntarily and constructively) in the
determination of its full complement of powers and perfections.

The transition from natural animal to human animal has been both
painful and protracted, and it is by no means complete. In order to impress
consciousness into service as a guide to living within the walls of civilization, human beings are obliged to direct *inward* the instinctual energy
that they would "naturally" discharge toward the external world:

> All instincts that do not discharge themselves outwardly *turn
> inward*—this is what I call the *internalization* of man: thus it
> was that man first developed what was later called his "soul."
> . . . Hostility, cruelty, joy in persecuting, in attacking, in change,
> in destruction—all this turned against the possessors of such
> instincts: *that* is the origin of the "bad conscience." (GM II:16)

The introjection of instinctual energy thus results in the pain of the "bad
conscience," which Nietzsche views as the non-negotiable, non-refundable
cost incurred by all human animals upon entering the shelter of civilization.[4] The onset of this "illness" initiates the ongoing transition from
natural animal to human animal, forcibly investing human beings with
the interiority that alone "makes them interesting."[5]

In addition to the insecurity of relying on a relatively inefficient organ
of internal regulation, human animals must also secure for themselves

some measure of relief from the affliction of their bad conscience. This relief usually arrives via the ascetic ideal, which bids human beings to accept the pain of the bad conscience as a just (albeit partial) punishment for their persistent incompleteness. The ascetic ideal thus "relieves" the pain of the bad conscience by pronouncing the guilt or indebtedness [Schuld] of all human animals. Yet this moral/metaphysical interpretation of the bad conscience only exacerbates the suffering of the "guilty" parties, who must attempt to repay their debts through the practice of self-inflicted cruelty. Under the aegis of the ascetic ideal, human beings *blame* themselves for their misery, compounding the (involuntary) suffering of the bad conscience with the (voluntary) suffering of guilt. The ascetic ideal thus pretends to still the *existential* suffering associated with the bad conscience by superposing upon it the *surplus* suffering associated with guilt (GM III:15).[6] Through the necromancy sponsored by the ascetic ideal, innocent sufferers are summarily transformed into guilty sinners.

Having nurtured the weakling human animal throughout its protracted childhood and arrested adolescence, the ascetic ideal has now outlived its usefulness to the continued development of the species. The surplus suffering of guilt has crippled the human animal to the extent that it can no longer tolerate the existential suffering of the bad conscience. Riddled with guilt, its will now aimed at securing final release from the torment of existence, the human animal once again contemplates the "suicidal nihilism" from which the ascetic ideal originally saved it (GM III:28). Having survived thus far its quantum leap into civil society, the human animal must now somehow survive civil society itself. In order to complete the transition from natural animal to human animal, the human species must wean itself from the metaphysical comforts dispensed by the ascetic ideal.

As a consequence of their renunciation of the "instinctual" regulation provided by Nature—an apostasy without precedent or parallel in the animal kingdom—human animals must determine for themselves what they ought to will. Once wrenched from its natural, instinctual moorings, the human will has no natural or proper object to pursue. It consequently attaches itself to *any* goal whose pursuit promises to deliver the threshold level of affective engagement, or feeling of power, that confirms the vitality of the human organism. Nietzsche thus cautions that "the basic fact of the human will" is its "*horror vacui: it needs a goal*—and it would rather will *nothingness* than *not* will" (GM III:1). If bereft of life-affirming alternatives, an enervated will would eventually embrace the goal of self-annihilation, for any goal is better than none at all. This "will to nothingness" constitutes the "last will" of humankind, the will never to will again, and its advent signifies the impending demise of modernity itself.

The haunting specter of the "will to nothingness" thus exposes the grave danger involved in all measures designed to permit (and even encourage) the indiscriminacy of the will. Because the will has grown too weak to bear the yoke of external legislation, some political thinkers now celebrate the ochlocratic plurality of objects to which the will promiscuously attaches itself. While it has become popular in late modernity to entrust to each will the task of determining its own goal, thereby obviating the legislative role of the lawgiver, this trust is egregiously misplaced. If each will is left to its own witless devices, if lawgivers fail to provide and enforce a sustaining goal, then the enhancement of humankind will continue to occur, if at all, only by accident. More importantly, in light of the peculiar exigencies of late modernity, an unguided will may eventually constitute itself as the "will to nothingness." Lawgivers must consequently legislate against the indiscriminacy of the human will, subjecting to their own design that which "naturally" falls to chance.

As Nietzsche sees it, exemplary human beings inadvertently assist lawgivers in correcting for the indiscriminacy of the human will. He regularly figures great human beings as intrepid navigators, who unwittingly serve as advance scouts for the drifting bark of humanity. These heroes turn the indiscriminacy of the will to the advantage of the species as a whole, experimenting with myriad, diverse goals and thereby testing the limits and plasticity of the human soul. From these dangerous experiments the species as a whole compiles a store of common wisdom, upon which the lawgiver draws in order to spare less robust souls the perils of similar experimentation. The extramoral genius consequently performs an indispensable political service, unknowingly providing lawgivers with the knowledge they need in order to compensate for the indiscriminacy of the human will.

Nietzsche thus advances both a general and a specific warrant for the production of those exemplary human beings who engender a renewed confidence in the future of humankind. He now realizes that Zarathustra's greatest fear, the somnambulant reign of the nodding, blinking "last man" (Z P5), has been eclipsed by a more ominous peril: the advent of the "will to nothingness," whereby humankind orchestrates its own annihilation in a final, apocalyptic frenzy of Dionysian expenditure. While the legislation of a permanent object for the will remains the highest priority overall, Nietzsche defers this task to the "philosophers of the future." His own task is to safeguard the endangered will until such time as new commanders and legislators arrive on the scene.

Toward this more modest end, he experiments with novel objects for the crippled will, gambling that virtually any constitution of the will is preferable to the "will to nothingness." He thus advocates a politics of resistance rather than a politics of redemption or revolution. Although he hopes to contribute to the eventual legislation of a permanent object or goal for humankind, he can do no more than preside over the survival of the will in the twilight of the idols.

The Use and Abuse of Christian Morality

Nietzsche can do nothing to assuage the existential suffering of the bad conscience, and he evinces no inclination to do so. The "sovereign individuals" whom he envisions will not only endure the pain of the bad conscience, but also cherish it as yet another seduction to Life. His perfectionism thus aims at nothing less than the (eventual) production of human beings who require no external, metaphysical justification for their meaningless existence. He consequently aims to diminish, and eventually to eliminate, the surplus suffering (or guilt) that attends the dominant, Christian interpretation of the bad conscience.

Nietzsche regularly links the survival of the will with the self-overcoming of Christian morality, which he also claims as his ownmost task (D P4). The self-reflexive nature of this task is crucial to an understanding of his perfectionism, for his vision of the "sovereign individual" actually incorporates some powers and faculties that have been perfected under the discipline of Christian morality. It was under the aegis of Christian morality, after all, that the "sovereign individual" briefly and accidentally emerged, in whose chiseled visage Nietzsche spies a glimpse of a post-Christian future:

> [L]ike only to himself, liberated again from morality of custom, autonomous and supramoral (for "autonomous" and "moral" are mutually exclusive), in short, the man who has his own independent, protracted will and the *right to make promises*— (GM II:2)

He thus associates the self-overcoming of morality with the "breeding" of individuals who stand security for their own future, who acknowledge (and repay) debts only to themselves (GM II:2). Christianity has made such individuals possible, and they will in turn abolish Christian morality and its emphasis on irremediable guilt.

Because Nietzsche envisions the completion (rather than the transcendence) of the all-too-human, his perfectionism aims not to absolve the indebtedness of the human animal, but to exploit it. The death of God does not absolve all human debts—*pace* Feuerbach—but it may, in some extraordinary cases, allow for "sovereign individuals" to assume full responsibility for the definition and payment of their debts. Just as Kantian autonomy delivers freedom not from the moral law itself, but from the *constraint* of the moral law, so Nietzschean "sovereignty" promises absolution not of indebtedness *per se*, but only of the constraint of one's indebtedness.[7] The sovereign individuals he foresees thus augur the self-overcoming of Christian morality: they are debtors, to be sure, but only to themselves. Hence they are *also* creditors, for they stand security for their own "guilt." The transition from natural animal to human animal will be complete only when humankind is able to produce these sovereign individuals as a matter of design. It is to this end that Nietzsche devotes the political thinking of his mature, post-Zarathustran period.

For all of his enthusiasm, however, the cultural production of sovereign individuals is simply incompatible with the diminished resources at the disposal of his age. What modernity calls an "individual," the pride of the Enlightenment, is nothing more than a "moral milksop," a domesticated animal that has internalized the demands of culture and consequently operates under the illusion of self-legislated freedom. Even the "sovereign individual," who possesses "the *right to make promises*," owes his "rare freedom" to his "*conscience*," which, Nietzsche shows, is itself an implant of socially enforced heteronomy (GM 2:2). The conscience, a fiercely vigilant homunculus responsible for reckoning one's debts and obligations, represents the final—and most forbidding—barrier to genuine sovereignty.

Nietzsche snickers at the idea that the right to make promises stands as sufficient evidence of one's sovereignty, for he views the conscience as the internalized, mnemonic distillation of socially enforced punitive and carceral practices. Whereas the noble savage and blond beast require sturdy cages or constant external surveillance, "men of conscience" are sufficiently docile to police themselves. Even Nietzsche himself, the self-styled immoralist and Antichrist, continues to wear this "venerable long pigtail," which makes him "seem old-fashioned and grandfatherly-honorable" (BGE 214). The closest thing we know to genuine, supramoral sovereignty is not the debt-paying, promise-keeping, originally positioned author of the social contract, but the criminal, the monster devoid of conscience, who personally shoulders the entire burden of his existential suffering. Nietzsche thus defines "the criminal type" as "the type of strong human being under unfavorable circumstances: a strong human being made sick" (TI IX:45).

Under the influence of Christianity, the institutions of Western civilization have for the most part implemented what Nietzsche calls "moralities of taming" (TI VII:3). Social practices of self-formation have succeeded in sickening (and thus domesticating) those individals whose "virtues are ostracized by society." The conscience thus prevents individuals from straying far from the internalized norm, while the institutions of modernity marginalize or stamp out those singular, exotic plants that do manage to blossom. On a rare occasion, however, "a man proves stronger than society: the Corsican, Napoleon, is the most famous case" (TI IX:45).

Napoleon thus represents the closest approximation known to Nietzsche of genuine sovereignty, for Napoleon approached the task of lawgiving (relatively) unconstrained by conscience and tradition. He consequently describes Napoleon as a "return to Nature," which he defines as "an *ascent*—up into the high, free, even terrible Nature and naturalness where great tasks are something one plays with, one *may* play with" (TI IX:48). Just as the taming disciplines of Christianity inadvertently made possible the emergence of the amoral criminal, who, in the person of Napoleon, returned to Nature, so the "philosophers of the future" may someday breed sovereign individuals by appropriating and adapting the signature practices of Christian morality. Until his nomothetic successors arrive, however, Nietzsche will take advantage of the demise of modernity to experiment with untested constitutions of the will, some of which may be successful in postponing the descent of the "will to nothingness."

The *Übermensch*

Nietzsche's perfectionism attains its apotheosis in his enigmatic conception of the *Übermensch*, or "over-man." While the relevant textual evidence is simply too slight to authorize any particular interpretation of this difficult teaching, the *Übermensch* is best understood within the context of Nietzsche's enduring admiration for heroic individuals and "higher humanity." He thus conceives of the *Übermensch* as embodying the perfection, rather than the transcendence, of humankind. The *Übermensch* is any human being who actually advances the frontier of human perfectibility.

Immediately after posing the problem of "breeding" superlative human beings, Nietzsche explains that this "higher type" of human being stands "in relation to humankind as a whole, [as] a kind of *Übermensch*" (AC 4). The central task of politics, then, is to produce (as a matter of design) those individuals who stand, "in relation to humankind as a whole," as exemplary human beings. The production of the *Übermensch* thus contributes to the enhancement of humankind, for the *Übermensch* in turn embodies a perfection of the soul from which others may draw courage and inspiration. In a remark that dispels much of the mythology that popularly surrounds Nietzsche's teaching of the *Übermensch*,[8] he immediately adds that

> Such fortuitous accidents of great success have always been possible and *will* perhaps always be possible. And even whole families, tribes, or peoples may occasionally represent such a *lucky strike* [*Treffer*]. (AC 4)

While it is ordinarily irresponsible to privilege a single passage from Nietzsche's books, this brief discussion of the *Übermensch* strikes me as decisive, and for several reasons. First of all, the *teaching* of the *Übermensch* more properly belongs to Zarathustra. Nietzsche himself mentions the *Übermensch* in only a few passages outside the text of *Zarathustra*, most of which shed no direct light on his political thinking. Indeed,

Zarathustra's evolving doctrine of the *Übermensch* often deviates significantly from the account Nietzsche provides in *The Antichrist(ian)*, and
we have good reason to believe that Zarathustra did not fully understand
the teachings entrusted to him.[9] Especially when pandering to obtuse audi-
tors throughout Parts I and II of his *Bildungsgang*, Zarathustra regularly
presents the *Übermensch* as the transcendence, rather than the completion or perfection, of the all-too-human "fragments and cripples" littered
about him (Z II:20). He thus lapses regularly into idealism, allowing his
prodigious resentment of modernity to invest his teaching of the *Übermensch* with the particular content and determination that he expressly
disallows. Zarathustra is a valuable guide through the labyrinths of
Nietzsche's teachings, but he too must be subjected to critical scrutiny.
We would do well not to confuse or conflate Nietzsche's account of the
Übermensch with Zarathustra's parabolic teaching.

Second, these telegraphic remarks in *The Antichrist(ian)* contain
Nietzsche's single most fully developed statement of his conception of the
Übermensch. In contrast to Zarathustra's ambiguous teaching, Nietzsche's
sketch of the *Übermensch* in *The Antichrist(ian)* is consistent with (and
explicitly linked to) his more familiar discussions of the political role of
exemplary human beings. On those rare occasions when he uses the term
Übermensch, he apparently has in mind the apotheosis of those specimens
of "higher humanity" to whom he more regularly refers. While it may
be important in certain contexts to distinguish between the *Übermensch*
and this "higher humanity,"[10] we are justified in treating the two concepts
as continuous within the economy of Nietzsche's thought. Indeed, the only
salient difference between the *Übermensch* and other, more familiar specimens of this "higher humanity" is that the emergence of the *Übermensch*
is *willed* by those commanders and legislators who undertake the task of
perfecting the all-too-human.

Third, this brief sketch of the *Übermensch* is further distinguished by
the political import Nietzsche attaches to *The Antichrist(ian)*, as the statement of his "revaluation of all values." Nietzsche is well aware that his
conception of the *Übermensch* has been widely misunderstood (EH III:
1),[11] and he knows that the political fate of his revaluation hinges in part
upon the reception of his remarks on the *Übermensch*. *The Antichrist(ian)*
thus affords him an opportunity to clarify—for some readers, at least—
the relation of his conception of the *Übermensch* to the impending event
of revaluation.[12] Attempting to avoid (some of) the misleading connota-
tions of the term *Übermensch*, he employs it only sparingly in his
post-Zarathustran writings, explicitly distancing himself from the idealism
that distorts Zarathustra's teaching (EH III: 1).

Nietzsche seems especially keen to disabuse his readers of the popular
interpretation of the *Übermensch* as a moral ideal, for he views all forms
of "idealism" as antithetical to the "realism" he champions:

> The word "*Übermensch*" . . . has been understood almost every-
> where with the utmost innocence in the sense of those very values
> whose opposite Zarathustra was meant to represent—that is, as
> an "idealistic" type of a higher man, half "saint," half "genius."
> (EH III: 1)

This commitment to realism, which informs all of his writings from 1888,
not only governs his laconic remarks on the *Übermensch*, but also
expresses the singular achievements of the *übermenschlich* type:

> this type of man . . . conceives reality *as it is*, being strong
> enough to do so; this type is not estranged or removed from
> reality but is reality itself and exemplifies all that is terrible and
> questionable in it—*only in that way can man attain greatness*.
> (EH XIV: 5)

The *Übermensch* is not simply another moral ideal, but a concrete, empirical type [*Typus*] or kind [*Art*].[13] An ideal suggests to Nietzsche a "flight
from reality," a theoretical construct that may or may not admit of
concrete instantiation, and which, in any event, implies an indictment of
reality (EH III: 1; XIV:3). As an opponent of idealism, he thus maintains
that

> What justifies man is his reality—it will eternally justify him.
> How much greater is the worth of the real man, compared with
> any merely desired, dreamed-up, foully fabricated man? with any
> ideal man? (TI IX:32)

Lest he slip into the unwanted idealism of Zarathustra, Nietzsche refrains
from offering any antecedent designation or defining characteristics of the
übermenschlich type, suggesting simply that we "should sooner look even
for a Cesare Borgia than a Parsifal" (EH III: 1). He explains that the
word "*Übermensch*" designates "a type of supreme achievement" and that
the *Übermensch* stands in opposition to "'modern' men, to 'good' men,
to Christians and other nihilists" (EH III: 1).

For Nietzsche, then, the *Übermensch* operates as an extremely (if not
perfectly) "thick" ethical concept, which can be grasped only through an
empirical study of the highest human types that actually have emerged.
He provides no abstract theory or account of *Übermenschlichkeit*, and he
relies almost exclusively on concrete examples—Cesare Borgia, for
instance—to convey the meaning he attaches to the concept. Following
his lead, we might profitably employ a strictly functional (or formal) designation of the *übermenschlich* type: *Übermenschen* are simply those
individuals who embody the "supreme achievements" of any culture or

epoch—regardless of the moral or aesthetic qualities they do or do not possess.

Nietzsche explicitly claims that "such fortunate accidents of great success have always been possible" (AC 4), which implies that *Übermenschen* have existed throughout human history. Even a passing familiarity with Nietzsche's books yields a fairly impressive list of the exemplary historical figures he has in mind: Caesar, Pilate, Cesare Borgia, Napoleon, Goethe, Frederick II, and so on. Nietzsche also expresses his hope that such superlative human beings "will perhaps always be possible," which implies that he may (or should) expect to encounter *Übermenschen* even in late modernity. Although his contempt for modernity escalates his skepticism of the generative powers of the age, he certainly proceeds in his post-Zarathustran political deliberations as if some such exemplars might someday emerge from the gloaming; his continued advocacy of perfectionism would otherwise make little sense. Indeed, he describes these *übermenschlich* types as "fortunate accidents" precisely because they embody an enhancement of humankind, which is the end to which he directs his own energies.

Nietzsche describes these *übermenschlich* types as standing "relative to," rather than independent of, "humanity as a whole" (AC 4). This description not only militates against defining the *Übermensch* in absolute or ideal terms, but also directs our attention to the relationships that obtain between *Übermenschen* and "humanity as a whole."[14] In fact, if these *übermenschlich* types stood independent of "humanity as a whole," estranged altogether from the ethical life of the communities that produce them, then they could play no role in the permanent enhancement of humankind. It is within the domain of these (admittedly unique) relations that the distinctly ethical content of Nietzsche's perfectionism resides. His attention to these relations furthermore indicates that he understands the *Übermensch* as constituting the perfection, rather than the transcendence, of humankind.

Throughout the post-Zarathustran period of his career, Nietzsche portrays the "genius" as strictly an economic type, characterized by a relatively expanded range of vitality and affective expression:

> The genius, in work and deed, is necessarily a squanderer: that he squanders himself, that is his greatness. The instinct of self-preservation is suspended, as it were; the overpowering pressure of outflowing forces forbids him any such care or caution. (TI IX:44)

The order of rank among individuals and types is thus determined by a measure of the relative capacity of excess affect that one can afford to reserve and expend. Nietzsche thus proffers a strictly formal account of the great individual, as an economic type endowed with a relatively *über-menschlich* capacity for reserve and expenditure: "He shall be greatest who . . . is overrich in will. Precisely this shall be called *greatness*: being capable of being as manifold as whole, as ample as full" (BGE 212). He consummates this economic designation of the *übermenschlich* type by defining the genius as "one who either *begets* or *gives birth*, taking both terms in their most elevated sense" (BGE 206). As we shall see later in more detail, he entrusts the future of humankind to these *übermenschlich* types precisely because they alone can afford to squander themselves in the catalysis of culture; for this procreative task, they need only be relatively greater than the humanity that surrounds them.

In fact, it is precisely the relations between exemplary human beings and "humanity as a whole" that make ethical life and moral development possible at all. The ethical life that springs up around *übermenschlich* types does not sustain a universal ethical community, nor a community founded on rational principles of legislation, nor a community sufficiently inclusive to mollify Nietzsche's liberal critics, but it sustains a thriving community nonetheless, complete with its own signature morality. As we shall see more clearly later on, the founding labors of the *Übermensch* create a community of friends in the peculiarly Nietzschean sense, of fellow travelers who share a common aesthetic sensibility, who mutually elevate one another through conflict and contest.[15]

As we have already seen, Nietzsche claims that entire communities of such exemplars—"families, tribes, peoples"—are possible (AC 4). This claim contradicts the popular caricature of the *Übermensch* as an autarkic nomad who willfully estranges himself from all traditions, communities and shared tables of value.[16] We therefore need not assume that Nietzsche imagines the *Übermensch* as some sort of abomination or monstrosity unknown to the ethical community. Indeed, since Nietzsche defines the *Übermensch* "in relation to humankind as a whole," rather than in some absolute or ideal terms, we may furthermore expect these exemplary figures to reflect in certain respects the relative character of their respective epochs.

Nietzsche is often criticized for portraying these *übermenschlich* types on the model of the amoral, world-historical conqueror.[17] While his romanticization of extramoral monsters *is* often childish and offensive, it does not constitute the core of his political thinking. As the textual evidence indicates, he defines exemplary figures solely in terms of their embodied justification of the future of humanity, a political task for which they need be neither world-historical nor particularly monstrous. He praises artists, poets and thinkers as lavishly and as frequently as he praises commanders, lawgivers and beasts; depending on the people or epoch in question, either type may represent the highest expression of vitality.[18] Healthy peoples and ages tend to produce world-historical commanders and lawgivers as their highest specimens, while decadent peoples and ages tend to produce philosophers and critics as their representative exemplars. We should therefore not be surprised to discover that the heroes of one epoch bear little external resemblance to those of another. Just as "we moderns" appear weak and impoverished in comparison with "that lavishly squandering and fatal age of the Renaissance" (TI IX:37), so the "higher men" of late modernity would seem sickly and pale beside the overflowing health of a Cesare Borgia.

The distinctly ethical role of the *Übermensch* becomes even clearer if we unearth the Emersonian roots of this exotic plant. Nietzsche apparently models the *Übermensch* on Emerson's notion of "representative men," who, in their own private pursuits of self-reliance, display (and thereby represent) the potentialities for perfection resident within the human soul.[19] By virtue of their embodied practices, representative men "remind" some others of the soul's natural (if ultimately futile) aspirations to transcendence. Representative men straddle the intersection of the human and the divine, of the temporal and the eternal, and they represent to some others the "forgotten" perfections attainable by all human beings.

Their contribution to ethical life is consequently predicated on their practice of aversion. They stand as living rebukes—"critics in body and soul" (BGE 210)—to the conformity and mediocrity into which human beings all too readily sink. Their pursuits of self-perfection stir similar longings within the souls of some others, thus galvanizing the ethical life of the community. In an early passage that conveys the extent of his debt to Emerson (as well as the provenance of his fascination with the prefix *über*), Nietzsche writes, "[y]our real nature lies . . . immeasurably high above [*über*] you, or at least above [*über*] that which you usually take yourself to be" (SE 1). Completing this Emersonian parallel, we might think of the *Übermensch* as a "representative individual," whose achievements in self-perfection illuminate the linkage between invidual human souls and the transpersonal oversoul of humankind.[20]

In light of these decisive passages from *The Antichrist(ian)*, we need not endorse Zarathustra's gnomic claim that there has never been an *Übermensch* (Z II:4), nor relegate the *Übermensch* to a distant and continually receding future,[21] nor confine the *Übermensch* exclusively to modernity,[22] nor imagine the *Übermensch* as an unattainable, strictly regulative ideal. Having separated Nietzsche's teaching from Zarathustra's, we may confidently interpret the *Übermensch* in concrete terms, as the historically instantiated, fully attainable, concrete embodiment of human perfectibility— an empirical type rather than a theoretical ideal—around whom the ethical life of any thriving culture revolves. The *Übermensch* is any higher human being whose "private" pursuit of self-perfection occasions an enhancement of the species as a whole, thus contributing to the perfection (rather than the transcendence) of the all-too-human. The *Übermensch* thus instantiates a justification of humankind grounded in its reality, rather than in some abstract ideal.

The *Übermensch* thus constitutes Nietzsche's general answer to the founding question of politics: "we" should undertake to breed a type of individual whose pursuit of self-perfection contributes to the enhancement of humankind and thereby justifies our own existence. "We" should undertake the establishment of a political regime that will in turn envision the *Übermensch* as its unimaginable, singular product. Indeed, the single most salient characteristic of this type of regime is that *Übermenschen* are produced by design. Nietzsche places extraordinary emphasis on the overt act of willing to assume responsibility for the future of humankind. Heroic human beings have emerged before to refresh the parched landscape of humanity, but always as "lucky strikes" on the part of an indifferent Nature. Never before have *übermenschlich* types been willed into existence, as the primary, overarching aim of a political regime.

It is important to note, however, that this interpretation of the *Übermensch* deviates from Nietzsche's teaching in an important respect. Whereas I have cast the *übermenschlich* type as the highest achievement realized by any people or epoch, Nietzsche tends to reserve the title *Übermensch* only for the representative exemplars of superlative peoples and epochs, and thus of humanity itself. It is entirely possible, then, that he would bristle at my suggestion that even the anemic, twilight cultures of late modernity might unwittingly produce *übermenschlich* types of their own. The ethical exemplars of late modernity are a far cry, admittedly, from the "lightning" and "frenzy" (Z P3) prophesied by Zarathustra, as well as from the redemptive man of the future—the "victor over God and nothingness" (GM II:24)—for whom Nietzsche romantically yearns.

In light of Nietzsche's abundant resentment of modernity, however, it is quite likely that he occasionally compromises his own teaching. Like Zarathustra, in fact, Nietzsche tends to depict the *Übermensch* in traditionally personal terms, as a charismatic individual endowed with superlative nomothetic powers.[23] He thus favors a model of agency that naturally lends itself to the redemptive and messianic interpretations that he claims to repudiate. Rather than take literally his (and Zarathustra's) pronouncements on the *Übermensch*, we might instead attempt to situate this difficult teaching within the economy of Nietzsche's thought as a whole. We might then view the *Übermensch* not as an individual agent *per se*, but as a historically specific vortex of generative powers and transformative possibilities. His vision of the *Übermensch* could be realized in a community, a discourse, a confluence of traditions, a network of social institutions, a constellation of cultural practices, an unanticipated mutation in the human phenotype—perhaps even a cyborg mechanism.

If we apply to Nietzsche his own guiding insights, then we can compensate somewhat for the distortions imposed on his political thinking by his own decadent yearnings. Indeed, if we succeed in filtering out his own prejudices, then there is no need to anticipate the completion of his thought in the advent of a prophet, messiah, charismatic leader, conqueror, commander, dictator or *Führer*. "*Übermensch*" could simply refer to a propitious confluence of social, historical and material conditions, such as those that presided over the birth of tragedy in ancient Greece. This interpretation of the *Übermensch*, which I will embellish in due course, is not only more faithful than the popular caricature to the (scant) textual evidence available, but also more promising as an interpretation of Nietzsche's ethical teaching.

2
The Uses and Disadvantages of Morality for Life

The genius, in work and deed, is necessarily a squanderer: that he squanders himself, that is his greatness . . . Yet, because much is owed to such explosives, much has also been given them in return: for example, a kind of higher morality. After all, that is the way of human gratitude: it *misunderstands* its benefactors.

—*Twilight of the Idols*, IX:44

The ethical core of Nietzsche's perfectionism is often eclipsed by his scathing attack on the Western moral tradition. But his critique of morality is not inhospitable to all forms of morality, and it in fact clears a space for the "morality of breeding" that motivates his perfectionism. He actually intends his perfectionism to shelter a moral pluralism, informed by an order of rank, which yields a hierarchical organization of ethical communities.

Nietzsche's Defense of Moral Pluralism

Although Nietzsche's perfectionism lies at the very heart of his political thinking, it remains one of the most obscure elements of his philosophy. His critics routinely dismiss his perfectionism, often assuming that he proposes a crude eugenics project, which will culminate in the savage, unprincipled rule of some blond beast or barbarian caste. John Rawls, for example, attributes to Nietzsche a version of "teleological perfectionism" that is not even worthy of consideration in the "original position."[1] The closest Rawls comes to a critical assessment of this "teleological perfectionism" is his terse observation that "[t]he absolute weight that Nietzsche sometimes gives the lives of great men such as Socrates and Goethe is unusual."[2] Rather than elaborate, Rawls moves on to consider the merits of a "more moderate doctrine" of perfectionism, which "has far stronger claims," but which he rejects nonetheless as a source of viable principles of justice.[3]

Rawls's response is typical in its summary rejection of the ethical claims of Nietzsche's perfectionism. Like Rawls, many readers conclude that Nietzsche's political thinking shelters virtually no ethical content whatsoever. Nietzsche himself is certainly responsible for much of the misunderstanding surrounding his perfectionism, for he often presents himself as an uncompromising opponent of morality *simpliciter*. He proudly describes himself as an "immoralist," and he congratulates himself for being the "first" of this noble breed (EH XIV:6). Fully representative of his rhetorical excesses is the following "definition of morality":

> Morality—the idiosyncrasy of decadents, with the ulterior motive of revenging oneself against life—successfully. (EH XIV:7)

Continuing this telegraphic line of argumentation, he submits the following summary epigram: "Morality as vampirism" (EH XIV:8).

Especially when viewed from the broadly historical perspective that Nietzsche favors, however, the enterprise of morality encompasses far more than the universal prescriptions and metaphysical fictions that he so famously debunks. In fact, he regularly reminds his readers that the type of morality he opposes is only one among several possible moralities:

> *Morality in Europe today is herd animal morality*—in other words, as we understand it, merely *one* type of human morality beside which, before which, and after which many other types, above all *higher* moralities, are or ought to be, possible. But this morality resists such a "possibility," such an "ought" with all its power: it says stubbornly and inexorably, "I am morality itself, and nothing besides is morality." (BGE 202)

Continuing this critique of moral monism in his next book, *On the Genealogy of Morals*, he declares that contemporary morality, despite its claims to universality, is in fact descended from a "slave" morality, which in turn emerged only in response to the hegemony of a logically and historically prior "noble" morality. The history of morality, encrypted in the "long hieroglyphic record" that Nietzsche aims to decipher (GM P:7), thus contradicts the claim of *any* morality, including the ubiquitous "herd animal morality," to a privileged, monistic prerogative as the arbiter of ethical life. In his "review" of the *Genealogy*, he explicitly identifies the "slave revolt in morality" with "the birth of Christianity out of the spirit of *ressentiment*" (EH XI).

Rather than reject the enterprise of morality itself, Nietzsche instead rejects the claim of any single morality to universal scope and application.

A universally binding morality would necessarily erect a monolithic moral ideal, thereby reducing a plurality of human types and kinds to a lowest common denominator. Ethical laws should (and do) bind collectively, but only across a limited number of individuals, such as constitute a people, race, tribe, or community. As Zarathustra puts it, "I am a law only for my kind [*die Meinen*], I am no law for all" (Z IV:12). The dream of an ethical community comprising all human beings, or all sentient beings, thus spells political nightmare. The laws of an omni-inclusive ethical community would express only the commonalities and banalities of the individuals involved, rather than their unique strengths and virtues. Morality should always serve the enhancement of the ethical life of a particular people, and not the other way around:

> *Morality*—no longer the expression of the conditions for the life and growth of a people, no longer its most basic instinct of life, but become abstract, become the antithesis of life—morality as the systematic degradation of the imagination, as the "evil eye" for all things. (AC 25)

Nietzsche's critique of Christian morality is best understood within the context of his political opposition to moral monism. He has no quarrel, for example, with Christian morality in its "pure" forms, which he applauds for providing comfort and solace to the demotic strata of hierarchically organized societies. He goes so far as to praise the contributions of Christian morality to the "hygienic" maintenance of intramural political boundaries, readily acknowledging the value of moralities that serve the inwardly destroyed (BGE 62). As his commitment to moral pluralism would suggest, he objects to Christian morality only in its most virulent political form, insofar as it arrogates to itself a universal application across all of humankind; as we have seen, this objection is sustained strictly on political, rather than epistemological or theological, grounds. He consequently aims to disabuse his readers of the belief that Christian morality is coextensive with morality itself: "I negate a type of morality that has become prevalent and predominant as morality itself—the morality of decadence or, more concretely, *Christian* morality" (EH XIV:4). He thus explains that his self-awarded title, "the immoralist," designates an opposition specifically to *Christian* morality, which in his day held (or so he believed) a virtual monopoly over ethical life throughout the diverse cultures of Western civilization (EH XIV:6).

As an alternative to the moral monism he detects at the rotten core of Christianity, Nietzsche espouses a moral pluralism that reflects the rich diversity of human types, while reminding us that these moralities vary in worth as widely as the individuals whose needs and perfections they express:

> Moralities must be forced to bow first of all before the *order of rank*; their presumption must be brought home to their conscience—until they finally reach agreement that it is *immoral* to say: "what is right for one is fair for the other." (BGE 221)

Indeed, a primary aim of Nietzsche's perfectionism is to promote the design of hierarchically organized political regimes, each of which would simultaneously sustain several grades of morality. The aristocratic regimes he favors would shelter a pyramidal hierarchy of ethical communities, each equipped with a distinctive morality that reflects its unique needs and strengths.[4] At the pinnacle of this pyramidal structure would stand the community of agonistic "friends" founded by the *Übermensch*.

As modernity nears exhaustion, the pyramidal structure of this hierarchy of moral communities becomes deformed accordingly, flattened by the glacial advance of decadence. In times such as these, Nietzsche recommends a renewed vigilance to the order of rank that separates human types:

> The more normal sickliness becomes among men . . . the higher should be the honor accorded the rare cases of great power of soul and body, humankind's *lucky strikes*; the more we should protect the well-constituted from the worst kind of air, the air of the sickroom. (GM III:14)

In order to resist collectively the decadence of late modernity, he urges his "friends" to band together, seeking strength in numbers and prophylaxis in seclusion:

> And therefore let us have good company, *our* company! . . . So that we may, at least for a while yet, guard ourselves, my friends, against the two worst contagions that may be reserved just for us—against the *great nausea at man!* against *great pity for man!* (GM III:14)

While it is not entirely inaccurate to portray Nietzsche as an amoral champion of autarkic individualism, we might think of him more precisely as a moral pluralist, who eschews the claims of any morality to a universal compass across the (potentially) wide expanse of human types:

> what is fair for one *cannot* by any means for that reason alone also be fair for others; . . . the demand of one morality for all is detrimental for the higher men; in short, . . . there is an order of rank between man and man, hence also between morality and morality. (BGE 228)

The most exacting moralities, those which assign the greatest privileges *and* responsibilities, are operative in the lives of the rarest and most exotic human beings. As evidence of his own exemplary standing relative to most of his contemporaries, Nietzsche reserves a "stricter" morality for himself and his unknown "friends" (BGE 219, 226).

Just as he opposes the moral monism of Christianity, so he refuses to prescribe his own "stricter" morality to those who are not of his kind. While he would clearly welcome the renascence of some descendant strain of the recessive "noble" morality, he just as clearly understands that any such morality would appeal only to a limited number of human beings. Indeed, although the ethical dimension of his perfectionism is not intended to serve demotic interests, it *is* fully compatible with a demotic morality that is properly bounded in scope and application. He consequently prefers those aristocratic political regimes that shelter multiple moralities simultaneously, including a demotic morality designed to alleviate the suffering of the incurably sick and infirm.

Nietzsche's love of solitude is well known. The specific form of solitude he praises, however, derives its appeal from its dependence on a logically prior ethical community. As Zarathustra discovers only after repeated *Untergänge*, solitude independent of community is indistinguishable from loneliness. Nietzsche speaks fondly and repeatedly of his unknown "friends," precisely because they represent a community from which his self-imposed exile involves only a temporary respite. These "friends," many of whom he draws from the pages of history or from the nether reaches of his febrile imagination, inspire him to persevere in his solitary task. The imaginary "free spirits," for example, were summoned in order that their "brave companionship" might "keep [him] in good spirits while surrounded by ills" (H I:P:2).

These communitarian and pluralist currents in Nietzsche's political thinking furthermore reflect his lifelong yearning for a community in which he might realize his destiny as a philosopher and lawgiver. Here we recall his founding membership in Germania and the Leipzig Philological Society; his complicated Oedipal alliance with the Wagners in Tribschen; his fantasies (including Peter Gast, his friend and amanuensis) of a Knightly Brotherhood of the *gaya scienza*; his proposal to Lou Salomé and Paul Rée of an intellectual *ménage à trois*; and his imagination in 1887–88 of a "subterranean" Nietzsche cult growing among "radical parties" in Europe (excepting Germany) and North America.[5]

As these examples indicate, however, Nietzsche's impulse toward community is characteristically deflected by his tendency to identify only with imaginary communities, including those of the mythical past and future. Availing himself freely of his prodigious powers of imagination, he regularly identifies himself as party to a contrived or fictitious collective: "we scholars," "we free spirits," "we Hyperboreans," "we Europeans of the day after tomorrow," "we philologists," "we psychologists," "we revaluers," and so on. He readily admits, for example, that he invented the "free spirits" to whom he dedicated *Human, All Too Human*, explaining that "these brave companions and familiars" served "as compensation for the friends [he] lacked" (H I:P2).

Since he never specifies an existing audience with which he identifies his most basic hopes and desires (a luxury unavailable to his rival, the phonocentric Socrates), his ethical thinking operates at a level of generality and abstraction that is inimical to the creation of new communities and the cultivation of existing ones. Like (Groucho) Marx, Nietzsche would never deign to join a community that would have him as a member. Rather than identify his aims and aspirations with those of any existing community, he saves himself for a transhistorical community that is worthy of the allegiance of his beautiful soul.

While this strategy of endless deferral surely involves a romantic flight from the present and the concrete, it also illuminates some of the perils of community, which Nietzsche's critics occasionally neglect to reckon accurately. His prolonged solitude clearly exacts a heavy toll, but it also enables him to resist the (decadent) impulse to seek recognition from those "beneath" himself. Since he cannot rely on the hygienic stratification of a hierarchical society to insulate him from the resentment of the weak and bedraggled, he must protect his pursuit of self-perfection by imposing his own regimen of prophylactic solitude. He thus identifies the refusal of community as a prerequisite of his own moral growth (EH II:8), and he observes that the preference for solitude over unworthy company often constitutes a sign of health (EH I:2).

Rather than treat solitude as necessarily a privation, to be recuperated by the flowering of community, Nietzsche views community as an accidental, outward extension of one's ownmost self, which, under the best of conditions, honors and commemorates the self-sufficiency of the noble soul. Healthy individuals thus value community not as the precondition of their redemption and becoming whole, but as an opportunity to revel in the externalized emanations of their own virtue and character. Hence only weak, corrupt souls, whose constitutive misery leads them to crave the distractions and diversions of facile companionship, need be alone in solitude: "a well-turned-out person . . . is always in his own company, whether he associates with books, human beings, or landscapes: he honors by *choosing*, by *admitting*, by *trusting*" (EH I:2). A thriving moral community that requires no other living human members: perhaps no image conveys more accurately than this the peculiar ethical content of Nietzsche's perfectionism. As we shall see later on in more detail, he defends this principled aversion to unworthy community as a corollary to his highest (and sole) moral obligation.

There is no prima facie warrant, then, for excluding Nietzsche's perfectionism from consideration as the source of a bona fide ethical position. The point of his perfectionism is to shelter the delicate resources of ethical life and to preserve the possibility of the sort of moral development that constitutes an enhancement of humankind as a whole. The ethical content of his perfectionism may be objectionable to liberal critics, but these objections are themselves open to philosophical scrutiny and evaluation. Nietzsche himself would maintain that all such objections bespeak the pre-philosophical prejudices of his critics; as such, they would reveal much more about these critics than they do about his perfectionism.

Nietzsche and Manu: Moralities of Breeding

Nietzsche's discussion of a kindred political thinker sheds clarifying light on the ethical content of his perfectionism. Both in *Twilight of the Idols* and *The Antichrist(ian)*, he expresses his admiration for Manu, the legendary Hindu lawgiver. Nietzsche recommends the law of Manu not as a blueprint for political reform in late modernity, but as evidence of the importance "noble" cultures have traditionally attached to the morality of breeding. While the restoration of political aristocracy is simply out of the question for late modernity, a (modified) morality of breeding, as established by Nietzsche's perfectionism, is not.

On Nietzsche's reconstruction, Manu successfully enforced a political regime that enabled several distinct social classes to flourish simultaneously. Manu understood that the enhancement of Hindu culture would require the prophylaxis supplied by a fairly rigid social stratification. His regime effectively quarantined the relatively "sick" from the relatively "healthy," while providing for the relative well-being of all social classes. The ethical motivation behind Manu's system is the perfectionism that Nietzsche too advocates: "To set up a code of laws after the manner of Manu means to give a people the chance henceforth to become master, to become perfect—to aspire to the highest art of life" (AC 57).

Nietzsche consequently credits Manu with designing a political organization and social structure that reflect the order of Nature itself:

> The *order of castes*, the supreme, the dominant law, is merely the sanction of a *natural order*, a natural lawfulness of the first rank, over which no arbitrariness, no "modern idea" has any power . . . The order of castes . . . is necessary for the preservation of society, to make possible the higher and the highest types. (AC 57)

Following Manu (and Nature), Nietzsche endorses the pyramidal caste system, or "natural aristocracy," as the supreme form of political regime.

His characterization of the three "castes" of Nature—distinguished, respectively, by pre-eminent spirituality, pre-eminent strength "in muscle and temperament," and by mediocrity (AC 57)—bears a remarkable resemblance to Socrates' sketch of his pyramidal "city in speech" in the *Republic*.[6] As we shall soon see, Nietzsche also follows Socrates (and Manu) in furnishing a "noble lie" about the origins and justification of the political regime he recommends.

Nietzsche admires Manu for his commitment to *the morality of breeding*, wherein the lawgiver establishes the social preconditions of a plurality of types, from which in turn rare and exotic specimens are most likely to emerge (TI VII:3). Like Manu, Nietzsche tracks the enhancement of humankind to the proliferation of unanticipated, unimagined human types, and he endorses the political project of "breeding" these exemplary human beings. He contrasts this approach to political legislation with the *morality of taming*, of which he cites Western Christianity as representative. Whereas "breeding" encourages the simultaneous flourishing of a plurality of forms of life, "taming" imposes upon all forms of life a single ideal, with respect to which the higher, more exotic types must be broken down:

> Physiologically speaking: in the struggle with beasts, to make them sick *may* be the only means for making them weak. This the church understood: it *ruined* man, it weakened him—but it claimed to have "improved" him. (TI VII:2)

These competing approaches to political legislation are predicated on diametrically opposed ethical principles. A morality of taming structures society in accordance with a predetermined ideal, while a morality of breeding establishes a political order in which a plurality of forms of life is pursued—including, for the highest types, a form of life that is unfettered by all known ideals. He dismisses "idealism" in any guise as "cowardice," as a "flight from reality" (EH XIV:3), for ideals invariably place preordained constraints on the range of human types that a society might produce. Like Manu, Nietzsche is an "immoralist." He refrains from proposing a single ideal in accordance with which all types must be domesticated; instead he encourages an untamed proliferation of rare and exotic individuals.[7]

If a morality of breeding is to succeed in producing exemplary specimens, then the lawgiver must eventually exclude those types that pose an immediate threat to the flourishing of the society as a whole. Hence the ethical arch-principle that engenders Nietzsche's admiration for hierarchically organized political regimes: "That the sick should *not* make the healthy sick . . . should surely be our supreme concern on earth" (GM III:14). The implementation of this hygienic principle thus affords each stratum of society the prophylactic luxury of *not* associating with lower, pathogenic strata (GM I:10).

Manu understood, as few since have, that only structure and stratification beget the fecund plurality from which rare specimens spring forth; the more exacting the discipline, the more exotic the emergent fruits and blossoms.[8] Unlike Nature, which can afford to be a "bad economist" (SE 7), the lawgiver must legislate the terms of exclusion and expenditure.[9] As a means of ensuring the success of the morality of breeding he implemented, Manu legislated the exclusion of the impure chandalas, whom his political regime simply could not accommodate. Manu understood the need both to exclude the chandalas *and* to render them politically impotent, lest their exclusion strengthen and embolden them (TI VII:3).

The cruelty of Manu's exclusionary legislations is palpable, for the chandalas are in no way responsible for falling outside the arbitrary class designations that he enforces; nor do they deserve the harsh, inhuman treatment they receive.[10] Yet some such cruelty is necessary if the morality of breeding is to succeed, and Manu's appeal to the purity of social caste furnishes his political regime with the sustaining myth it needs in order to "justify" the cruelty it inflicts. While it may be possible for modern lawgivers to temper the cruelty of Manu's legislations—through improvements in technology and distributive justice, or through the invention of more humane forms of exclusion—the practice of exclusion is itself unavoidable.

Nietzsche does not personally advocate the caste system developed by Manu, but he fully endorses the willed practice of political exclusion, which Manu's system was designed to convey. With respect to this precise point, he does not mince his words:

> The essential characteristic of a good and healthy aristocracy, however, is that it . . . accepts with a good conscience the sacrifice of untold human beings who, *for its sake*, must be reduced and lowered to incomplete human beings, to slaves, to instruments. (BGE 258)[11]

Nietzsche thus presents slavery as a necessary, indispensable practice in those hierarchically organized societies that contribute to the permanent enhancement of humankind (BGE 44), a practice he associates with spiritual husbandry: "Slavery is, as it seems, both in the cruder and in the more subtle sense, the indispensable means of spiritual discipline and cultivation, too" (BGE 188).

Although it turns out that he is more interested in the sort of "slavery" that one imposes on oneself in the cultivation of one's soul, his peculiar, metaphorical use of the term "slavery" is itself a concession to the besetting decadence of his epoch. If *real* slavery were possible in late modernity—that is, if the establishment of an aristocratic political regime were a viable option in the twilight of the idols—then he would surely, and unabashedly, endorse it as a precondition of the perfectionism he advocates. And although he might prefer the practice of slavery in its "more subtle sense," allowing the "slaves," for example, an (illusory) feeling of their freedom and self-determination, he also justifies the institution of slavery by appealing to the "moral imperative of Nature," which is directed, he insists, at humankind itself (BGE 188).

Nietzsche thus views the practice of exclusion as an inescapable element—a "necessary evil," as it were—of political legislation in any regime. In order for a society to produce a few whole human beings, it must legislate and enforce the fragmentation of countless others. Only by virtue of this exclusion is culture—an artificial subsystem sheltered within the indifferent economy of Nature—possible at all. He thus insists that "the greatest of all tasks, the attempt to raise humanity higher, includ[es] the relentless destruction of everything that [is] degenerating and parasitical" (EH IV:4). It is simply the nature of politics, he believes, that all regimes must practice exclusion, whether or not they do so knowingly and resolutely. Despite their visceral aversion to Manu's grisly decrees, modern lawgivers are no more at liberty to dispense with political exclusion than to reprise his specific practice of it. The morality of taming too practices a form of exclusion, insofar as it forces all higher, singular types to lie in a Procrustean bed of its own mediocre design (TI IX:43); it too justifies its exclusionary practices by appealing to a sustaining myth, that of "*equal* rights for all" (CW 7).

While Manu is by no means alone in practicing exclusion, he distinguishes himself—at least in Nietzsche's mind—by subjecting this practice to willful legislation. Manu does not require the implementation of exclusionary stratifications; Nature does (AC 57). But Manu *wills* the practice of exclusion, furnishing it with a particular aspect and *modus operandi* within the caste system he designs; he unflinchingly inscribes the canon of Nature into the constitution of his political regime. Rather than consign to chance the regulation of his political regime, Manu legislates the exclusionary practices that will best promote his morality of breeding. Nietzsche consequently admires Manu not for practicing exclusion *per se* (which all lawgivers must do), nor for the specific practices he implements, but for doing so as a matter of design.

Nietzsche is no champion of democracy, but he believes that demotic interests are best served in hierarchical political regimes devoted to the breeding and production of exemplary human beings. All members of a thriving community are, and should be, elevated by the "immoral" exploits of its highest exemplars. While this elevation is least visible (and least appreciated) within the demotic stratum of a hierarchical society, he nevertheless insists, like J.S. Mill, that some attenuated benefits of perfectionism trickle down to everyone.[12] Unlike the "flathead" Mill, however, Nietzsche does not propose the benefits of involuntary cultural elevation as a justification for the perfectionism he legislates. With reference to the "higher" human types, he declares that

> Their right to exist, the privilege of the full-toned bell over the false and cracked, is a thousand times greater: they alone are our *warranty* for the future, they alone are *liable* for the future of humankind. (GM III:14)

A utilitarian defense of perfectionism, such as the one Mill concocts, would not only yoke political legislation to the tyrannical whims of ochlocratic taste—a problem Mill never adequately solved—but would also presuppose that the *demos* can in fact recognize and pursue its own best interests, which Nietzsche expressly denies.[13] It is an unalterable fact of political life that most individuals fail to discern, much less appreciate, the spiritual and material elevation they derive from their involuntary contributions to the production of exemplary human beings. This fact is not sufficient, however, to deter Nietzsche from his promotion and defense of perfectionism.

In order to obviate the disaffection of the demotic stratum of a hierarchical society, and thereby attend to its genuine (as opposed to its perceived) self-interest, the lawgiver must always reinforce the perfectionist aims of the regime with a sustaining myth. Toward this end, Nietzsche recommends the use of state-sponsored religions to elevate the *demos* against its will:

> To ordinary human beings, finally—the vast majority who exist for service and the general advantage, and who *may* exist only for that—religion gives an inestimable contentment with their situation and type, manifold peace of the heart, an ennobling of obedience, one further happiness and sorrow with their peers and something transfiguring and beautifying, something of a justification for the whole everyday character, the whole lowliness, the whole half-brutish poverty of their souls. Religion and religious significance spread the splendor of the sun over such ever-toiling human beings and make their own sight tolerable to them. (BGE 61)

State-sponsored religions thus furnish and perpetuate the sustaining myths of a hierarchically organized society, which in turn supply "ordinary human beings" with the solace and comfort they need. It should be noted, moreover, that state-sponsored religions also function to co-opt the disaffections that invariably suffuse the barren souls of "ordinary human beings," thereby preventing, or at least dampening, explosive outbreaks of resentment within the lowest strata of society.

Nietzsche often associates the perfectionism he advocates with aristocratic political regimes, which, as his critics observe, are incompatible with the depleted vitality he attributes to late modernity. If his perfectionism required the structure and discipline that aristocratic regimes alone can supply, then his ethical and political thinking would be hopelessly anachronistic; his vision of the future of humankind would be incompatible with his critique of modernity. He may yearn for the halcyon days of the Roman Empire and the Florentine Republics, but he is not so foolish as to confuse those days with his own. He unabashedly admires Manu as a lawgiver, but he neither recommends nor advocates Manu's aristocratic regime as a viable solution to the unique political problems of modernity. The institutions of modernity are simply too corrupt to impress into service as he would have us believe Manu did, and he is too decadent to supply the requisite nomothesis in any event. The "philosophers of the future" may someday successfully emulate Manu, Caesar or Napoleon in their political lawgiving, but Nietzsche cannot.[14]

The *Pathos* of Distance

In order to account for the legislative predilections that he shares with Manu and other "noble" souls, Nietzsche occasionally alludes to a "*pathos* of distance" resident within himself. Although he usually associates this *pathos* of distance with the aristocratic regimes he expressly admires, its existence is not dependent on any particular form of political regime. Indeed, his own *pathos* of distance not only suggests the viability of his perfectionism in the twilight of the idols, but also secures his claim to the hyperopic perspective of the "immoral" lawgiver.

Nietzsche introduces the *pathos* of distance as definitive of the "noble" mode of evaluation, describing it as

> the protracted and domineering fundamental total feeling on the part of a higher ruling order in relation to a lower order, to a "below"—*that* is the origin of the antithesis "good" and "bad." (GM I:2)

This *pathos* of distance, he later explains, is "characteristic of every strong age," for it expresses "the cleavage between man and man, status and status, the plurality of types, the will to be oneself, to stand out" (TI IX:37). As we shall see, a diminished "*pathos* of distance" not only is possible in decadent epochs like late modernity, but also may sustain in these twilight epochs a modest morality of breeding.

The *pathos* of distance signifies an enhanced sensibility for, or attunement to, the order of rank that "naturally" informs the rich plurality of human types. According to Nietzsche, the *pathos* of distance animates those aristocratic regimes that he most admires:

> Every enhancement of the type "man" has so far been the work
> of an aristocratic society . . . that believes in the long ladder of
> an order of rank and differences in value between man and man,
> and that needs slavery in some sense or another. (BGE 257)

He furthermore associates the absence or diminution of this *pathos* of distance with decadence and decline: "Today nobody has the courage any longer for privileges, for masters' rights, for a sense of respect for oneself and one's peers—for a *pathos of distance*" (AC 43).

While Nietzsche usually discusses the *pathos* of distance in the context of his praise for aristocratic political regimes, the motivation for his celebration of this *pathos* of distance—and of aristocracy itself, for that matter—is distinctly ethical. His perfectionism, which shelters the ethical core of his thought, not only is separable from the particular structure provided by political aristocracy, but also operates independently of this and any other particular form of political regime. As he explains, it is not the aristocratic political regime itself that stimulates human flourishing, but the *pathos* of distance sustained therein:

> Without that *pathos of distance* which grows out of the ingrained
> difference between strata . . . that other, more mysterious *pathos*
> could not have grown up either—the craving for an ever new
> widening of distances within the soul itself, the development of
> ever higher, rarer, more remote, further-stretching, more compre-
> hensive states—in brief, simply the enhancement of the type
> "man," the continual "self-overcoming of man," to use a moral
> formula in a supra-moral sense. (BGE 257)

In this passage, Nietzsche discloses the ethical core of his perfectionism. The permanent enhancement of humankind is attributable to the attainment of ever rarer states of the soul. This "aristocracy of the soul" is in turn the product of an internal *pathos* of distance, a "mysterious" craving for multiplicity and stratification within the soul itself. Nietzsche thus believes that the internal *pathos* of distance is itself instilled (or nourished) by the external *pathos* of distance evoked by any stable political aristocracy. As we shall see later on, this mysterious craving for internal distance either is, or is related to, *erōs*.

The attraction for Nietzsche of aristocratic regimes thus lies in their capacity to accommodate and implement human design. The rigid hierarchical stratification that he generally recommends is maximally effective at insulating political legislation from accident and chance. Aristocratic political regimes enable the lawgiver to intervene in Nature, to correct for Nature's indifference, and to assume (limited) dominion over the continued enhancement of the species. He consequently favors aristocratic political regimes, but only because they preserve and embellish the *pathos* of distance, which he in turn reveres for its evocation of a craving for "self-overcoming." As we shall see, "self-overcoming" is Nietzsche's preferred term for the moral content of his perfectionism.

Our attention to the *pathos* of distance thus reveals the ethical basis of Nietzsche's perfectionism. Natural aristocracy is the best form of political regime *not* in the sense that all peoples and epochs ought to aspire to its grandeur, but in the sense that it expresses the highest degree of strength and vitality known to humankind. With few exceptions, political regimes will accurately reflect the vitality of the peoples and ages they serve; for the most part, human beings establish the best political regimes they can also afford to sustain. While aristocracy is grander than democracy as an expression of an epoch's vitality, it is not a better regime for those epochs that can afford only democracy. Nature always requires the pyramidal organization that aristocracy attains most perfectly, but it does not always supply the lawgiver with the tools and materials to fashion an aristocratic political regime. In that event, lacking the macropolitical resources needed to reprise the law of Manu, the lawgiver must aspire instead to reproduce Nature's pyramid in diminished miniature.

Nietzsche consequently defends aristocratic regimes, but only insofar as they nurture (or preserve) the *pathos* of distance that alone enables moral development. His notorious fascination with the morality of breeding is similarly grounded in ethical concerns: by preserving the stratification of types—and the *pathos* of distance it evokes—the morality of breeding sustains the possibility of moral progress. The morality of taming, on the other hand, elides the difference between types, thus threatening to extinguish the *pathos* of distance that genuine moral progress necessarily presupposes.

As a political thinker, then, Nietzsche is a consequentialist, for he aims to impress politics into the service of ethics. Political regimes are valuable only insofar as they enable psychic regimes, rather than the other way around. He favors political aristocracy as the form of institutional organization that is most conducive to the "aristocracy of soul" that he associates with nobility, but it is by no means a necessary condition of self-perfection.[15] The essential element of his political thinking lies not in his yearning for an institutionally reinforced hierarchy, but in his perfectionism. While the former requires a degree of strength and vitality unknown to late modernity, the latter is in principle compatible even with the depleted resources of Nietzsche's own epoch.

We need not conclude, then, that his political thinking is either hopelessly anachronistic or irrelevant to the peculiar conditions of late modernity, for his perfectionism *can* operate independently of his romantic yearnings for political aristocracy. So long as a culture preserves some minimal *pathos* of distance, expressed however faintly in some trace of pyramidal structure, the permanent enhancement of humankind remains possible. Isolating the ethical content of his perfectionism is crucial to our understanding of his project, for in the event that an aristocratic regime were no longer possible (as is the case in late modernity), he could still advocate the perfectionism that lies at the heart of his political thinking.

Nietzsche offers no further defense of his preference for the morality of breeding, and the reason for his silence is simple: the *pathos* of distance does not admit of further, theoretical justification. Lawgivers are "justified" not by virtue of some epistemic privilege, divine decree, natural right or Promethean insight, but simply by virtue of their audacious desire to subject to design what naturally falls to chance. The sole justification for a lawgiver's decrees resides exclusively in the vision of humankind that informs them. Nietzsche consequently does not pretend to offer any further justification for his morality of breeding than the products of such "breeding" personally embody. One either shares his attunement to the *pathos* of distance that motivates his perfectionism, or one does not.

The perceived need to advance or receive a theoretical justification of political legislation is symptomatic, he believes, of the decadence of modernity. A healthy people or age neither demands nor requires a discursive justification for its legislations:

> What must first be proved is worth little. Wherever authority
> still forms part of good bearing, where one does not give reasons
> but commands, the dialectician is a kind of buffoon: one laughs
> at him, one does not take him seriously. (TI II:5)

Nobility is expressed simply in the attempt to create or preserve an order of rank in the face of the indifference of Nature; the noble soul consequently requires no prior or independent justification of its creations. A decadent people or age, on the other hand, which cannot afford to squander its dwindling resources, generally resolves to expend itself only if given good reason to do so, usually in the form of a discursive justification. Only decadent peoples need to justify the practices and policies whereby they express their signature virtues, and only decadent peoples bemoan the absence of such justifications. The conspicuous failure of Nietzsche's critics to satisfy the very conditions of justification to which they hold him suggests that he may have a point.

3
Perfectionism in the Twilight of the Idols

> The whole of the West no longer possesses the instincts out of which institutions grow, out of which a *future* grows: perhaps nothing antagonizes its "modern spirit" so much. One lives for the day, one lives very fast, one lives very irresponsibly: precisely this is called "freedom." That which makes an institution an institution is despised, hated, repudiated: one fears the danger of a new slavery the moment the word "authority" is even spoken out loud.
>
> —*Twilight of the Idols*, IX:39

In response to his own diagnosis of the decadence of modernity, Nietzsche rethinks his endorsement of political perfectionism. While he would like nothing better than to contribute to the establishment of an aristocratic regime, he also realizes that the depleted vitality of modernity is simply incompatible with the political perfectionism he envisions. His subsequent shift in emphasis to *moral* perfectionism not only is consistent with his critique of modernity, but also conveys the priority he has always assigned to ethics over politics. In order to assess more precisely the moral content of his perfectionism, I turn now to examine his post-Zarathustran critique of modernity.

Nietzsche's Critique of Modernity

Nietzsche originally conceived of the production of exemplary human beings as a macropolitical task, which would mobilize (and justify) the political institutions of the modern nation state. Although he isolates the "disease" of modernity in its senescent educational institutions, he nevertheless believes that they can be rejuvenated sufficiently "to establish a permanent alliance between German and Greek culture" (BT 20). He actively opposes any political solution on the part of the newly established

Reich, but he nevertheless recommends a reorganization of German educational institutions, such that they might produce as a matter of design the exemplary individuals who have emerged heretofore only as accidents of Nature.

While his public lectures on "The Future of Our Educational Institutions," which he delivered early in 1872, warn of the creeping mediocrity of higher education, and of the yawning gulf that separates education from genuine culture, they collectively sound a call to arms rather than a requiem.[1] The political macrosphere is still a salvageable shelter for ethical life, provided that he and Wagner can infuse the new *Reich* with a tonic appreciation for tragedy:

> Let no one try to blight our faith in a yet-impending rebirth of
> Hellenic antiquity; for this alone gives us hope for a renovation
> and purification of the German spirit through the fire magic of
> music. (BT 20)

As this passage demonstrates, the young, professorial Nietzsche exudes the very optimism that *The Birth of Tragedy* disparagingly attributes to Socrates.

Following his "discovery" of the decadence of modernity, however, Nietzsche realizes that his earlier faith in the salvageability of modern institutions was egregiously misplaced. He consequently withdraws his plans for macropolitical reform, and he does so in two identifiable steps. First, he acknowledges that the institutions of modern Europe are simply too corrupt to serve in the macropolitical capacity he had mistakenly reserved for them.[2] Although he argues that institutions have functioned historically as the crucibles of culture, wherein human animals have been forcibly "civilized," cruelly implanted with memories and painfully invested with "the right to make promises" (GM II:2), he also insists that the institutions of Western civilization, those "bulwarks of political organization" (GM II:18), have gradually usurped the task of consecrating individuals to culture. The institutional reinforcement of the morality of taming, euphemistically known as the "improvement-morality," now threatens to extinguish the *pathos* of distance upon which culture is founded.

The institutions of bygone epochs may have been amenable to the production of exemplary human beings, but the macropolitical resources of modernity are arrayed in a manner inimical to this task. "In present-day Germany," he laments, "no one is any longer free to give his children a noble education" (TI VIII:5). Modernity is marked as an age by the cold, refined efficiency, the debilitating anonymity, of its sustaining institutions, which militate ever more perfectly against the emergence of singular human types. Great individuals now emerge only in opposition to institutional design, only in spite of the decadence of the age that spawns them (TI IX:44).

Second, he acknowledges that, independent of the macropolitical resources at his disposal, he is in no position to orchestrate the redemption of modernity. His critique of modernity may focus on the corruption of modern institutions, but it locates the cause or source of this corruption in an underlying cultural decadence, of which he interprets the demise of these institutions as symptomatic. He consequently observes that

> Our institutions are no good any more: on that there is universal agreement. However, it is not their fault but ours. Once we have lost the instincts out of which institutions grow, we lose institutions altogether because we are no longer good for them . . . The whole of the West no longer possesses the instincts out of which institutions grow, out of which a *future* grows. (TI IX:39)

Any attempt to bolster our sagging political institutions, independent of addressing the decadence they manifest, thus betrays a disastrous confusion of cause and effect:

> What will not be built any more henceforth, and *cannot* be built any more, is—a society [*Gesellschaft*] in the old sense of the word; to build that, everything is lacking, above all the material. *All of us are no longer material for a society*; this is a truth for which the time has come. (GS 356)

We must not underestimate the enormity of Nietzsche's claim that the "slave morality always first needs a hostile external world" (GM I:10). This means that any campaign to change, reform, or meliorate this "hostile external world" would also threaten to strip the "slaves" of their ownmost identity. As a consequence, the "slave" type, which supposedly dominates decadent epochs like late modernity, always maintains a vested interest in *not* reforming the "hostile external world" that it identifies as the source of its victimization and oppression.

In his post-Zarathustran writings, Nietzsche acknowledges the complicity of his original call for political reform with the decadence it presumed to combat. The fatal anachronism of his plan to reawaken the tragic muse lay in his conviction that he was somehow immune to the cultural disarray he detected. Armed with a moral ideal of his own to purvey—and a romantic ideal to boot—he unwittingly installed himself as yet another "improver of mankind." Arrogating to himself the privilege of the physician of culture, he blithely prescribed redemptive measures designed to cure the ills of modernity. His prescription of a Wagnerian rebirth of tragic culture thus marked one more expression of the advancing decadence of modernity.

He consequently concludes that presently there exists no macropolitical solution to the problem of decadence in late modernity. The "philosophers of the future" may someday arrive at one, but Nietzsche himself, rooted inextricably in the decadence he so despises, cannot. His writings of 1888 candidly pronounce his own decadence (EH I:2; CW P), thereby discrediting his presumed credentials as a physician of culture. In fact, his perception of a *need* in late modernity for exemplary human beings, who generally arise as an expression of surfeit rather than of lack, itself confirms that they are unlikely to appear as the willed products of a morality of breeding. He thus concedes that neither he nor the political institutions that fashioned him are likely to produce anything but alternate permutations of decay:

> It is a self-deception on the part of philosophers and moralists if they believe that they are extricating themselves from decadence when they merely wage war against it . . . [T]hey change its expression, but they do not get rid of decadence itself. (TI II:11)

Nietzsche thus regards the macropolitical agenda sketched in his early writings as historically naive, as woefully ignorant of the source of the decay of modern institutions:

> I now regret . . . that I appended hopes where there was no ground for hope, where everything pointed all too plainly to an end! . . . That on the basis of the latest German music I began to rave about "the German spirit" as if that were in the process even then of discovering and finding itself again—at a time when the German spirit, which not long before had still had the will to dominate Europe and the strength to lead Europe, was just making its testament and *abdicating* forever . . . (BT AS:6)

While he continues to voice his yearnings for a macropolitical "cure" for the decadence that besets modernity, he usually defers all such speculations to the "philosophers of the future" who will succeed him, or to his unreliable mouthpiece, Zarathustra. On topics such as these, to which he has no "right," it behooves him "only to be silent" (GM II:25).

How can Nietzsche so calmly document the demise of the very political institutions in which he had originally invested his hopes for the future? Is this withering critique of modernity not inhospitable to his vision of the future of humankind? He understands, and frequently reiterates, that the corruption of modern institutions is not the cause of decadence, but its most telling symptom. That "we are no good" for these institutions thus signals the advance, rather than the advent, of decadence.[3] He consequently ridicules the idea that we might combat decadence simply by easing the discomfort that attends it:

The supposed causes of degeneration are its consequences. But the supposed remedies of degeneration are also mere palliatives against some of its effects: the "cured" are merely one type of the degenerates. (WP 42)

In other words, the crisis of modernity is even more acute than he originally imagined, when he called for a rebirth of tragic culture. As a physiological affliction indelibly inscribed into the bodies of modern agents, decadence is encoded within the (disintegrating) ethos of modernity itself.

Yet the ethical resources of late modernity are not yet exhausted. The catalysis of culture continues, as evidenced by Nietzsche's own reliance on Schopenhauer as an *Erzieher*. The diffusion of the *pathos* of distance, of which he interprets the pandemic spread of democratic reforms as symptomatic, is not yet sufficiently entropic to preclude the possibility of the continued enhancement of humankind. Since a form of ethical life has survived the demise of the sustaining institutions of late modernity, future enhancements of humankind remain possible. While it is true that Nietzsche must modify his political agenda to accommodate the decadence of late modernity, there is no need yet for him to abandon politics altogether. Here, he believes, he differs from Socrates, who could not afford to sustain his own personal war against decadence in the absence of institutional support (TI II:12).

Rather than attempt directly to produce the redemptive exemplars who will warrant the future of the species, he undertakes to play a more modest and indirect role in the permanent enhancement of humankind. The overarching goal of his politics is to preserve the diminished *pathos* of distance that ensures the possibility of ethical life and moral development in late modernity. It is his specific task to convoke a gathering of those individuals who are best suited to survive the twilight of the idols, and to train these unlikely "heroes" in the experimental disciplines that are most likely to stave off the will to nothingness. This revised task requires fewer macropolitical resources, but it shifts the (diminished) burden of political legislation squarely onto his own stooped shoulders.

The Political Microsphere

Nietzsche's odyssey on the "open seas" ultimately transports him to the political microsphere, a destination unknown to him in his pre-Zarathustran career. While involved in his campaign to orchestrate the redemption of modernity, he characteristically restricted his focus to the political macrosphere, to the dying institutions he hoped to resuscitate. In response to the self-referential implications of his critique of modernity, however, he subsequently relocates his political program from the macrosphere to the microsphere.

In order to convey a sense of Nietzsche's revised role in the production of superlative human beings, I distinguish between the macropolitical (or institutional) and micropolitical (or infra-institutional) incarnations of his perfectionism. The political macrosphere comprises the network of relations that obtain between a people's institutions and its representative exemplars, while the political microsphere comprises those relations between a people and its representative exemplars that are *not* mediated by social institutions. Macropolitics governs the production of great human beings through the organization of institutional resources, while micropolitics governs the production and illumination of great human beings outside (or beneath) the institutional frameworks of civilization. Whether prosecuted in the macrosphere or in the microsphere, politics contributes to the enhancement of humankind through the legislative deployment of the ethical resources of the community.

We might think of the political microsphere on an organic model, as the vital core that engenders the signature legislations of a people or community, from which the political macrosphere extends outward as an involuntary, spontaneous outgrowth. The microsphere thus shelters the fund of vital resources upon which a people draws as it expresses (and memorializes) itself in the creation of institutions. Autochthonous folkways, tribal rituals, ethnic customs and memory traces, familial habits and mores, hieratic regimens of diet and hygiene: all contribute to the delicate, capillary network of ethical life in the political microsphere, from which the macrosphere emerges as a natural shell or mantle. These are the smoldering embers from which the Promethean fire of civilization draws its wondrous flame.

In a strong age overflowing with vital energy, externalized in the institutions and festivals of a healthy people, lawgivers would have neither the need nor the inclination to restrict their legislations to the political microsphere. But in a decadent age unable to sustain the vitality of a people's signature institutions, lawgivers have no choice but to legislate from within the political microsphere. If necessary, the micropolitical lawgiver must strategically inhabit the disintegrating institutions of the political macrosphere, parasitically draining their residual vitality for use in husbanding the resources of the microsphere. Indeed, Nietzsche's favorite "simile" for decadence is that of a vital core mantled within a dead husk or shell, such that "The whole no longer lives at all: it is composite, calculated, artificial, and artifact" (CW 7).

Nietzsche thus realizes that his contribution to the enhancement of humankind need not presuppose the macropolitical support of modern institutions. His perfectionism is compatible with cultures of virtually any degree of vitality, and it consequently requires only minimal institutional support. His retirement from macropolitics therefore does not signal the termination of his program to contribute to the production of superlative human beings. Rather than abandon entirely the idea of producing such exemplars by design, he relocates the site of this production to the political microsphere, where he and his fellow "free spirits" must foster the emergence of genius without the assistance of (and in fact in opposition to) institutional reinforcement. Indeed, his diagnosis of decadence suggests that the degeneration of modernity might actually contribute to the emergence of (a peculiar breed of) exemplary human beings:

> Great men, like great ages, are explosives in which a tremendous force is stored up; their precondition is always, historically and physiologically, that for a long time much has been gathered, stored up, saved up, and conserved for them—that there has been no explosion for a long time. (TI IX:44)

Ethical life continues to flourish in late modernity, but only in microcommunities that spring up around those representative exemplars whose self-perfections inscribe the canon of the law. Amid the collapse of the political macrosphere, these exemplars have assumed the mediating role traditionally played by political institutions. As we have seen, the relation between great human beings and "humanity as a whole" reflects the *pathos* of distance that suffuses a people or epoch. So long as the *pathos* of distance survives, an age will produce exemplary specimens, and so long as these heroes continue to perfect themselves, the *pathos* of distance will survive. The representative exemplars of late modernity are perhaps obnubilated by the twilight, or overlooked amid the rubble of fallen idols, but they remain capable nonetheless of contributing to the permanent enhancement of humankind.

The central role of these exemplary individuals in Nietzsche's perfectionism is not affected by his emigration to the political microsphere. Perhaps more confidently than ever, he appeals in his post-Zarathustran works to the importance of those individuals who embody the perfectibility of the human soul. He consequently shifts the burden of his perfectionism, which he originally expected macropolitical institutions to bear, entirely onto the microspheric legislations of the representative exemplars of late modernity. He now understands that it is the micropolitical responsibility of individual philosophers to produce such specimens by design—to become them if possible, and to invent them if necessary. Unable to rely on the macropolitical reinforcement of an aristocratic regime, he gambles that the "aristocracy of soul" exhibited by these exemplary types is sufficient to sustain and nurture an ethical community of unknown friends and followers.

It would be misleading, however, to suggest that Nietzsche's turn to micropolitics coincides with a wholesale disavowal of his investment in the macropolitical redemption of modernity. His "longing for total revolution,"[4]

and for its world-historical architects, persists to the conclusion of his productive career.[5] In his "review" of *The Birth of Tragedy*, for example, he
renews his "promise" of a tragic age, though he postpones its advent to a
more distant remove from the present; he also diverts the credit for this coming age from Wagner to himself (EH IV:4).

Nietzsche's attention to the political microsphere may occasionally
neutralize these romantic yearnings, but it neither erases nor eliminates
them. As expressions of his own decadence and resentment, however, his
political sentiments are of considerably less interest than the form in which
he presents them. Rather than recoil in horror from his retrograde elitist
yearnings, we might more fruitfully inquire: of what relevance to micropolitics is his admiration for the morality of breeding? As we shall see,
he (partially) recuperates his macropolitical yearnings by enlisting them
in his campaign to acquaint his readers with the ethical resources of the
microsphere.

Nietzsche's shift to the political microsphere also reprises a similar
dislocation in his personal life. In order to become a philosopher and reclaim the task [*Aufgabe*] reserved for him, he withdrew from the political
macrosphere as he understood it, resigning his professorship at Basel and
vanishing into a lonely, nomadic existence. Genuine philosophy, it would
seem, requires an immersion in the quotidian contingencies and fragile
relations of the microsphere. The real work of the philosopher is
performed not in stuffy lecture halls and musty archives, but on long,
solitary walks in the mountains, in poorly heated pensions, in deserted
train stations, on unfamiliar beaches. Rather than harangue university
students and continue to campaign for macropolitical reform, he courts
anonymity as a wanderer and sun-seeker, connected to the "world" he
leaves behind only through an erratic regimen of correspondence.

Nietzsche's immersion in the political microsphere thus reflects the
experimental nature of his own life and work. In order to see himself as
a political agent, he first had to situate himself within the microsphere of
late modernity and discipline himself to acknowledge the ethical resources
arrayed therein. He relocates his perfectionism to the political microsphere
only after personally testing it for himself. This proved to be an extremely
painful experiment, one which may have contributed significantly to his
eventual breakdown. It is perhaps no coincidence that Nietzsche returns
to the political macrosphere, promising to assassinate the religious and
secular leaders of Western Europe, only under the delusions of grandeur
wrought by his incipient madness.[6]

Light Amid the Shadows: An Attempt at Aesthetic Education

Nietzsche's perfectionism thus remains viable even in the twilight of the
idols, and we should expect superlative human beings to flourish even in

the gloaming of late modernity. These twilight "heroes" will remind no one of the world-historical conquerors who populate Nietzsche's fantasies, for they must reflect the decadence of the age they represent. They may nevertheless contribute to the ongoing catalysis of culture.

While it need not be the case, as Zarathustra seems to think, that late modernity is "too late" to produce *Übermenschen* of its own, the "higher men" of our epoch are not readily apparent to us. Nietzsche and Zarathustra may be partially responsible for our faulty vision, for they have trained us to look out for the beasts and heroes who represent vital epochs rather than the fools and invalids who stand for dying epochs. In order to educate the sensibilities of his readers and prepare them to partake of ethical life in the political microsphere, Nietzsche must isolate and illuminate those queer *Übermenschen* who labor in the twilight of the idols. As we shall see, the twin tasks of *creating* and *discovering* exemplary human beings are not readily distinguishable in the shadows of late modernity.

As a preparation for his revised political project, Nietzsche must refine somewhat the aesthetic sensibilities of his readers, thereby discouraging them from deferring to the world-historical heroes whom he and Zarathustra have led them to anticipate. He thus warns that

> [O]ne misunderstands great human beings if one views them from the miserable perspective of some public use. That one cannot put them to any use, that in itself may belong to greatness. (TI IX:50)

He consequently attempts to illuminate the ethical resources of the political microsphere, and to acquaint his readers with the "useless" squanderers who currently preside over the catalysis of culture.

Because "genuine philosophers" live "unphilosophically" and "unwisely" (BGE 205), however, they may also live obscurely. Eclipsed by the twilight of the idols, their pursuits of self-perfection go largely unnoticed, along with the micropolitical legislations they enact. In light of his critique of modernity, in fact, the micropolitical exemplars he has in mind must necessarily appear to us as buffoons, fools, misfits, miscreants, criminals, rogues, creatures of *ressentiment*, and anyone else who can muster even a minimal resistance to the decadence of modernity. In bringing to light the ethical resources of the microsphere, as we shall see, Nietzsche must become his own test case: the viability of his relocated perfectionism rests on his success in creating/discovering himself as an *Übermensch*.

Throughout his career, his perceived contribution to politics was dominated by the historical necessity of a prelude or preparation. As a young scholar, he presented *The Birth of Tragedy* as a prelude to a Wagnerian rebirth of tragic culture, and *Schopenhauer as Educator* as a blueprint for German educational reform. He later advertised *Beyond Good and Evil* as the "prelude to a philosophy of the future," describing his task in general as a preparation for the mysterious "philosophers of the future." His commitment to perfectionism similarly reflects this preparatory emphasis, for it obliges him to educate his readers to discern any *Übermenschen* who might roam the microsphere. While he is certainly not a "philosopher of the future," however, he must also beware of simply busying himself with the preparations for the future as he speculates on the advent of his successors. Once he relocates his political perfectionism within the microsphere, he must recover for himself the legislative role that he carves out for other micropolitical *Übermenschen*. Toward this end, he legislates his own self-creation as an exemplary human being.

This conclusion may prove difficult to accept, however, for Nietzsche obviously falls far short of the world-historical *Übermenschen* whom he and Zarathustra have led us to anticipate. When casting about for exemplary human beings, Nietzsche's readers customarily search for world-historical redeemers and conquerors, and he is largely responsible for fostering this false expectation. In order for us to see this cranky, infirm hermit as an exemplary human being, and thereby partake of the catalysis of culture to which he contributes, we must consequently revise our opinions of both Nietzsche and the *Übermensch*. Such a revision would require the precise reversal of perspective—wrought by an cultivation of aesthetic sensibilities—that he hopes to induce in his readers.

Moral Perfectionism

Nietzsche's shift in emphasis to the political microsphere places into sharper relief the moral perfectionism at work in his thought. While the depleted vitality of his epoch is admittedly inimical to the *political* perfectionism he wishes to pursue, the adverse conditions of late modernity are nevertheless compatible with his related project of *moral* perfectionism. Indeed, he can sustain the (revised) political dimension of his philosophy only because his project of moral perfectionism requires no greater political support than the microsphere can in fact furnish.

In an explicit response to John Rawls, Stanley Cavell has recently attempted to recover the distinctly ethical dimension of Nietzsche's perfectionism.[7] In defense of the position he calls *moral perfectionism*, Cavell interprets both Emerson and Nietzsche as

> calling for the further or higher self of each, each consecrating himself/herself to self-transformation, accepting one's own genius, which is precisely not, it is the negation of, accepting one's present state and its present consecrations to something fixed, as such, "beyond" one.[8]

Cavell thus presents Nietzsche's moral perfectionism as an unintended (and unacknowledged) casualty of Rawls's refusal to weigh the claims of perfectionism in his original position. In rejecting Nietzsche's perfectionism as a potential source of viable principles of justice, Rawls inadvertently vetoes a program of moral education that is uniquely suited to the training of citizens in a democratic society:

> [T]he view Emerson and Nietzsche share, or my interest in it, is not simply to show that [moral perfectionism] is tolerable to the life of justice in a constitutional democracy but to show how it is essential to that life . . . I understand the training and character and friendship Emerson requires for democracy as preparation to withstand not its rigors but its failures, character to keep the democratic hope alive in the face of disappointment with it.[9]

Cavell thus contends that moral perfectionism alone provides the "democratic training" required of all citizens who must abide by (though never consent to) the imperfect justice delivered by contemporary democracies.

Cavell's eloquent response, however, does not directly address Rawls's specific objections to Nietzsche's perfectionism. While it is not the case that Cavell conflates the moral perfectionism he champions with the political perfectionism Rawls rejects, he does fail to distinguish sharply between the two positions; as a consequence, the precise relationships that obtain between the two forms of perfectionism are left unarticulated and unclear.[10] In any event, it seems abundantly clear that liberals like Rawls should *always* beware of political theories and regimes that promise to curtail individual freedoms, irrespective of the "democratic" moral sentiments indirectly expressed by their founders and champions. In this limited sense, then, Rawls's misunderstanding of Nietzsche is irrelevant, for *no* moral teaching is sufficiently democratic to compensate for the illiberal excesses of Nietzschean perfectionism. In light of his pre-established allegiance to liberal ideals, Rawls is surely right (if not philosophically justified) to bar Nietzsche's perfectionism from consideration in the original position.

Although Cavell fails to address, and so to deflect, Rawls's suspicions of Nietzschean perfectionism, he nevertheless succeeds in transplanting the tangled debate into a more fertile field of inquiry. Indeed, by diverting our attention to the ethical core of Nietzsche's political thinking, Cavell implicitly limns a distinction between Nietzsche's *political* perfectionism and his less familiar *moral* perfectionism. While Rawls prudently rejects the former position, as patently illiberal, his undisclosed recoil from the latter position constitutes the most glaring fault in the foundation of his theory of justice. As we have seen, Nietzsche's political perfectionism is largely a vehicle or conveyance for the moral perfectionism that lies at the very heart of his philosophical enterprise. In denying Nietzsche entry into the original position, Rawls may rid political philosophy of some very murky bathwater, but only by expelling the only baby for whom the construction of a "theory of justice" is warranted. Although Cavell presents his account of "moral perfectionism" as a friendly amendment to Rawls's theory of justice, it seems likely that Rawls's original position is constructed precisely to obviate the moral education and "democratic training" that Cavell applauds in Nietzsche and Emerson.

Following Cavell's cue, we are now in a position to distinguish between the political and moral perfectionisms operative within Nietzsche's thought. Political perfectionism, as we have seen, provides for the rigid stratification and hierarchical organization of society and its resources, with the aim of producing, as a matter of design, those exemplary human beings whose exploits alone warrant the future of humankind. The aims of political perfectionism are best served by pyramidal aristocratic regimes, which not only reflect and preserve the natural order of rank among human types, but also encourage moral development by engendering a robust *pathos* of distance. On Nietzsche's account, the priority of political perfectionism resides in its justificatory capacity, for no political arrangement can better protect citizens from the perceived meaninglessness of their existence.

Nietzsche's moral perfectionism is perhaps best characterized in terms of the conviction that one's primary, overriding—and perhaps sole—ethical "obligation" is to attend to the perfection of one's ownmost self. Any "obligations" that one might choose to observe to others are strictly derivative of, and secondary to, the imperative to perfect oneself. While this general imperative appears in many diverse forms and formulations in the history of moral thought, it is typically conveyed via the language of *autonomy* and *authenticity*. Borrowing from Pindar, a predecessor moral perfectionist, Nietzsche exhorts himself and (some of) his readers with the slogan that he incorporates into the subtitle of his "autobiography": *become what you are*.[11]

As this Pindaric slogan suggests, the project of moral perfectionism involves cultivating one's native endowment of powers and faculties; eliciting from within oneself the perfections that lie dormant, undiscovered, or incomplete; and so fortifying one's soul with the virtues constitutive of a sterling character. One is obliged, in short, to strive to produce oneself as an *übermenschlich* human being. All moral "obligations" to others are simply illusory, either because they are in fact continuous with the project of perfecting one's ownmost self (as in many cases of charity and gift-giving, such as potlatch), or because they are fabricated by the creative resentment of those who cannot abide the successful self-perfection of others.

These two forms of perfectionism do not logically entail one another. While it is true that some political thinkers—Plato, Hegel and Nietzsche, for example—cleave to both forms of perfectionism, other thinkers defend only one or the other. Emerson, Mill, Wittgenstein, Sartre, and Berlin, for example, enthusiastically endorse versions of moral perfectionism, but they all vehemently refuse the palpable tyranny of political perfectionism. On the other hand, political thinkers such as Machiavelli and Dostoevsky's Grand Inquisitor, whose insights into human "nature" have been brutally implemented by totalitarian dictators, embrace the project of political perfectionism, while holding little hope for the general project of moral perfectionism. In an interesting hybrid case, Richard Rorty endorses the project of moral perfectionism (which he calls the pursuit of autonomy), but he relegates it to the private sphere; this may be tantamount to proscribing all vital forms of moral perfectionism. Still other theorists, such as Rawls, reject the claims of both forms of perfectionism, as inimical to the "freedom from shame" that is ideally enjoyed by self-respecting citizens of liberal democratic societies.[12]

In Nietzsche's own case, political perfectionism serves in a largely instrumental capacity, as a vehicle for his more basic project of moral perfectionism. Although he publicly endorses both forms of perfectionism, he defends political perfectionism only because, and insofar as, it promises to deliver the social conditions that are most conducive to moral perfectionism.[13] In decadent epochs like late modernity, however, which cannot muster the resources needed to sustain the hygienic stratification inherent in a stable aristocratic regime, the project of political perfectionism must be modified significantly, if not abandoned altogether. Nietzsche's critique of modernity thus occasions a shift in emphasis from political to moral perfectionism; while the former project is simply incompatible with the advanced decay of late modernity, the other is not.

The logical independence of these two forms of perfectionism is crucial to an understanding of Nietzsche's post-Zarathustran political thinking, especially in light of his withering critique of modernity. As Cavell observes, those critics who, like Rawls, oppose Nietzsche's political perfectionism generally fail (or refuse) to detect its distinctly moral warrant and motivation. Though perhaps damaging in some way to his political perfectionism, their criticisms consequently fail to touch, much less to damage, his project of moral perfectionism.

Nietzsche himself does not use the term "moral perfectionism." He describes Schopenhauer, whom he never met and with whom he later would express profound disagreement, quite simply as his "teacher and taskmaster [*Lehrer und Zuchtmeister*]" (SE 1). This rare combination of virtues (galvanized by a chance visit to a Leipzig bookshop) ordains Schopenhauer as Nietzsche's *Erzieher*—his educator. Indeed, the perfectionism for which Nietzsche is routinely vilified in fact shelters a program of moral education, which is supposed to produce as a matter of design those exemplary individuals who unintentionally and unwittingly preside over the catalysis of culture.

Nietzsche does not have in mind here the sort of Gradgrindian education that transforms people into "machines" by teaching them "to be bored" (TI IX:29). His understanding of moral education, as of the nature of ethical life in general, evinces his substantial intellectual debt to Emerson. The term *erziehen* suggests a process of eliciting, or drawing out, the "hidden" powers and perfections resident in oneself and a few others. His political perfectionism thus establishes the social conditions that are most conducive to an education of the highest human types, while his moral perfectionism comprises this education itself. By provoking its greatest exemplars to embody perfections hitherto unknown to humanity, an educational program of this scope would contribute to the permanent enhancement of humankind itself.

As an aspiring *Erzieher* in his own right, Nietzsche writes only for those who share his aesthetic sensibilities, and for those who *may* someday accede to this lofty rank if properly educated. In both cases the pedagogical aim of his writing is neither to convert nor to "improve" his readers, but to announce himself to kindred spirits and fellow squanderers. His moral pedagogy is designed not to "cure" the sick and infirm, but to embolden and encourage the healthy—much as his "friends," the fictitious free spirits, served as "brave companions and familiars" during his own convalescence (H I:P:2). He not only addresses those readers who might be exemplary human beings, but also encourages anyone who can afford to do so to appreciate these exotic and endangered plants wherever they might bloom.

Moral Perfectionism and/as Ethical Egoism

Nietzsche's moral perfectionism may very well amount to a version of ethical egoism, as critics often charge. Yet he is keen to purge "egoism" of the taint foisted upon it by Christian morality and other vehicles of resentment:

> Rather it was only when aristocratic value judgments *declined* that the whole antithesis "egoistic"/"unegoistic" obtruded itself more and more on the human conscience—it is, to speak in my own language, the *herd instinct* that through this antithesis at last gets its word (and its *words*) in. (GM I:2)

Taking up this defense of egoism, Zarathustra distinguishes between the selfishness [*Selbstsucht*] born of health, which is marked by the "thirst to pile up all the riches in [one's] soul," and that born of sickness, which "sizes up those who have much to eat . . . and always sneaks around the table of those who give" (Z I:22.1). Echoing his loquacious "son," Nietzsche declares that

"Selflessness" has no value either on heaven or on earth. All great problems demand *great love*, and of that only strong, round, secure spirits who have a firm grip on themselves are capable. (GS 345)

This proposed rehabilitation of "selfishness" accounts for the only others to whom Nietzsche recognizes ethical obligations: one's "friends," those members of one's "kind" or "type," whose virtues and perfections mirror one's own. Following Aristotle, Nietzsche conceives of a friend as another "I," as an external instantiation of one's own virtuous character.[14] Friendship thus affords one the unique opportunity to behold—and celebrate—one's ownmost perfections from an "external" standpoint, as individuals possessed of sterling character are naturally inclined to do. Building on the pagan narcissism he applauds in Aristotle's thought, Nietzsche depicts friendship as a mutually empowering *agon*, in which select individuals undergo moral development through their voluntary engagement in contest and conflict. On this agonistic model of friendship, one has no ethical obligations to those who cannot contribute to one's own quest for self-perfection, those for whom Zarathustra reserves the disap-probative term *neighbor*. One may, of course, acknowledge various politi-cal obligations to one's "neighbors," but genuine ethical obligations to those outside one's "kind" are strictly ruled out. In fact, friends of high character must always guard their virtues jealously, lest vampiric "neigh-bors" insidiously distract them from the difficult task of self-perfection.

A formidable obstacle to this project of moral perfectionism lies, in fact, in the difficulty involved in undertaking an honest inventory of one's native endowment of virtues and faculties. Those who would perfect them-selves must first dare to stand beyond good and evil, for the conventional moral standpoint available to them will invariably discount their richest stores of affect, passion and fantasy. They will be urged to perfect them-selves in the virtues and talents that constitute a conventional definition of "goodness," regardless of any natural affinities or predilections they may or may not possess. Those who would remain true to their ownmost selves must consequently free themselves first from the constraints of convention and conformity.

For a moral perfectionist like Nietzsche, solipsism is, and must remain, a constant danger of ethical life. Especially in a decadent age, one must fiercely protect one's (diminished) store of ethical resources and assume only those ethical obligations that will truly enhance one's own character. To lapse occasionally into solipsism is far preferable to expending oneself in the service of bogus ethical obligations. Although the project of moral perfectionism need not presuppose the political perfectionism of an aris-tocratic regime, the absence of such a regime means that the project of elevating the *demos* must be abandoned. One can afford to attend to the moral development only of oneself and of one's kind. In a decadent age, in which solipsism may indeed be inevitable, it is far nobler to consign oneself to loneliness and solitude than to surrender oneself to the parasitic ethical obligations that characterize the "herd" of humankind. Indeed, this is the philosophical motivation behind Nietzsche's experiment with self-imposed solitude, which may in the end have cost him his sanity.

Nietzsche's sketch of the mythical "noble morality" furnishes a broad-brushed blueprint for his moral perfectionism. The noble morality begins with the "I"—embodied in its "powerful physicality"—and moves outward, conferring "goodness" upon everyone and everything it touches or possesses; all else is "other-than-I" and therefore "base" (GM I:2). In the rudimentary moral vocabulary of the noble, the term "good" is roughly equivalent to the term "mine," while the designation "bad" is roughly equivalent to "not-mine," or "other." These crude evaluative terms thus admit of no independent reference and no antecedent meaning. For the nobles, the "I" is the ultimate, unchallenged arbiter and generative source of all goodness in the world; they consequently recognize no moral "obligations" to those who are unlike themselves. Nietzsche's sketch of the noble morality may be simplistic, and perhaps even childish at times, but it raises an important, and often neglected, ethical question: what is properly called *mine*?

In order to answer this question, Nietzsche, like Plato before him, employs the model of the *oikos*, or household, to convey his commitment to the project of moral perfectionism.[15] Human beings naturally seek to maintain that which is uniquely theirs, that which they call and make their "home," which is the generative core from which all "experiences" ramify outward. Nietzsche thus introduces himself and his fellow "men of knowledge" by confiding that "there is one thing alone we really care about from the heart—'bringing something home'" (GM P:1). One's sole moral "obligation" lies in regulating the economy of one's own soul, providing oneself with the care and nourishment needed to preserve and expand one's native holdings of virtue.

In order to maintain its self-imposed principle of internal regulation, a strong household will inevitably squander its lesser holdings, in the interest of continued growth and expansion. Although these squanderings are often mistaken, especially by poorer households, for alms and altruisms, they are in fact the inevitable waste products and excreta that issue forth from an efficiently regulated *oikos*:

> Morally speaking: neighbor love, living for others, and other things *can* be a protective measure for preserving the hardest self-concern. This is the exception where, against my wont and conviction, I side with the "selfless" drives: here they work in the service of *self-love*, of *self-discipline*. (EH II:9)

Even the "gift-giving virtue" extolled by Zarathustra (Z I:22) falls within the contours of this regimen of self-perfection, creating a potlatch economy to ensure that one receives ever greater treasures in return for one's gifts.

Altruism is consciously practiced only by those impoverished households that have no remaining native stores to protect. Having allowed, and even encouraged, the plunder of its ownmost holdings, a barren soul must attach itself parasitically to other souls, under the insidious, neighborly pretense of "helping" them to protect their remaining stores. Decadent souls are failed householders, for they give away what is truly precious and resolve to stand guard only over empty households. They cannot distinguish friend from foe, kin from stranger, virtue from vice, or triumph from collapse. Under the guise of "altruism" and "neighbor-love," they involuntarily infect other, unsuspecting households with their constitutive disarray, urging these "neighbors" similarly to divest themselves of their ownmost holdings.

Nietzsche thus traces the ultimate origin of altruism to the constitutive illness that compels individuals—he studiously avoids calling it a "choice" or "decision"—to endure the indignities of unfreedom. That one instinctively prefers slavery to death is not the *cause* of a broken soul, but its primary symptom or effect. The "slave morality" arises precisely to preside over these barren souls, suffusing their bankrupt households with the prepotent (albeit transient) affects of hatred and resentment. Slave morality thus begins with a "hostile external world" and moves inward, designating as "evil" everything it encounters. While this gambit does not (directly) succeed in renewing the barren larders of the slave's soul, it generates sufficient affect to distract the slaves from their poverty and disarray. Through their blinding resentment of the "evil" external world, they gain temporary release (which they call "goodness") from the self-contempt that defines their agency. Of course, since their *faux* "goodness" is secured only in contradistinction to the "evil" resident within the "hostile external world," the slaves can never genuinely wish to reform the world that holds them hostage.

Like Socrates, Nietzsche amplifies the single imperative of his moral perfectionism by figuring the soul as a treasury, whose precious holdings are naturally coveted by all.[16] In his recommendation of the "gift-giving virtue," Zarathustra thus teaches:

> This is your thirst: to become sacrifices and gifts yourselves; and that is why you thirst to pile up all the riches in your soul. Insatiably your soul strives for treasures and gems, because your virtue is insatiable in wanting to give. You force all things to and into yourself that they may flow back out of your well as the gifts of your love. (Z I:22.1)

Echoing these sentiments, Nietzsche later introduces himself and his fellow "men of knowledge" with a similar image: "It has been rightly said: 'Where your treasure is, there will your heart be also'; our treasure is where the beehives of our knowledge are" (GM P:1).

Much as Socrates spins his "noble fiction" of souls naturally veined with gold, silver or bronze, so Nietzsche figures the (healthy) soul as a treasure-laden citadel, which is under constant attack by clever, scheming vulgarians. Explaining his strategy for guarding his own fertility and reproducing his store of precious "metals," he observes,

> One must avoid chance and outside stimuli as much as possible;
> a kind of walling oneself in belongs among the foremost instinc-
> tive precautions of spiritual pregnancy. Should I permit an *alien*
> thought to scale the wall secretly? (EH II:3)

Unlike an impoverished or plundered household, a treasury is generally considered to be well worth the effort required to protect its boundaries and expand its *oikos*. Whether or not a particular soul actually harbors anything resembling treasure remains to be seen, but Nietzsche's intent is clear. As his noble lie indicates, the project of moral perfectionism need not presuppose a static, metaphysical conception of the self. In order to embark upon the painful project of moral perfectionism, one must first *believe* that one's soul contains the aretaic equivalent of precious metals; souls can become treasure-houses only if they are treated as such. As in the case of Socrates' "myth of the metals," Nietzsche's *pia fraus* is justified, and ennobled, by its contribution to the project of moral perfectionism.

4
Regimens of Self-Overcoming:
The Soul Turned Inside Out

> For believe me: the secret for harvesting from existence the greatest fruitfulness and the greatest enjoyment is—to *live dangerously*! Build your cities on the slopes of Vesuvius! Send your ships into uncharted seas! Live at war with your peers and yourselves!
>
> —*The Gay Science*, 283

> *Nitimur in vetitum*: in this sign my philosophy will triumph one day, for what has been forbidden so far as a matter of principle has always been—truth alone.
>
> —*Ecce Homo*, Preface, 3

It remains to be seen how Nietzsche can possibly afford to forgo the (admittedly scarce) macropolitical resources of late modernity. The relocation of his perfectionism to the political microsphere would seem to require him to abandon the legislative component of his perfectionism, which apparently presupposes the support of macropolitical institutions. According to Nietzsche, however, philosophers will continue to pursue this nomothetic task, even within the political microsphere, legislating the conditions under which great human beings would most likely emerge. In order to compensate for the creeping decay of modernity, he restricts the production of exemplary human beings to self-production, and the legislation of values to self-legislation. In the twilight of the idols, philosophers contribute to the enhancement of humankind by producing themselves as repesentative exemplars.

"*Thus* It *Shall* Be!" The Philosopher as Legislator

The legislative role of the philosopher is an enduring theme of Nietzsche's political thinking. As early as 1874, he insists that "it has been the proper task of all great thinkers to be lawgivers as to the measure, stamp and weight of things" (SE 3). In praising philosophers, however, he does not have in mind those narrow specialists, bookish scholars and petty "laborers" who are popularly identified as "philosophers." Genuine philosophers are those intrepid thinkers who legislate a vision of human perfectibility, a goal toward the attainment of which the resources of humankind might be profitably gathered and directed.

Nietzsche's post-Zarathustran writings thus point ever more dramatically (and ever more autobiographically) to the philosopher as a lawgiver:

> Genuine philosophers, however, are commanders and legislators: they say, "thus it shall be!" They first determine the Whither and For What of man, and in so doing have at their disposal the preliminary labor of all philosophical laborers, all who have overcome the past. With a creative hand they reach for the future, and all that is and has been becomes a means for them, an instrument, a hammer. Their "knowing" is creating, their creating is a legislation, their will to truth is—will to power. (BGE 211)

Alluding to this legislative capacity, he thus describes the philosopher "as a terrible explosive [Explosionsstoff], endangering everything" (EH V:3). This description in turn calls to mind his general account of "great men" as "powerful explosives [Explosiv-Stoffe]" (TI IX:44), and it thus implies that he conceives of the philosopher-commander as a superlative human being. Invoking his designation of the Übermensch as an economic type or kind, he directs our attention to "the noble riches in the psychic economy of the philosopher" (BGE 204).

In a healthier age, perhaps, these philosopher-commanders could marshall macropolitical resources to support their legislations, and this is precisely the image Nietzsche cultivates of the "philosophers of the future." Philosophers in a decadent age, however, cannot expect to receive institutional reinforcement for their legislations. In fact, Nietzsche's uplifting sketch of the philosopher is usually judged to be self-congratulatory at best, and risible at worst. One is hard-pressed to summon any historical examples of the daring commanders he attempts to call to mind, and one need look no further than to his own writings for a definitive inventory of the cowards, frauds, con artists, valets, charlatans, demagogues, invalids, decadents, and buffoons who are characteristically accorded the title of "philosopher." Indeed, if we are to appreciate his hagiographic portrait of these philosopher-commanders, then we must investigate more closely the unique nomothetic activity he attributes to them.

Throughout his career, Nietzsche places unusual emphasis on the antagonistic relationship that prevails between philosophers and their respective epochs. In his Untimely Meditation on Schopenhauer, he explains,

> I profit from a philosopher only as he can be an example . . . .
> [T]he genius must not fear to enter into the most hostile relation-
> ship with the existing forms and order if he wants to bring to light
> the higher order and truth that dwells within him. (SE 3)

As his thinking matures, he comes to propose this "hostile relationship"
as the destiny of genuine philosophers, which they are free neither to
refuse nor to repeal:

> More and more it seems to me that the philosopher, being *of*
> *necessity* a man of tomorrow and the day after tomorrow, has
> always found himself, and *had* to find himself, in contradiction
> to his today: his enemy was ever the ideal of today. So far all
> these extraordinary furtherers of humankind [*Förderer des*
> *Menschen*] whom one calls philosophers . . . have found their
> task . . . in being the bad conscience of their time. (BGE 212)

In this passage, he explicitly links the iconoclasm of philosophers with
the enhancement of humankind, which we know to be the goal he sets
for politics as a whole. Following Emerson, he believes that ethical life
and moral progress—culture in the broadest sense—are dependent upon
the "aversive thinking" of the philosopher.[1]

Although Nietzsche often describes the philosopher's "hostile relationship" and "bad conscience" in terms of outwardly directed rebellions of
potentially macropolitical consequence, his later writings consistently characterize the goal of aversive thinking as the deliberate escalation of conflict
within the philosopher's own soul.[2] The philosopher's aversion to the
reigning idols of the age should not be confused with a direct attempt to
implement social reforms, even in the event that some such reforms eventually result as unintended by-products of his aversion. The primary targets
of the philosopher's aversion are the manifestations and reflections of the
age that prevail within himself:

> What does a philosopher demand of himself first and last? *To*
> *overcome his time in himself*, to become "timeless [*zeitlos*]." With
> what must he therefore engage in the hardest combat? With
> whatever marks him as a child of his time. (CW P, emphasis
> added)

The enduring value of the philosopher's aversion thus lies in its capacity
to promote his own "timelessness," which is the goal of Nietzsche's moral
perfectionism. From this "timeless" perspective the philosopher may
"objectively" survey the historical idols that spawned and sustain him,
and thus, through a ruthless regimen of self-examination, take the measure

of the age he involuntarily represents. Nietzsche consequently locates the
genius of Schopenhauer in his campaign to "conquer his age in himself"
(SE 3).

Following Emerson, Nietzsche prizes aversion, resistance, and opposition because they contribute to the production of the philosopher's "next"
self, each incarnation of which affords the philosopher a clearer glimpse
of the truth of his age:

> By applying the knife vivisectionally to the chest of the *very
> virtues of their time*, [philosophers] betrayed what was their own
> secret: to know of a *new* greatness of man, of a new untrodden
> way to his enhancement. (BGE 212)

Although bound like his contemporaries by the horizons of understanding
that define their age, the antagonistic "genius" is able to illuminate the
"higher order and truth" of the age as a whole. The philosopher gains
an immanent critical perspective on his age by resisting those of its emanations that reside within himself. We consequently may learn from the
philosopher how to take the measure of an age: "through Schopenhauer
we are all *able* to educate ourselves *against* our age—because through
him we possess the advantage of really *knowing* this age" (SE 4).

The precise target of the philosopher's aversion is not, strictly speaking,
the indelible imprint of his age upon his soul, but his *consent* to the reigning idols and values of his day.[3] Although one cannot alter the concatena-
tion of historical contingencies that have collectively fashioned one's present
self, one *can* oppose the particular constitution of one's present self, thereby
refusing to consent to prevailing standards of human flourishing. The
philosopher practices aversion not by "coming to terms" with his histor-
icity, nor by meekly assenting to his historical destiny, nor by fatuously
mouthing the Zarathustran refrain "Thus I willed it!," but by railing against
his voluntary participation in the signature prejudices of the age.

While self-contempt is ordinarily quite destructive, a certain form of
self-directed hatred is not only compatible with moral development, but
absolutely indispensable to its successful fruition. When directed toward
one's consent to the historical conditions of one's identity (rather than
toward these conditions themselves), *shame* can play a powerful role in
one's moral growth, especially if it is inspired by the aversive labors of
a great human being:

> [T]he sign of [one's consecration to culture] is that one is ashamed
> of oneself without any accompanying feeling of distress, that one
> comes to hate one's own narrowness and shrivelled nature, that
> one has a feeling of sympathy for the genius who again and again
> drags himself up out of our dryness and apathy. . . (SE 6)[4]

Shame frees the aversive philosopher not from the historical conditions that define him, but from the constraint of these conditions. By eliminating the constraint of his age upon himself, the philosopher may now turn his historical destiny to his advantage, as the condition of his accession to the "next" selves that await him. While the philosopher's "next" selves remain timely, necessarily reflecting the reigning forms and order of the age, they are also "timeless," insofar as they are born of an aversion to these forms and order.

Nietzsche's controversial appeal to shame as a catalyst of moral development derives from his economic designation of human genius. While virtually any soul (and especially those that are already inwardly destroyed) can muster sufficient shame to drown the pain of the bad conscience in a flood of resentment, this familiar gambit signifies (rather than causes) the irreversible corruption of the soul in question. One may enjoy the analgesic properties of self-contempt only if one first construes one's continued existence as a ghastly, grotesque punishment; this desperate addiction must certainly end in suicidal nihilism. In order to produce and harbor sufficient self-hatred to propel oneself beyond the perceived limitations of one's present self, one must already possess a robust soul, informed by multiple striations of internal difference and rank. More importantly, only a fortified soul can withstand the explosion of self-hatred that is needed to wrench oneself from the inelastic moorings of conformity and convention; impoverished souls cannot afford to turn self-hatred to their constructive advantage. As we shall see, Nietzsche consequently recommends the generative power of shame only to those rare, *übermenschlich* individuals who can also afford to endure the delusional madness induced by *erōs*.

Self-Overcoming

Nietzsche proposes "self-overcoming" as his preferred model for the aversive activity that constitutes a regimen of moral perfectionism. As he understands it, self-overcoming comprises a discipline of self-perfection based on a principle of assimilation or incorporation. The goal of self-overcoming is to gain for oneself a measure of freedom from the limitations of one's age, in order that one might command an expanded range of affective engagement and expression.

Anticipating his readers' desire for him to name for them the philosopher's regimen of self-directed aversion, Nietzsche remarks,

> You want a word for it?—If I were a moralist, who knows what
> I might call it? Perhaps *self-overcoming* [*Selbstüberwindung*].—
> But the philosopher has no love for moralists. Neither does he
> love pretty words. (CW P)

Nietzsche may not love "pretty words" like *self-overcoming*, but he is "moralist" enough to suggest this term for the moral perfectionism he advocates. As his reluctance indicates, however, the term "self-overcoming" is ripe for misunderstandings and misappropriations, many of which are fostered by his own confusions and indirections.

The concept of *self-overcoming* plays a uniquely complex role in the economy of Nietzsche's thought, encompassing both the psychological mechanism of personal moral development *and* the logical transformation of transpersonal structures, historical movements and political institutions. Indeed, our attention to the *macrocosm* of self-overcoming, and its logic of historical self-transformation, may shed clarifying light on the *microcosm* of self-overcoming and its logic of personal self-perfection.

Nietzsche commonly employs two terms that are often translated as "self-overcoming": *Selbstüberwindung* and *Selbstaufhebung*. While the former term appears more frequently throughout his writings (especially so in *Zarathustra*), the latter term appears in passages of great importance to his post-Zarathustran project of self-presentation (cf. GM III:27; D P:4). Since he appeals to the logic of self-overcoming within both the macrocosm of transpersonal self-transformation and the microcosm of personal self-transformation, we might be tempted to designate the former process by *Selbstaufhebung* and the latter process by *Selbstüberwindung*. While some such distinction clearly conveys the spirit of his post-Zarathustran political thinking, his actual use of these terms does not provide adequate textual evidence to support the distinction in question.[5]

He apparently adapts the term *Selbstaufhebung* from his dim understanding of Hegel, who similarly employed the term *Aufhebung* to describe the logic of immanent self-transformation. Despite his admission that the facile dialectics of *The Birth of Tragedy* emit "an offensively Hegelian" odor (EH IV:1), he nevertheless appeals to the saving logic of *Selbstaufhebung* at crucial junctures throughout his productive career. He apparently intends to mark his distance from Hegel by juxtaposing the terms *Selbstüberwindung* and *Selbstaufhebung*, often in close proximity within a single passage. Witness, for example, his invocation of the quasi-dialectical "law of Life":

> All great things bring about their own destruction through an
> act of self-overcoming [*Selbstaufhebung*]: thus the law of Life
> will have it, the law of the necessity of "self-overcoming"
> [„*Selbstüberwindung*"] in the nature of Life—the lawgiver
> himself eventually receives the call: "*patere legem, quam ipse
> tulisti.*" (GM III:27)

Nietzsche customarily treats the logical process of self-overcoming not only as inexorable—thereby raising, once again, an "offensively Hegelian" stench—but also as natural. Designating "Life" (rather than Hegel's *Geist*) as the ultimate subject of self-overcoming, he charts the transformations that ensue when any "great thing" attempts to constitute itself in accordance with its favored account of its nature and destiny. The process of self-overcoming is complete when the "great thing" in question, having failed to articulate itself as originally promised, triumphantly constitutes itself as its opposite or "other." Justice, for example, "overcomes itself" when, through a series of failed attempts at self-articulation, it finally constitutes itself as mercy (GM II:10).

Within this process of self-transformation, moreover, the destruction and creation of "great things" are inextricably linked. For example, although Christian morality "must end by drawing its *most striking inference*, its inference *against* itself" (GM III:27), its demise will give birth to the "other" of Christian morality, which Nietzsche associates with himself (EH XIV:4). He thus intends the term *self-overcoming*, despite its undeniably destructive connotation, to convey a sense of generative power and promise.

Moving seamlessly from the macrocosm of "great things" to the microcosm of individual souls, he similarly treats personal self-overcoming as a complex process of destruction and creation. Nietzschean self-overcoming is not to be confused with the oleaginous tolerance and vapid affirmation that grip modernity in a suffocating stranglehold. The project of moral perfectionism requires that one repudiate one's current self as it comes to manifest the extent of one's odious complicity in conformity and convention. Yet the fashioning of a "new" or "next" self involves no act of creation independent of one's merciless aversion to one's current self.

Indeed, because the promise of one's "next" self arises only in the practice of one's refusal of one's current self, the project of moral perfectionism is both risky and indeterminate. Those who set out on the path of self-overcoming are obliged to raze their old "homes" before new ones are yet in sight. Yet it is precisely the prospect of this "homelessness" that confers upon moral perfectionism its peculiar urgency and attraction:

> Every time [philosophers] exposed how much hypocrisy, comfortableness, letting oneself go and letting oneself drop, how many lies lay hidden under the best honored type of their contemporary morality, how much virtue was *outlived*. Every time they said: "We must get there, that way, where *you* today are least at home." (BGE 212)

The philosopher's aversion thus enables the process of assimilation or incorporation that Nietzsche associates with self-overcoming. Whereas the practice of Christian morality operates on a principle of castration or elimination, self-overcoming incorporates as many, and as diverse, capacities as possible. One overcomes one's age, for example, not by obliterating from one's soul all traces of the prevailing idols and allegiances, but by integrating all such traces into one's identity, by appropriating them for one's own designs. This process of incorporation and integration lends depth and complexity to the economy of the soul, and it is constrained only by the vitality at the philosopher's disposal, which is in turn determined by the relative health of his epoch. "The price of fruitfulness," Nietzsche intimates, "is to be rich in internal opposition" (AC 3).

The philosopher's self-overcoming thus exploits the plasticity of the human soul to engender internal difference and variegation. The greater the distances created within the soul, the greater the range of perspectives the philosopher can entertain and command. Rather than define "objectivity" in terms of disinterested contemplation from an abstract, disembodied standpoint, Nietzsche recommends that the philosopher command as many "perspectives" as possible:

> There is *only* a perspectival seeing, *only* a perspectival "knowing"; and the *more* affects we allow to speak about one thing, the *more* eyes, different eyes, we can use to observe one thing, the more complete will our "concept" of this thing, our "objectivity," be. (GM III:12)

The philosopher may not aspire to a privileged, external perspective on his age, but he may venture an immanent critique of his age if he can afford to occupy a representative range of affects and "perspectives." By engaging in aversive activity, the philosopher lends voice to the affective chorus resident within himself, overcoming his age by reprising its signature cacophony.

Self-overcoming thus presupposes the capacity to accommodate ever greater degrees of difference, opposition and contradiction within one's soul.[6] Proffering a self-referential example of his model of self-overcoming, Nietzsche proclaims,

> Facing a world of "modern ideas" that would banish everybody into a corner and "speciality," a philosopher . . . would be compelled to find the greatness of man, the concept of "greatness," precisely in his range and multiplicity, in his wholeness in manifoldness. He would even determine value and rank in accordance with how much and how many things one could bear and take upon himself. . . (BGE 212)

Unlike those who seek simplicity, unity and uniformity of soul, the genuine philosopher courts the *monstrum in animo*, whose propinquity prompted

Socrates's cowardly obeisance to the "counter-tyrant" reason (TI II:9). Once freed from the constraint of his historical identity, the philosopher may turn his "timeliness" to the advantage of his own "untimely" moral development.

As a general formula for the self-overcoming he has in mind, Nietzsche recommends turning the soul inside out. This is a painful, invasive process, which requires the philosopher to take up an evaluative standpoint beyond good and evil (GS 380). A project of self-overcoming obliges the philosopher to reclaim the previously estranged "evil" and "sin" resident within himself, by transforming vices into virtues and afflictions into advantages. Self-overcoming thus provides one with the opportunity to re-structure the "commonwealth" that informs one's soul (BGE 19), as one fashions a novel order of rank to accommodate the drives, impulses, pathologies, and homunculi that one has most recently exhumed.[7] In order to contribute to the perfection of humankind, that is, the philosopher must experiment with various interpretations of its innocence, always asking himself, "How can one spiritualize, beautify, deify a craving?" (TI V:1).

The reclamation of previously disowned drives and impulses does not return them to their "original" place within the economy of the mortal soul, for the soul is itself transformed in the process of self-overcoming. Self-overcoming neither restores a lost innocence, nor sanctions a "return to nature" in the romantic sense that Nietzsche (mistakenly) associates with Rousseau (TI IX:48).[8] The very reliance of the philosopher on (self-directed) aversion ensures that his self-overcomings will contribute to the production of a "new," second nature rather than to the restoration of an authentic, original nature. Just as a volcanic eruption augments the landscape it disfigures, so self-overcoming increases the dimensionality and surface area of the soul, allowing for an expanded range of capacities and expressions. Self-overcoming thus informs the philosopher's soul with an order of rank, but only by placing at risk the current psychic regime. An overflowing will necessarily destroy or sublate its previous configurations, thus fashioning a "next" self at the considerable expense of the integrity of one's current self.

Nietzsche apparently models the aversive mechanism of self-overcoming on the *agon* or contest, which he proposed in an early (unpublished) essay as emblematic of the health and nobility of Homeric Greece.[9] As a self-styled "warrior" who lives only to test himself in "battle," Nietzsche strives not so much to win his quixotic contest with modernity—which would, if it were possible, extinguish the *agon*—as to prolong its duration while continually raising the stakes of participation. His model here is probably the tragic hero, whose struggles against an uncompromising fate elicit our sympathy not because they promise success, but because they express a heroic strength of will. At least on Nietzsche's reconstruction of the *agon*, aspiring "warriors" compete not so much to vanquish upstart opponents or to alter an ineluctable destiny, as to enact their overflowing, *übermenschlich* power. The *agon* furnishes a public space within which contestants are invited to exceed themselves, to transform themselves momentarily into *signs* of the superfluous vitality that courses through them. As we shall see, it is precisely this significatory capacity that enables the political dimension of Nietzsche's moral perfectionism.

Self-Creation vs. Self-Discovery

A precise determination of Nietzsche's moral perfectionism is complicated by his apparent recommendation of two separate models of self-overcoming. On some occasions he deploys a set of strongly cognitive images and terms, urging us to *discover* our true, authentic selves, while on other occasions he prefers a distinctly voluntarist vocabulary, exhorting us to *create* the selves we wish to become. By relying on both sets of images, he indicates that the "discovery" and "creation" of one's "next" self are inextricably linked.

Nietzsche is best known for apparently promoting a volitional model of self-creation, which entrusts the project of self-overcoming to a titanic act of will. Speaking on behalf of his unknown "friends," he proclaims, "We, however, *want to become those we are*—human beings who are new, unique, incomparable, who give themselves laws, who create themselves" (GS 335). As a general rule, he tends to convey this model of self-overcoming via a cluster of aesthetic metaphors. In an oft-cited passage, he recommends the project of self-creation by issuing an "imperative" to fashion one's life into a work of art:

> To "give style" to one's character—a great and rare art! It is practiced by those who survey all the strengths and weaknesses of their nature and then fit them into an artistic plan until every one of them appears as art and reason and even weaknesses delight the eye. Here a large mass of second nature has been added; there a piece of original nature has been removed—both times through long practice and daily work at it. (GS 290)

This strongly voluntaristic model of self-overcoming is further reinforced by his ridicule of the Socratic/Enlightenment ideal of self-knowledge or self-discovery, which presupposes that a true, authentic self lies within, waiting to be discovered. He counters the Delphic injunction by calling into question the very possibility of a definitive self-knowledge:

> "Everybody is farthest away—from himself;" all who try the reins know this to their chagrin, and the maxim "know thyself!" addressed to human beings by a god, is almost malicious. (GS 335)

Every gain in self-knowledge contributes to who or what one is, thus continually displacing one's "true" self and indefinitely postponing a conclusive self-discovery. The putative "object" of self-discovery continually changes as a result of the investigation itself: "Learning changes us; it does what all nourishment does which also does not merely 'preserve'— as physiologists know" (BGE 231). Proponents of this volitional model of Nietzschean self-overcoming thus conclude that, because we can discover no authentic selves to which we might be true, it must be the case that we create our ownmost selves.[10]

For all the textual support in its favor, however, this volitional model of self-overcoming fails to capture Nietzsche's full account of moral perfectionism. First of all, the project of self-creation runs aground on the shoals of idealism. Any attempt to fashion a more authentic self necessarily involves a "cowardly" flight from the empirical to the ideal. The determination that one's empirical self is inadequate, unsatisfactory, or defective in some respect potentially implicates one in the metaphysics of morals that Nietzsche's "immoralism" ostensibly opposes. Second, this model of self-creation is overly voluntaristic, for it fails to take into account the general limitations of one's creative capacities. One does not "become what one is" *simply* by dint of an act of will; to preach otherwise verges upon cruelty.[11] Third, the excessive voluntarism of this model of self-overcoming betrays the "confusion of cause and effect" that is pandemic among philosophers. What some philosophers call "self-creation" may be the effect, rather than the cause, of the accession to regency of a novel configuration of one's soul. Challenging the voluntarism that informs both Platonic and Christian ethics, Nietzsche observes that

> [A] well-turned-out human being, a "happy one," *must* perform certain actions and shrinks instinctively from other actions; he carries the order, which he represents physiologically, into his relations with other human beings and things. In a formula: his virtue is the *effect* of his happiness. (TI VI:2)

For these reasons, perhaps, Nietzsche also promotes a distinctly *cognitive* model of self-overcoming, which sanctions a program of self-discovery. Especially in his post-Zarathustran works, he cautions against the misleadingly voluntaristic models of self-overcoming, warning that "at the bottom of us, really 'deep down,' there is, of course, something unteachable, some granite of pure spiritual *fatum*, of predetermined decision and answer to predetermined selected questions" (BGE 231). Nietzsche's fatalism, which plays an increasingly important role in his post-Zarathustran writings, thus mitigates the optimism and exuberance conveyed by his rhetoric of self-creation.[12] This "spiritual *fatum*" comprises those intractable, relatively permanent elements of one's identity that one cannot readily change. It is crucial that one limns the contours of this spiritual *fatum*, for it effectively restricts the sphere of self-overcoming, thereby limiting the range of "next" selves one can become. On this strongly cognitive model, the task of self-overcoming will apparently require a healthy reverence for that *fatum* within oneself that proves resistant to aesthetic rehabilitation. In deference, perhaps, to the importance of this project of self-discovery, Nietzsche proposes *amor fati* as his "formula for greatness in a human being" (EH II:10).

While Nietzsche may appear simply to vacillate between these models of human flourishing, his actual goal is to propose a synthesis or composite of the two. One "becomes what one is" by overcoming oneself, which always involves elements of both self-creation and self-discovery. As we have seen, his readers customarily define his moral perfectionism through a process of elimination: self-overcoming is a matter either of creation or discovery, and we have good reasons for eliminating one of these options. Proponents of the model of self-creation, for example, arrive at their determination of Nietzschean self-overcoming not by way of actually creating themselves anew, but by way of their doubts concerning the possibility of self-discovery. Champions of the model of self-discovery similarly point not to their obvious success in gaining a definitive self-knowledge, but to the facile idealism involved in any campaign to create oneself anew. It is Nietzsche's intention, however, to expose the distinction between self-creation and self-discovery as sheltering a false dichotomy.[13] While his voluntaristic rhetoric suggests the construction of selfhood, his fatalism recommends the discovery of an authentic self. One "becomes what one is" only by combining elements of cognition and volition, discovery and creation.

The composite nature of Nietzsche's moral perfectionism is crucial to his political thinking, for only the combination of self-creation and self-discovery engenders the *cruelty*—both to oneself and to others—that ensures the nomothetic impact of self-overcoming. On their own, self-creation and self-discovery both fail to fascinate and to arouse. Both are eminently safe (and fatuous) strategies for "becoming what one is," and they are likely to seduce no one. Only the volatile mixture of volition and cognition, which the philosopher's experiments cruelly detonate, can engender that dimension of Dionysian excess that simultaneously quickens and jeopardizes the economy of the soul. As we shall see in the next chapter, this potentially mortal expenditure in turn guarantees the self-inflicted violence that some others find so erotic. In order to become nomothetic, and thus political, a regimen of self-overcoming must combine elements of both volition and cognition.

Self-Overcoming and Self-Experimentation

Owing to the inherent risks involved in self-overcoming, Nietzsche regularly recommends his moral perfectionism as an exercise in self-experimentation. Through self-experimentation, the "genuine philosopher" accedes to those "next" selves that enable an immanent critique of the age as a whole. But the philosopher who seeks to overcome his time in himself possesses no recipe or formula for becoming "timeless." He must consequently experiment with a variety of aversive activities, all of which potentially place his soul at mortal risk.

The rebellion sanctioned by Nietzsche's model of self-overcoming is not merely theoretical or ideological in nature. In order to take the measure of their age, philosophers must always place themselves in grave danger, insofar as they unleash toward themselves the destructive power of self-contempt. The "philosophers of the future" are thus described as "critics in body and soul," whose "passion for knowledge force[s] them to go further with audacious and painful experiments than the softhearted and effeminate taste of a democratic century could approve" (BGE 210).

Genuine philosophers experiment with themselves not in the sense of trying on exotic fashions, causes and poses, but in the sense of turning *against* themselves the excess affect that defines their destiny: "the genuine philosopher . . . risks *himself* constantly, he plays *the* dangerous game" (BGE 205). The project of moral perfectionism thus involves the philosopher in an ever-escalating regimen of reconstituting himself through the implementation of novel ascetic disciplines. As we shall see in Chapter 6, Nietzsche actually attempts to hijack the ascetic ideal for his own political campaign to secure the survival of the will.

While Nietzsche often ridicules the limitations of human interiority, exposing the "growth of consciousness" as a "danger" and "disease" (GS 354), diagnosing the "bad conscience" as a potentially terminal illness (GM II:16), and disparaging consciousness as a feeble organ of relatively recent development (AC 14), he nowhere advocates a renunciation of interiority or a flight from conscious activity. He likens the "disease" of the bad conscience to a "pregnancy," which may someday culminate in the "birth" of the sovereign individual (GM II:2). His political project aims at the perfection (rather than the transcendence) of humankind, a task that requires the completion (rather than the reversal) of the transition from natural animal to human animal. The completion of this transition in turn involves perfecting the interiority upon which the human animal necessarily relies. Despite its inherent limitations, then, consciousness remains our best means of resisting the decadence of late modernity.

The eventual perfection of humankind may entail a selective amnesia of particular patterns of acquired behavior, but this forgetting will more closely resemble an active "inpsychation" than the *vis inertiae* that is desperately embraced in late modernity (GM II:1).[14] Rather than abandon consciousness and embrace its "other," the philosopher must seize control of the cultural production of interiority and guide this production to a more satisfactory conclusion. While Nietzsche reserves this larger task for the "philosophers of the future," he also contributes to its fruition by pursuing his project of moral perfectionism. The orientation of his own self-experimentation is prospective rather than retrospective, pointing forward to the creation of new, undiscovered selves.

Nietzsche occasionally registers a preference for aesthetically pleasing souls, which has prompted some readers to ascribe to him a strictly formal, Apollinian model of self-overcoming.[15] For example, he identifies the "one thing needful" as the "constraint of a single taste," which "gives style" to one's character (GS 290). On its own, however, a formally coherent soul might signify an incapacity to accommodate the internal contradictions that distinguish a healthy soul. Regardless of the "style" it displays, a two-dimensional, self-restrained soul is ill-suited to the self-overcoming Nietzsche recommends, for it cannot withstand the internal conflict on which moral perfectionism is predicated. In fact, he endorses "the constraint of a single taste" not for its own sake, nor for the aesthetic pleasure it may precipitate, but only insofar as it better prepares the soul to accommodate an ever excessive, overflowing will. By virtue of their aesthetically pleasing constitution, then, two-dimensional souls are probably safe from the dangers of self-overcoming, but only because their temperate "style" bespeaks an irrecuperable decay.

Nietzsche's model of self-overcoming *is* strongly Apollinian, insofar as it promotes the mastery within a single soul of as many tensions and contradictions as possible. But this model is also undeniably Dionysian, for it promotes internal mastery only as a means of further expanding the capacity of the soul, an ever-escalating process that must eventually culminate in the destruction of the soul. The inherent dangers of self-overcoming are therefore great, for the human soul does not admit of an infinite degree of plasticity. The incorporation into the soul of additional distance and contradiction may secure the philosopher's claim to take the measure of his age, but it also exerts a potentially mortal strain on the economy of his soul. Indeed, the immediate goal of any regimen of self-overcoming is simply to secure the conditions of future self-overcomings; the philosopher cultivates and disciplines his soul only in order to place it at ever greater risk. The philosopher who constantly overcomes himself thus "builds his city on the slopes of Vesuvius" (GS 283), for he voluntarily stations himself on the brink of Dionysian excess and disintegration.

Nietzsche's model of self-overcoming thus suggests a hospitable context for his otherwise audacious claim that "*genuine philosophers . . . are commanders and legislators*" (BGE 211). He locates the essence of lawgiving *not* in the redaction of positive law, but in the act and enactment of aversion itself. The outward signs of political legislation will vary in accordance with the vitality of the people or the age in question, but the internal mechanism of lawgiving remains constant throughout all epochs. Decadent philosophers too are lawgivers, even though their legislations are not reflected in the positive law of real cities, for they too engage in aversive activity. The seemingly idle declamations of Socrates and Nietzsche thus differ "only" in outward expression from the world-historical decrees of Manu, Caesar, and Napoleon.

Nietzsche thus conceives of philosophers as commanders and legislators, but only insofar as they stand in open contradiction to the reigning idols and values of their age. He also suggests that the sphere of the philosopher's legislative jurisdiction is strictly bounded by these enacted aversions. We should therefore expect these "legislations" to take the form of iconoclastic proclamations against the epoch as a whole. In order to discern and appreciate the legislations of decadent philosophers, we must attend not to the outward forms and expressions of their lawgiving, but to the nomothetic activity of aversion itself. The political consequences of this activity generally correspond to the residual vitality of the age in question.

The Case of Nietzsche

The case of Nietzsche provides us with an instructive, self-referential example of the model of self-overcoming he recommends. While he readily concedes his own decay, he also distinguishes between himself and another famous decadent: "Well, then! I am, no less than Wagner, a child of this time; that is, a decadent: but I comprehended this, I resisted it. The philosopher in me resisted" (CW P).

Although it may be tempting to conclude that "the philosopher" in Nietzsche enabled him to *escape* the decadence that besets modernity, this is not what he says. His relation to decadence, encapsulated in his enduring "need" for the loathsome Wagner, more closely resembles an involuntary affliction than a voluntary (and corrigible) affiliation:

> When in this essay I assert the proposition that Wagner is harmful, I wish no less to assert for whom he is nevertheless indispensable—for the philosopher. Others may be able to get along without Wagner; but the philosopher is not free to do without Wagner. (CW P)

Just as a principled opposition to racism need not free an inveterate bigot from his defining prejudices, so Nietzsche's aversion to decadence fails to deliver him from the besetting affliction of modernity as a whole. To resist decadence is not to free oneself from decadence, but to become a specific type of decadent. His regimen of self-overcoming does not eliminate his "periodic" lapses, but it may enable him to express his decadence in the form of a "timeless" resistance to the decadence of his age. He consequently overcomes his decadence not by eliminating or reversing it, but by resisting it, by opposing it even as it constitutes his identity.

In order to overcome his decadence, Nietzsche implements a "special self-discipline" that requires him "to take sides against everything sick in [him]" (CW P). His "convalescence" takes the form of a gradual estrangement from the practices, customs, manners, idols, and people who either aggravated or prolonged his illness. Because he does not enjoy the anchoritic luxury of Zarathustra's mountaintop retreat, he must become a "cave" unto himself, into which he might withdraw to gain a critical distance from the signature forms and order of his day.[16] Ensconced in virtual solitude, he declares war on his consent to the emanations of modernity lurking within himself.

On Nietzsche's (self-serving) account, this regimen of solitude has been a resounding success. He subsequently congratulates himself for having achieved the internal *pathos* of distance that he associates with the noble soul:

> For the task of a *revaluation of all values* more capacities may have been needed than have ever dwelt together in a single individual—above all, even contrary capacities that had to be kept from disturbing, destroying one another. An order of rank among these capacities; distance; the art of separating without setting against one another; to mix nothing, to "reconcile" nothing; a tremendous variety that is also the opposite of chaos . . . (EH II:9)

As in all cases of self-overcoming, the proof of Nietzsche's success lies in his capacity "to turn even what is most questionable and dangerous to [his] advantage and thus to become stronger" (EH II:6). He proudly describes himself as both a "decadent" and "the *opposite* [*Gegenstück*] of a decadent," explaining that he always instinctively chooses "the *right* means against wretched states" (EH I:2). This dual experience with decadence has enabled him to "master" the art of reversing perspectives (EH I:2). Although he remains a decadent, he now commands an immanent critical perspective on the decadence of modernity, such that he can take the measure of the age as a whole.

The logic of self-overcoming thus diverts our attention from the external targets of Nietzsche's polemics to their internal manifestations. The outwardly directed polemics for which he is famous—against moralists, priests, dogmatists, and decadents—are best understood as occasions for galvanizing an internal resistance to the moralists, priests, dogmatists, and decadents who inhabit his own polycentric soul. His resistance thus informs his crowded soul with an order of rank, which secures the "happiness" of the psychic "commonwealth" as a whole (BGE 19).[17] His legislations too are best understood as primarily self-directed, and all of his post-Zarathustran writings bear the unmistakable stamp of an author cheerfully at odds with himself. These writings become the sites of his own political legislations, wherein he enacts his own self-overcomings.

Nietzsche resists the idols of modernity not in order to vanquish his decadence—this disastrous gambit earlier plunged him into pessimism and despair (H I:P:3)—but in order to transform himself into a more resilient type of decadent. Whereas the virile heroes of the Homeric myths would customarily test their strength against external opponents, such as enemies, gods or fate itself, Nietzsche is limited by his decadence to internal contests against the prevailing idols and values. He resists and opposes his own decadence simply to prove to his unknown friends that the will is still (relatively) strong in him, that his dying sun still burns bright. He consequently seeks to ensure that his self-overcoming does not reach a premature conclusion, lest his contribution to the enhancement of ethical life come to an end as well.

In order to transform himself into a sign, and thereby attract the audience he needs, he must adopt a regimen of self-overcoming that places his soul at mortal risk: "[We] modern men, like semi-barbarians . . . reach *our* bliss only where we are most—*in danger*" (BGE 224). When properly cultivated, that is, the soul becomes an internalized version of a heroic battlefield, onto which "civilized" warriors dare not tread.

5
The Philosopher's
Versucherkunst

But lest I should mislead any when I have my own head and obey my whims, let me remind the reader that I am only an experimenter . . . I unsettle all things. No facts are to me sacred; none are profane; I simply experiment, an endless seeker with no Past at my back.
—Ralph Waldo Emerson, "Circles"

A moral view can never be proven right or wrong by any ultimate test. A man falling dead in a duel is not thought thereby to be proven in error as to his views. His very involvement in such a trial gives evidence of a new and broader view. The willingness of the principals to forgo further argument as the triviality which it in fact is and to petition directly the chambers of the historical absolute clearly indicates of how little moment are the opinions and of what great moment the divergences thereof. For the argument is indeed trivial, but not so the separate wills thereby made manifest.
—Cormac McCarthy, *Blood Meridian*

It remains to be seen to what political end philosophers can turn their self-experimentation. Does Nietzsche's account of self-overcoming amount to anything more than a self-serving sketch of an unpolitical man? In order to understand how his project of moral perfectionism contributes to the enhancement of humankind, we must investigate the affinities that he detects between self-experimentation and the expenditure of excess vitality.

An Attempt at an Invitation to Temptation

Nietzsche's passion for wordplay and *double entendre* furnishes some crucial insights into the nature of self-overcoming. The "genuine philosopher," we know, is a *Versucher*—an experimenter and quester (BGE 205).

He further explains that

> We opposite men, having opened our eyes and conscience to the
> question where and how the plant "man" has so far grown most
> vigorously to a height—we think that . . . the art of experiment
> [*Versucherkunst*] and devilry of every kind . . . serves the
> enhancement of the species "man" as much as its opposite does.
> (BGE 44)

Here he identifies the practitioners of this "art of experimentation" as
contributing to the enhancement of humankind. He thus implies that the
philosopher's self-experimentation is irreducibly political in nature. This
Versucherkunst engenders the superlative human beings who alone
warrant the future of the species.

But a *Versucher* could also be a tempter, and the *Versucherkunst* the
art of seduction. The *Versuch einer Selbstkritik*, for example, which
Nietzsche prefixed to *The Birth of Tragedy* in 1886, is obviously an
"attempt at self-criticism," but it might also comprise a *temptation* or
invitation to self-criticism. The same is true of *The Antichrist(ian)*, which
he advertised in his original subtitle as a *Versuch einer Kritik des
Christenthums*—an attempt at a critique of Christianity, to be sure, but
perhaps a temptation as well.[1] Indeed, his explicit association in the
passage cited above of the *Versucherkunst* with "devilry [*Teufelei*] of every
kind" overlays these "invitations" with the biblical evocation of leading
his readers into temptation.

After suggesting the name *Versucher* for the "new breed" of philosophers
he sees "coming up," Nietzsche confides that "This name itself is in the end
a mere attempt [*Versuch*] and, if you will, a temptation [*Versuchung*]"—a
name which confirms his own affinities with this "new breed" (BGE 42). He
goes on to insist that "the genuine philosopher . . . lives 'unphilosophically'
and 'unwisely,' above all *imprudently*, and feels the burden and the duty of
a hundred attempts [*Versuchen*] and temptations [*Versuchungen*] of life"
(BGE 205). Drawing attention to their "attempts [*Versuchen*] and delight in
attempts [*Lust am Versuchen*]," he proclaims that such philosophers "certainly . . . will be men of experiments," who "like to employ experiments in
a new, perhaps wider, perhaps more dangerous sense" (BGE 210). When
imagining his "perfect reader," he conjures those "bold searchers and
researchers [*Suchern, Versuchern*]" to whom Zarathustra relates his terrible
riddle (EH III:3; cf. Z III:2). Finally, the divided office of the *Versucher*—as
both experimenter and seducer—also boasts a divine lineage: Nietzsche
describes Dionysus as "that great ambiguous tempter-god [*jener grosse
Zweideutige und Versucher Gott*]" (BGE 295).

Nietzsche's wordplay furnishes an important clue to the psychological
mechanism involved in self-overcoming. In order to experiment on

themselves, philosophers must gather and discharge excess stores of expendable affect. He describes the great human being as a "calamity," and he likens the effects of self-overcoming to a river overflowing its banks and flooding the surrounding countryside (TI IX:44). Indeed, the swollen will of the genius obliterates its observed boundaries naturally and involuntarily, evincing no concern or consideration for its ineluctable effects on others. Born of excess, the philosopher's "private" experiments leak uncontrollably into the public sphere, where they are received as temptations and invitations. While the philosopher's legislations remain exclusively self-directed, inscribed "only" into the canon of his own self-overcomings, the enactment of these legislations involves an expenditure of affect that eventually exceeds the bounds of private self-legislation.[2] Insofar as they also comprise "invitations" and "temptations" to others, the philosopher's "attempts" and experiments function as outward signs of the healthy discord raging within his soul.

As a residue or by-product of his regimen of self-overcoming, the philosopher involuntarily generates an excess of expendable affect. This expenditure emanates outward from its center, thereby transgressing any conventional boundary between public and private domains, and it constitutes itself in the public sphere as a dialogical sign. While the philosopher's regimen of self-overcoming remains essentially "private," its sumptuary residue enters the public sphere as an invitation and temptation to others. On their own, independent of reception, these experiments are nomothetic only for the philosopher in question. They may eventually contribute to the founding of the positive law of a community, but only in the event that the recipients of this invitation endorse it as such.

When successful, this internecine struggle arouses in the philosopher the *pathos* of (internal) distance that only the well-ordered soul can afford to accommodate. Self-overcoming whets the "craving for an ever new widening of distances within the soul itself," contributing to the "development of ever higher, rarer, more remote, further-stretching, more comprehensive states" (BGE 257). Resistance to the reigning idols of the age thus informs the philosopher's soul with an "aristocratic" order of rank, which Nietzsche proposes as the hallmark of the noble soul (BGE 257). Because this aversive activity produces additional "next" selves and further displays the hidden perfections of the human soul, Nietzsche associates the philosopher's self-overcomings with the enhancement of humankind as a whole. In the process of overcoming themselves, philosophers expand the envelope of human perfectibility.

The philosopher's *Versucherkunst* not only informs his own soul with an "aristocratic" order of rank, but also, and unbeknownst to him, generates the significatory affect that tempts others to enter the "circle of culture" described by his expenditures. Schopenhauer, for example, is an educator, but only secondarily (and unwittingly) an educator of others.

He is an *Erzieher* primarily of himself, insofar as he elicits and brings to light the hidden perfections resident within his own soul. In the process of educating himself, the philosopher inadvertently provokes others, by tempting them to attempt experiments of their own design.³ Schopenhauer can therefore provoke others like Nietzsche only because he has already educated himself. The task of "creating" worthy disciples, in preparation for which Zarathustra seized his cruel hammer (Z II:2), has thus been radically recast: the philosopher "creates" a community only indirectly and unwittingly, through his expenditure of the excess affect required to turn the hammer on himself. He thus becomes a sign unto himself, irrepressibly projecting his self-directed legislations into the public space that surrounds him.

Hence it is the expenditure of excess affect that transforms the philosopher's experiments into temptations. Nietzsche's self-experimentation thus conveys both senses of the philosopher's *Versucherkunst*: *because* the philosopher's experiments are self-directed and self-inflicted, they are *also* temptations or invitations to others. While Nietzsche believes, following Emerson, that each invitation is radically singular in address, privately tempting *only* the solitary individual who receives the unintended calling, he also believes that the invitations received by the various members of one's community or "kind" may overlap significantly, especially with respect to the public consequences they entail. The resulting imbrication of kindred regimens of self-overcoming enables Nietzsche to derive a fairly rich field of intersubjectivity—a "we"—from the radically subjective temptations individually received by the community's founding members.⁴

The Manifold Genius: Philosopher, Artist, and Saint

In order to appreciate the political consequences of the philosopher's *Versucherkunst*, we must determine how and why an expenditure of excess affect transforms an experiment into a temptation. With respect to those witnesses who receive his experiments as invitations, the exemplary human being appears in the multiple aspects of philosopher, artist, and saint. Unlike the awkward suitors whom Nietzsche lampoons for their bungling pursuit of Truth (BGE P), *his* philosophers are always also artists and saints in their own right. Indeed, the coalescence of this triumvirate within a single soul accounts for the political dimension of self-overcoming. Hence it is in his conception of the manifold genius that he ultimately links politics and art, self-overcoming and self-creation.

The Philosopher

Nietzsche never adequately explains the psychological mechanism that renders political the self-overcomings of exemplary individuals, but his writings contain sufficient clues to support a plausible reconstruction. In a remarkable passage from his *Untimely Meditation* on Schopenhauer, he outlines the political role of the aversive genius:

> It is hard to create in anyone this condition of intrepid self-knowledge because it is impossible to teach love; for it is love alone that can bestow on the soul . . . the desire to look beyond itself and to seek with all its might for a higher self as yet still concealed from it. Thus only he who has attached his heart to some great man is by that act *consecrated to culture*. (SE 6)

Human communities are founded on any number of principles and pretexts, but culture originates only in the love excited by, and bestowed upon, a great human being. Only those who "attach their hearts" to an exemplary figure may enter the "circle of culture." Nietzsche thus identifies love not only as the impetus to self-overcoming, but also as the constitutive and unifying principle of culture itself. The existence of great human beings is therefore a precondition of culture, as are the measures required to produce them in any specific epoch. Hence his concern to continue his own regimen of self-overcoming in the face of the advanced decay that besets his age: even in the twilight of the idols, exemplary human beings are both possible and necessary, as objects of consecratory love.

While Nietzsche ventures no further elaboration of this important thesis, the love he proposes as constitutive of culture closely resembles Platonic *erōs*.[5] The consecratory properties to which he appeals suggest a love that is exclusive both in its attachments—only great individuals are its proper objects—and in its possession—for the lover too must become, if only temporarily, a squanderer. Only a great human being introduces others to the "next" selves they might become, and only those individuals who are touched by the madness of *erōs* dare to enter "the circle of culture" described by the self-overcomings of a representative exemplar. This love is furthermore as rare and precious as the "intrepid self-knowledge" that leads the soul "to look beyond itself." In a note from the spring of 1888, Nietzsche explicitly identifies love as the catalyst of self-perfection: "And in any case, one lies well when one loves, about oneself and to oneself: one seems to oneself transfigured, stronger, richer, more perfect [*vollkommener*], one *is* more perfect" (WP 808).[6]

Other forms of love, such as *agape*, the universal love, celebrated by some Christians, may certainly play an important role within specific cultural settings, but they cannot serve to found or constitute culture. The founding of culture requires as its catalyst nothing less than *erōs*, the most powerful, carnal, discriminating, and dangerous form of love known to humankind:

[L]ove as *fatum*, as fatality, cynical, innocent, cruel—and precisely
in this a piece of Nature. That love which is war in its means, and
at bottom the deadly hatred of the sexes! . . . Even God . . .
becomes terrible when one does not love him in return. (CW 2)

Ethical life may be enriched by *agape*, especially within the demotic
stratum of a hierarchical society, but it is sustained and nurtured only by
erōs. Only *erōs* furnishes the psychological motivation to overcome
oneself, to place one's soul at risk in the pursuit of self-perfection.

It is the business of politics, Nietzsche believes, to oversee the production of those rare, exotic individuals who, by virtue of their
übermenschlich beauty, excite in others the stirrings of *erōs*. Indeed, the
production of such individuals is coextensive with the production of
culture itself. He characteristically refers to such individuals as "lucky
strikes" (AC 4), for they emerge only rarely as a matter of design; this
means, then, that culture itself usually arises only as a fortunate accident
within the sumptuary economy of Nature.

Exceptions to the political rule of chance are indeed rare, for they issue
forth only from the untimely insight that genuine beauty, the source of
the erotic attraction that founds culture, is "no accident":

> The beauty of a race or family, their grace and graciousness in
> all gestures, is won by work: like genius, it is the end result of
> the accumulated work of generations . . . The good things are
> immeasurably costly; and the law always holds that those who
> *have* them are different from those who *acquire* them. (TI IX:47)

In order to oversee the founding of culture, the philosopher must first
legislate the production of a genuinely beautiful human being, one whose
perfections are sufficiently developed that others will "attach their hearts"
to him and thereby enter the "circle of culture."

Christianity, Nietzsche charges, has reinforced the rule of chance by
further complicating the task of producing exemplars of *übermenschlich*
beauty. In order to secure for *agape* a privileged place within culture,
Christian morality demonizes the generative power of *erōs*:

> Thus Christianity has succeeded in transforming Erōs and
> Aphrodite—great powers capable of idealization—into diabolical
> kobolds and phantoms by means of the torments it introduces
> into the consciences of believers whenever they are excited sexu-
> ally . . . And ought one to call Erōs an enemy? The sexual
> sensations have this in common with the sensations of sympathy
> and worship, that one person, by doing what pleases him, gives
> pleasure to another person—such benevolent arrangements are
> not to be found so often in nature! (D 76)

In a more succinct account of the fundamental antagonism between *Erōs* and the Crucified, Nietzsche charges that "Christianity gave *Erōs* poison to drink. He did not die of it but degenerated—into a vice" (BGE 168).

Although *erōs* enables the psychological mechanism of his moral perfectionism, Nietzsche nowhere ventures an account of its nature and genesis. Wary perhaps of relapsing into romanticism, he misplaces *erōs* behind the unwieldy "scientific" vocabulary that dominates his later writings. Whatever its provenance, his failure to identify explicitly the role of *erōs* in the psychological mechanism of self-overcoming has contributed to the distortion of his philosophy. From his post-Zarathustran writings, however, we can reconstruct with some confidence the signal psychological insight that governs his political thinking: *askēsis* begets *erōs*. That is, the experimental disciplines developed by the philosopher arouse in (some) others the erotic attachment that alone forges the "circle of culture."

The artist

Extremely conspicuous in its absence from Nietzsche's later writings, especially in comparison with *The Birth of Tragedy*, is an appeal to *art* as a potentially unifying cultural force. He retains an enduring interest in aesthetics, but he no longer believes that art can play in modernity the unifying macropolitical role he assigned to it in *The Birth of Tragedy*. He remains optimistic about art itself as a nomothetic medium, even suggesting that art may someday furnish an alternative to the ascetic ideal (GM III:25), but he no longer envisions art as a vehicle of macropolitical reform.

Although it may appear that he has simply abandoned his earlier interest in the political efficacy of art, in favor perhaps of an apolitical interest in the physiology of aesthetics, this development in fact reflects his turn to the political microsphere. Rather than divorce aesthetics from politics, he shifts his focus to the psychology of the artist. The outward, public expressions of artistic creation may vary from epoch to epoch, but the "physiological" preconditions of art remain constant.

Despite his uninspiring account of the political alternatives available to agents laboring in the twilight of the idols, he thus maintains his unshaken conviction that all art is irreducibly legislative in nature:

> A psychologist, on the other hand, asks: what does all art do? does it not praise? glorify? choose? prefer? With all this it strengthens or weakens certain valuations . . . Art is the great stimulus to life: how could one understand it as purposeless, as aimless, as *l'art pour l'art*? (TI IX:24)

He furthermore links the nomothetic properties of art to its capacity for creating beauty, whose appreciation furnishes the psychological basis for self-overcoming: "In the beautiful, man posits himself as the measure of perfection; in special cases he worships himself in it. A species cannot do otherwise but thus affirm itself alone" (TI IX:19). Even in peoples and ages marked by advanced decay, that is, great human beings function as artists, as the creators of surpassing beauty and the indirect founders of culture.

Nietzsche often speaks of self-overcoming in terms of *self-creation*, and this fecund metaphor conveys his sense of the nomothetic influence of exemplary human beings. Great individuals are always artists in Nietzsche's sense, for, in the course of their self-overcomings, they inadvertently produce in themselves the beauty that alone arouses erotic attachment. By virtue of their self-creation, exemplary figures come to embody "the great stimulus to life," unwittingly inviting some others to join them in the pursuit of self-perfection. Nietzsche consequently admires Goethe not so much for his creation of Werther and Faust, as for his *self*-creation, of which all else is derivative (TI IX:49). We should similarly admire Nietzsche for his creation of Zarathustra, but only if we understand this achievement as a symptom or expression of Nietzsche's own originary self-creation.

This capacity for self-creation is the common element that links all great human beings, whether they be the macropolitical redeemers of the past and future or the micropolitical philosophers of the present. It is only as artists, as producers of surpassing beauty, that exemplary human beings fulfill their social role as lawgivers.[7] Owing to the nomothetic effects of self-creation, exemplary human beings also produce themselves as *Übermenschen* and thus unwittingly contribute to the permanent enhancement of humankind.

The term "self-creation" also conveys the irresistibly public nature of the philosopher's self-overcomings. Independent of the philosopher's own aims and aspirations, his overflowing will enters the public sphere as a sign, presenting itself for reception by observers and witnesses who do not share his firsthand, artist's perspective. "The first distinction to be made regarding works of art," Nietzsche decrees, is that between "monological" and "dialogical" art (GS 367). Monological art is produced by the artist who has "forgotten the world," who disregards altogether the perspective of his likely audience, while dialogical art is produced by the artist who "looks at his work in progress (at 'himself') from the point of view of the witness" (GS 367).

This distinction is crucial to Nietzsche's political thinking, for it explains the difference between the philosopher's orientation to his own self-overcomings and that of his witnesses. A philosopher who maintains a monological orientation toward his own self-overcomings will inadvertently produce for his witnesses an incarnate work of art, whose dialogical significance remains unknown (and uninteresting) to him.[8] This means that the nomothetic influence and consecratory properties of exemplary human beings are, to a great extent, unwitting and involuntary; the dialogical use made of them need bear no correlation to their own monological aims.

From the dialogical perspective of the witness, in fact, the squanderings of the genius are often mistaken, especially by impoverished souls, for invitations and seductions. From the monological perspective of the artist, however, these same emanations appear (if at all) simply as the inevitable by-products of the philosopher's private pursuit of self-perfection. Indeed, the ethical life of any community is made possible only by the amoral self-creation of the exemplary human beings who found—and then desert—it.

Much as the young Nietzsche praised the transformative capacity of the tragic dithyramb, he now appeals to the transfigurative power of self-creation. Here his investigations into asceticism and aesthetics converge, for he also describes *art* as the product of a swollen will:

> If there is to be art . . . one physiological condition is indispensable: frenzy [*Rausch*] . . . What is essential in such frenzy is the feeling of increased strength and fullness . . . A man in this state transfigures [*verwandelt*] things until they mirror his power—until they are reflections of his perfection. (TI IX:8–9)[9]

The "frenzy of the will" is thus responsible not only for the artist's own "craving" for internal self-overcoming, but also, as reflected in the artist's external "transfigurations," for the *pathos* of distance that inspires others to overcome themselves.

Artists are defined, physiologically, by the involuntary, affective capacity to project outward their native vitality, to transform the world around them: "this *having to* transform into perfection is—art" (TI IX:9). Although this transformative capacity is most obviously reflected in the artist's externalized productions—paintings, sculpture, opera, and so on—Nietzsche cautions his readers not to equate the two. In fact, an artist's primary transformation, of which concrete aesthetic productions are "merely" outward expressions, pertains exclusively to himself. The artist always produces himself, albeit unwittingly and inadvertently, as an embodiment of *übermenschlich* beauty, and thus as an object of erotic attraction.

This insight is especially apposite in the case of decadent artists, who do not command the vital resources needed to transform the external world on a grand scale. Socrates, for example, never founds the city he so eloquently constructs in speech. Yet he remains an artist nonetheless, for in the process of "building" his "city in speech" he transforms himself into an incarnate work of art. His self-creation in turn awakens the *erōs* lying dormant in (some of) his interlocutors.[10]

In their private pursuits of self-perfection, exemplary human beings inadvertently produce themselves as works of art for public reception.[11]

This self-creation has the (unintended) effect on its witnesses of transfiguring—and thus redeeming—the suffering attendant to the ascetic practices deployed in self-experimentation. In a pioneering psychological insight, Nietzsche explains that

> Man, the bravest of animals and the one most accustomed to suffering, does *not* repudiate suffering as such; he *desires* it; he even seeks it out, provided he is shown a *meaning* for it, a *purpose* of suffering. (GM III:28)

Weaned on the ascetic ideal, the human animal avoids only "meaningless" suffering. If rendered purposeful within a context of interpretation, suffering actually enables the human animal to attain the threshold level of vitality associated with an enhanced feeling of power. A goal or aim is needed to galvanize an otherwise sclerotic will, and the ascetic ideal accomplishes this task by investing suffering with meaning.

The ascetic ideal provides meaning by proposing self-inflicted cruelty as constitutive of human flourishing. Our best, and perhaps only, access to the sublime consequently lies in our capacity to suffer meaningfully. The enduring erotic appeal of exemplary human beings thus derives from their power to transfigure, and thereby render meaningful, the otherwise meaningless suffering required by the ascetic ideal. The palpable suffering induced by the philosopher's self-inflicted cruelty is redeemed by the incarnate work of art he becomes in the eyes of his beholders. The philosopher's *Versucherkunst* thus ensures that each self-overcoming is also a self-creation, that every experiment is also a temptation.

Nietzsche entrusts the future of humankind to these higher human beings precisely because of their capacity to transfigure the pain and suffering that necessarily attend self-overcoming. In the eyes of their witnesses, exemplary figures redeem their own suffering, which in turn emboldens these witnesses to attempt painful self-overcomings of their own. The philosopher's self-creation thus "reminds" others of their expanded capacity for affective expression, thereby rendering (potentially) sublime the suffering involved in self-overcoming. Nietzsche's philosophers may not be world-historical redeemers, but their self-experimentation always culminates in an act of self-creation. They contribute to the permanent enhancement of the species by advancing the frontier of human perfectibility, which in turn stimulates in others the erotic impulse to engage in self-overcomings of their own.

The Saint

It remains to be seen, however, how the philosopher's self-creation might redeem the suffering of others. On precisely this point, Nietzsche's development as a psychologist is especially welcome, for his pre-Zarathustran works either overlook or underestimate the seductive attraction of ascetic practices. What initially alerted him to the Dionysian roots of tragedy, but what the "offensively Hegelian" argument of *The Birth of Tragedy* failed to capture, was the enticing appeal of the tragic hero, whose sublime self-destruction paradoxically ignites our passions and enflames our own futile aspirations to heroism. Similarly absent from Nietzsche's praise for the triumvirate of philosopher, artist, and saint was an account of the seductive appeal of their self-imposed disciplines. In fact, all of his pre-Zarathustran writings failed to explain adequately the psychological, or transformative, effects of the exemplary human being's labors of self-overcoming. The "aesthetic justification" delivered by tragedy, the precise influence of Schopenhauer as *Erzieher*, the promise of Wagnerian opera—all remained mysteries even to Nietzsche himself.

Returning afresh to the problem of tragedy, he issues the following amendment to his earlier findings: "What constitutes the painful voluptuousness of tragedy is cruelty; what seems agreeable in so called tragic pity, and at bottom in everything sublime . . . receives its sweetness solely from the admixture of cruelty" (BGE 229).[12] Having "reconsidered cruelty," he similarly revises his opinion of its self-inflicted manifestations:

> There is also an abundant, overabundant enjoyment at one's own suffering, at making oneself suffer—and wherever man allows himself to be persuaded to self-denial in the *religious* sense, or to self-mutilation . . . he is secretly lured and pushed forward by his cruelty, by those dangerous thrills of cruelty turned *against oneself*. (BGE 229)

While most individuals who are at war with themselves are merely enacting their fated dissolution, other souls are sufficiently robust that their internal struggles "have the effect of one more charm and incentive of life" (BGE 200).

Nietzsche thus believes that witnesses to the philosopher's self-creation are enticed to similar experiments of their own by the giddying prospect of *meaningful* self-inflicted cruelty. The philosopher's self-creation redeems the suffering of others by furnishing a context of enactment, within which his own suffering is transfigured. By redeeming the suffering involved in all self-overcoming, the philosopher inadvertently participates in the founding of culture:

> Almost everything we call "higher culture" is based on the spiritualization of *cruelty*, on its becoming more profound: this is my proposition. That "savage animal" has not really been "mortified"; it lives and flourishes, it has merely become—divine. (BGE 229)

Thus interpreted (and sublimated), self-inflicted cruelty becomes a source of an incipient erotic bond between the ascetic and his witnesses. The ascetic, who voluntarily embraces forms of suffering that most human beings would otherwise prefer to forgo, actually succeeds in arousing in some others an erotic attraction.

Because self-overcoming presupposes suffering, any attempt to "abolish" suffering in the name of "modern ideas" would spell disaster (BGE 44). Suffering is furthermore the art at which human animals excel most resoundingly. All that is valuable within the "circle of culture" represents the spiritualization of cruelty. Lest we disable the engine of moral progress, then, Nietzsche urges us not to indulge our pity "for 'the creature in man,' for what must be formed, broken, forged, torn, burnt, made incandescent and purified—that which *necessarily* must and *should* suffer" (BGE 225). Genuine *Erziehung* is both painful and dangerous, provoking and eliciting the uncharted plasticities of the human soul. Rather than abolish suffering, we must continue to fashion interpretive contexts in which the suffering endemic to self-overcoming becomes meaningful and sublime. For this reason, the ascetic, or saint, plays a central role in the founding of culture.

The erotic fascination inspired by the ascetic issues from his painful attempt to tame the will, a project that paradoxically requires of him a superhuman strength of will:

> For an ascetic life is a self-contradiction: here rules a *ressentiment* without equal, that of an insatiable instinct and power-will that wants to become master not over something in Life but over Life itself, over its most profound, powerful, and basic conditions; here an attempt [*Versuch*] is made to employ force to block up the wells of force... (GM III:11)

Ascetics awaken the *erōs* of others precisely insofar as they (appear to) squander themselves, for they are (believed to be) possessed of a strength of will that affords them the capacity to swallow even mortal doses of suffering. Nietzsche thus views the excitation of *erōs* as an unintended by-product or emanation of the swollen will, as exemplified by ascetics, and, at the extreme, by martyrs and saints.

Martyrs "convince" others only erotically—"*Is the cross an argument?*" (AC 53)—and only insofar as they derive intense (and unexpected) pleasure from their ascetic disciplines. Seemingly unaffordable feats of self-overcoming awaken in others the *erōs* that conformity and convention have put to sleep:

> So far the most powerful human beings have . . . sensed the superior force that sought to test itself in such a conquest,

the strength of the will in which they recognized and honored
their own strength and delight in mastery . . . [S]uch an enormity of denial, of anti-nature will not have been desired for
nothing, they said to themselves. (BGE 51)

Of course, not all ascetic disciplines are capable of arousing *erōs*, for not
all ascetics are genuine squanderers. For those ascetics who cannot afford
the requisite expenditure of affect, disciplines of self-denial engender a
sacrifice rather than a squandering. It is not uncommon, however, for
a sacrifice to be mistaken for a squandering; most martyrs are portrayed
not as decadents desperately embracing the "will to nothingness," but as
heroes who spend themselves in the tragic service of noble ideals. As unintended signs, in fact, the philosopher's "invitations" and "temptations"
are always ripe for misinterpretation. "Blood" is powerfully erotogenic,
but it is also "the worst proof of truth" (Z II:4). Nietzsche consequently
locates the stimulation of *erōs* not in ascetic practices themselves, which
may bespeak either a squandering or a sacrifice, but in the expenditure
of excess affect.

In a surprising revision of his argument in *The Birth of Tragedy*,
Nietzsche announces that "Socrates was also a great *erotic*," for "he
discovered a new kind of *agon*"—an *agon* he waged with himself (TI
II:8). Socrates beguiled the youth of Athens because he appeared to master
himself, subjecting his monstrous appetites to the cold, arresting glare of
hyperrationality. His self-inflicted cruelty, which aroused in some witnesses
ridicule, suspicion, and contempt, was welcomed by others as "an answer,
a solution, an apparent cure" for the instinctual disarray that had stricken
the citizens of Athens (TI II:9). Socrates eventually cast his erotic spell on
posterity by following his ascetic dicta to their logical conclusion.

According to Nietzsche, however, the erotic charm of Socrates is attributable to a grand misunderstanding. Socrates was no squanderer, and he
died not so much to honor noble ideals as to surrender to his consuming
decadence. Socrates in fact orchestrated his own demise, gratefully quaffing
a tonic draught of hemlock: "Socrates *wanted* to die: not Athens, but he
himself chose the hemlock; he forced Athens to sentence him" (TI II:12).
Other martyrs, including Jesus, have had a similarly erotic—and similarly
disastrous—influence on their witnesses, for they too have been mistaken
for squanderers: "The deaths of the martyrs, incidentally, have been a
great misfortune in history: they *seduced* . . . The martyrs have *harmed*
truth" (AC 53). The psychological genius of St. Paul lay in his political
appropriation of Christ as a martyr, in order that he might exploit the
erotogenic possibilities engendered by the unjust death of a Savior (AC
42). As a martyr or sacrifice, Christ awakened in countless others the *erōs*
that his life on its own terms inspired in only a few loyal disciples.

Like Plato, Nietzsche accounts for the excitation of *erōs* as a response to a perceived lack or deficiency:

> This one is hollow and wants to be full, that one is overfull and wants to be emptied—both go in search of an individual who will serve their purpose. And this process, understood in its highest sense, is in both cases called by the same word: love ...
> (D 145)

Erōs arises in response to the gulf that separates the exemplary human being from all others, and it naturally aspires to bridge this gulf. While the self-overflowing emanations of the will establish and preserve the *pathos* of distance, *erōs* strives to eliminate or minimize the distance between lover and beloved. The excitation of *erōs* in turn fortifies the lover's will, enabling him to accept his beloved's unintended invitation to enter the "circle of culture." (Although Nietzsche occasionally remarks favorably on heterosexual love, he typically favors male gender designations for both the lover(s) and the beloved.)[13]

As he explains in a note written in the spring of 1888, the excitation of *erōs* transfigures the lover, elevating him—if only temporarily—to the lofty station of his beloved:

> The lover becomes a squanderer [*Verschwender*]: he is rich enough for it. Now he dares, becomes an adventurer, becomes an ass in magnanimity and innocence; he believes in God again, he believes in virtue, because he believes in love; and on the other hand, this happy idiot grows wings and new capabilities, and even the door of art is opened to him. (WP 808)[14]

Blinded by *erōs* to his beloved's indifference, "this happy idiot" mistakes his beloved's need to disgorge himself for an invitation to permanent union. He consequently "grows wings" and ventures to bridge the gulf that ordinarily separates them. In so doing he becomes, like his beloved, a squanderer, leaving comfort, conformity, and good sense behind.

Inspired to unimagined heights by the madness of *erōs*, the bewinged lover becomes acquainted with various perfections resident within his own soul, some of which he temporarily shares with his beloved. Nietzsche thus locates in *erōs* the power to create sublime illusions, which alone enable human beings to endure the suffering involved in moral development:

> Love is the state in which man sees things most decidedly as they are not. The power of illusion is at its peak here, as is the power to sweeten and transfigure. In love man endures more, man bears everything. (AC 23)

The enraptured lover too transfigures the world around him, if only temporarily, for "even the door of art is open to him." The sublime illusions produced in the lover by *erōs* thus enable *nomos* (or human design) to perfect and complete *physis*. Only when engulfed in the madness of *erōs* will human beings ever attempt to overcome or transcend their natural limitations.

As *erōs* finally subsides, the temporary union of lover and beloved dissolves, and the "natural" gulf between them is restored, in accordance with the order of rank. Emptied once again of the superfluous affect that had burdened him, the beloved distances himself from his frustrated lovers and resumes his solitary pursuit of self-perfection. Lovers "attach their hearts" to a great human being and are thereby consecrated to culture, but their love is not reciprocated. Because *erōs* only strives ever upward, these exemplary figures never come to love those whose *erōs* they have inadvertently awakened. Their gaze fixed firmly on the shimmering horizon of human perfectibility, great human beings love only themselves and their "next" selves, which immediately vanish upon consummation. In a pithy statement of his own tragic view of the human condition, Nietzsche submits that all great love, by its very nature, stands unrequited.[15]

But the recession of *erōs* nevertheless leaves the lover changed, for the "circle of culture" has been forged around him. As the madness of *erōs* fades, a sense of shame suffuses the neglected lover, who now cannot help but see himself as mired in a life unworthy of his "next" self, which he momentarily glimpsed in the visage of his beloved. If this shame is attached directly to the lover's failures and incompleteness, then his opportunity for moral growth is soon crushed by a swelling tide of resentment and self-contempt; he will spend his life in penitent atonement for his momentary affliction of madness.

If this sense of shame is directed instead to the lover's consent to his incompleteness, to his willingness to remain unworthy of his beloved, to his voluntary complicity in his current imperfections, then it may succeed permanently where *erōs* itself has failed, in spurring the lover to attain his "next" self. If the spurned lover resists his plight, refusing to consent to the imperfections of his current incarnation, then he may overcome himself, despite the "melancholy" and "longing" he feels upon "discovering in himself some limitation, of his talent or of his moral will" (SE 3). Although stricken by the unspeakable suffering of an unrequited love, he may now redeem this suffering through the various strategies of "spiritualization" presented to him within the circle of culture. Nietzsche thus conceives of culture as the consolation prize that *Erōs* bestows upon his abandoned children—provided that they translate their numbing shame into aversion and moral growth.

As the founding catalyst of culture, *erōs* plays a central, if under-developed, role in Nietzsche's political thinking. It is in the excitation of *erōs* that he unites the twin senses of the philosopher's *Versucherkunst*. The philosopher's experiments are also temptations only if *erōs* is awakened by the self-directed violence involved in self-overcoming; the philosopher consequently tempts some others to attempt self-overcomings of their own. It is *erōs*, finally, that links the *pathos* of distance with "that other, more mysterious *pathos* . . . the craving for an ever new widening of distances within the soul itself" (BGE 257). If self-creation were not erotic, then the philosopher's attempts to nurture the *pathos* of distance would never arouse in others a similar craving for internal distance and rank.

Born of the expenditure of excess affect, *erōs* both drives the mechanism of self-overcoming and secures the consecration of culture. The *erōs* aroused in others by the squandering of these exemplary individuals is ultimately responsible for founding the communities that spring up around them. These communities are grounded neither in democratic consensus, nor in informed consent, nor in a social contract, nor in any other rational or discursive principle, but in a similar capacity for affective engagement and expression.[16] This capacity for squandering, which defines the community and its laws, is established through the self-directed legislations of the founding exemplars. The order of rank among such communities is similarly established by appeal to strictly economic considerations: how much squandering can the community afford and accommodate? How much suffering can the community redeem and transfigure? At the pinnacle of this order of rank, at least on Nietzsche's fanciful reconstruction, stand the ancient Greeks, whose tragic art expresses an affirmation of Life *as it is*, complete with its ingredient suffering, demise, and dissolution.

The advent of the "last will of humankind," the will to nothingness, marks the critical point of exhaustion at which the enervated will is no longer capable of awakening *erōs*, the point at which the *pathos* of distance vanishes altogether. The advanced decay of late modernity thus signifies a state of affective entropy, a disaggregation of the will into quanta so discrete that they can no longer generate the *erōs* needed to sustain the ethical life of the community (CW 7). A dissipation of will would result in the irrecuperable desuetude of *erōs*, and a cessation of *erōs* would nullify the temptations of the *Versucherkunst*. The decadence that besets late modernity thus comprises an assault on beauty itself, as potential objects of erotic attraction are systematically debased. Indeed, if it were no longer possible to "attach one's heart" to a great human being, in whom one sees reflected one's own prospects for self-perfection, then one would have no means of redeeming one's hatred of oneself. The future of humankind as a whole would no longer be warranted, and the teachings of Silenus would become wisdom once again.

An Unintended Experiment: Resentment as Expendable Affect

As a general theory of the seductive appeal of ascetic practices, Nietzsche's account of the excitation of *erōs* seems plausible. It would also seem, however, that this account only serves to reinforce the futility of any political response to the decadence that besets modernity. If *erōs* is awakened only by an expenditure of excess affect, then how can late modernity, an anemic epoch verging on exhaustion, possibly produce the squandering exemplars who consecrate others to culture? This question becomes crystallized in the case of Nietzsche's attempt to orchestrate a strategic expenditure of his own residual vitality. If he is "dynamite," then from whence does he derive his explosive force? He regularly portrays himself as a disciple of Dionysus, but where precisely might we locate the moment of excess in his own thought?[17]

As we have seen, Nietzsche's self-creation admits of important political consequences. Although he limits himself to self-experimentation, the overflowing will required for such endeavors eventually exceeds its circumscribed bounds and spills over into the lives of his readers. His aversion to modernity causes him to expend his excess affect, whereby he becomes a sign of the swollen will pulsating within him. This significatory excess in turn awakens the *erōs* that transforms an experiment into a temptation and eventually consecrates others to culture. He consequently identifies his own self-overcoming as his greatest contribution to the permanent enhancement of humankind: "my humanity does *not* consist in feeling with men how they are, but in *enduring* that I feel with them. My humanity is a constant self-overcoming [*Selbstüberwindung*]" (EH I:8).

In his own self-overcomings, then, Nietzsche embodies the redemptive triumvirate hailed in *Schopenhauer as Educator*: as a philosopher, he legislates the production of those exemplary individuals who alone warrant the future of humankind; as an artist, he creates beauty, which transfigures his own suffering; and as a saint, he seduces others to crave the suffering endemic to self-overcoming. In his resistance to decadence, he thus fulfills his destiny as a commander and legislator. Although he reminds no one of the modernity-crushing *Übermensch*, his limited sphere of legislative jurisdiction is nevertheless perfectly consistent with the depleted volitional resources of his age. Through his self-experimentation, he hopes not only to resist his twin temptations, nausea and pity, but also to furnish his unknown "friends" with aversive strategies designed to postpone the advent of the will to nothingness:

> We violate ourselves nowadays, no doubt of it, we nutcrackers
> of the soul, ever questioning and questionable, as if life were
> nothing but cracking nuts; and thus we are bound to grow day-
> by-day more questionable, *worthier* of asking questions; perhaps
> also worthier—of living? (GM III:9)

Nietzsche's pre-Zarathustran works failed, both individually and collectively, in their avowed campaign to restore the voice of Dionysus. Rather than eliminate the distortions imposed on Dionysus by the anti-affective practices of Christian morality, his books contributed additional distortions of their own. Of *The Birth of Tragedy* he remarks, "Here was a spirit with strange, still nameless needs, a memory bursting with questions, experiences, concealments after which the name of Dionysus was added as one more question mark" (BT:AS 3). From the retrospective Preface of 1886 issues a startling admission: the author of *The Birth of Tragedy* either misunderstood the Dionysian impulse or possessed a merely theoretical grasp of it. In either event, he was unable to apply his understanding to his own circumstances—an embarrassing lapse for a self-proclaimed disciple of Dionysus. As a consequence of this failure, *The Birth of Tragedy* characteristically confined Dionysus to the measured, restrained precincts of Apollo. The "music-practicing Socrates," for example, whom Nietzsche summoned in *The Birth of Tragedy* as a symbol for his own youthful hopes, was as cheerful, optimistic and Apollinian as his unmusical counterpart.[18]

In his post-Zarathustran writings, however, Nietzsche atones for his prior failure to isolate traces of the Dionysian impulse. True disciples of Dionysus, he now understands, affirm Life "even in its strangest and hardest problems" (TI X:5). Since the "strangest and hardest problem" facing him is the problem of history, of the "it was" (Z II:20), he must come to affirm not only modernity itself, but also his own resentment of modernity. In a remarkably autobiographical passage, he acknowledges that

> The human being . . . who wants to behold the supreme measures
> of value of his time must first of all "overcome" this time in
> himself—this is the test of his strength—and consequently not
> only his time but also his prior aversion and contradiction
> *against* this time, his suffering from time, his un-timeliness, his
> *romanticism*. (GS 380)

Nietzsche cannot eliminate his resentment of modernity, for it partially defines his destiny, but he *can* overcome it. If he is to take the measure of his age, then he must somehow turn even his own resentment to his advantage.

Here, it would seem, we have reached the outer limits of Nietzsche's experiment with self-overcoming, for his resentment of modernity would appear to defy incorporation into a healthy soul.[19] How could he make use of such vile stuff as resentment, especially the impressive store he harbors? In order to answer this question, and continue to pursue his experiment with self-overcoming, we must part company decisively with his own official account of himself as a philosopher. He overcomes his resentment as he overcomes any other affect, by harnessing it as expenditure.

Like any prepotent, expendable affect,[20] resentment can escalate and intensify a philosopher's self-overcomings, which may in turn elicit from others an erotic response. Nietzsche's abundant resent of modernity thus constitutes the elusive moment of excess within the economy of his soul and work. Here, in his unbridled ridicule of the puny aspirations and accomplishments of modern man, his vitality, power, and eroticism all attain their convergent heights. If it is true that "nothing burns one up faster than the affects of *ressentiment*," and that "no reaction could be more disadvantageous for the exhausted" (EH I:6), then perhaps his breakdown and collapse are best attributed to his self-enflamed resentment of modernity. Perhaps his vaunted "revaluation of all values," which he promises will alter the course of human history (AC P), is nothing more than an "explosion" of pent-up resentment. Indeed, if a cure for decadence is out of the question, then an accelerated decay may be most advantageous for his political aims.[21]

Although Nietzsche reserves his most caustic invective for "the man of *ressentiment*," he also grudgingly admits that *ressentiment* is not bereft of generative value.[22] *Ressentiment*, after all, "becomes creative and gives birth to values" (GM I:10). The man of *ressentiment* "understands how to keep silent, how not to forget, how to wait, how to be provisionally self-deprecating and humble," and "his spirit loves hiding places, secret paths and back doors" (GM I:10). "A race of such men of *ressentiment*," Nietzsche concludes, "is bound to become eventually *cleverer* than any noble race" (GM I:10). While the clandestine virtues of the "man of *ressentiment*" are not likely to put anyone in mind of the noble warrior or the blond beast, they may be the only productive tools available to the enfeebled representatives of a decadent, epigonic age. Moreover, if Nietzsche cannot rid himself of his own resentment, then his swooning admiration for "noble races" and "active forces" is, in the end, simply irrelevant; he must either overcome his resentment or capitulate to the decadence of modernity.

I do not mean to suggest that the appropriation of resentment represents a conscious or deliberate strategy on Nietzsche's part. He nowhere allows that he deploys any such strategy, and the success of his self-overcoming may in fact depend upon his ignorance of the nature of his own excesses. By his own account, the *worst* judge of excess is always the enthusiast in question. The monological perspective of the genius is singularly inappropriate for reckoning the dialogic reception of his expenditures. If his resentment of modernity *does* contribute to the signature excesses of his life and work, then we should not expect him to know very much about it. Because he is ignorant of the precise nature of his expenditures, his own account of his self-overcomings may deviate wildly from those offered by his witnesses.

Nietzsche consistently demonstrates in his self-reflective writings that he cannot accurately locate the moments of excess resident in his own life and work.[23] He knows that his excesses transform him into a sign, but his own interpretations of this sign amount to little more than idealized self-portraiture. He insists, for example, that he is both "free" from and "enlightened" about *ressentiment*, and he speaks proudly of the "Russian fatalism" that distinguishes him from the "man of *ressentiment*" (EH I:6). In an apparently autobiographical remark, he explains that

> *Ressentiment* itself, if it should appear in the noble man, consummates and exhausts itself in an immediate reaction, and therefore does not *poison*: on the other hand, it fails to appear at all on countless occasions on which it inevitably appears in the weak and impotent. (GM I:10)

In his account of the genesis of *Zarathustra*, moreover, he presents himself as a Dionysian vessel overflowing with spirit, health, inspiration, wisdom, beneficence, and other noble endowments (EH IX:6). He may need to believe, like Zarathustra, that his involuntary emanations are as salubrious as the sun's rays (Z P:1).

I see no prima facie reason to accept his account of himself in *Ecce Homo*, and I believe that we have strong Nietzschean reasons for subjecting it to further scrutiny. While he is clearly repulsed by acts and agents of resentment, his aversion to them *itself* usually takes the form of resentment. He thus represents a peculiar type of "man of *ressentiment*," and his sole mark of distinction within this ignoble lineage is his ability to turn his *ressentiment* against itself. Just as in the case of the original "slave revolt," which he vows to reverse, *ressentiment* "becomes creative" in his thought, giving birth to the values that inform his resistance to decadence. His resistance is neither heroic nor noble, but it transforms the "imaginary revenge" of *ressentiment* into a genuine deed [*That*], which he identifies as the "true [*eigentliche*] reaction" (GM I:10).[24] Although he never admits as much, he regularly harnesses as expenditure his own resentment of modernity—just as he has led us to expect any decadent philosopher must do.

His grandiose political aims furthermore *require* him to appropriate his resentment of modernity.[25] He is neither as wise nor as clever as he thinks himself, and his stores of love, courage, beneficence, and resolve are all precariously low. With the exception of his abundant resentment, he commands no other reservoir of combustible affect to expend. If we are to take seriously his frequent references to himself as "dynamite," then we must compile a realistic inventory of the "explosives" at his disposal.

Only in his resentment of modernity, and of Christianity, does he express the overflowing vitality that he regularly attributes to himself. His resentment of modernity, which earlier precipitated his plunge into romantic pessimism, now attests to the (relative) frenzy of his own swollen will, and so to his own decadent "health."

The secret hero of late modernity is none other than the reviled "man of *ressentiment*," who consumes himself in his own poisonous venom. While this assertion certainly contradicts Nietzsche's familiar rhetoric, his own critique of modernity confirms the failure of the epoch to produce more glamorous heroes. The "man of *ressentiment*" spawns many avatars amid the rubble of modernity, but none so intriguing as Nietzsche himself. His expenditure of excess resentment helps to sustain ethical life in the fragile microsphere of late modernity, but it also leaves its indelible stamp on those whom it attracts. His bizarre pursuit of his "next" self, which he alternately sees reflected in Zarathustra, Dionysus, the millennial Antichrist, the "philosophers of the future," and other "untimely" heroes, may be perverse, even obscene at times, but it might nevertheless lead to the founding of communities within the political microsphere. From Nietzsche's tragic fragmentation and self-division we may witness the excitation of *erōs* and the consecration of culture.

If successful in his experiments, he awakens in (some) others the dormant *erōs* that alone consecrates human beings to culture. His self-experimentation thus founds a community constituted by all those who can similarly afford to squander themselves in their aversion to the decadence of modernity. The public consequences of this *askēsis* are crucial to Nietzsche's political enterprise, for it is his self-experimentation that ostensibly draws others to him and founds communities of resistance within the microsphere. His expenditure of resentment, channelled by self-imposed disciplines of resistance, arouses the *erōs* that draws these fellow travelers to him. Seduced by his "tempting" self-experimentation, these "free spirits" join him in his efforts to sustain the *pathos* of distance and to survive the twilight of the idols.[26] Nietzsche's *real* "children," of course, are not the "noble warriors" who populate his fantasies, but the nook-dwelling creatures of resentment who have been consecrated to culture by a decadent philosopher. For this very reason, however, his real "children" may be uniquely suited to survive the demise of modernity.

The confusion surrounding the identity of Nietzsche's rightful heirs confirms the greatest danger involved in his own self-experimentation. From the dialogic perspective of their audiences, great human beings always appear, and function publicly, as *signs* of the (relatively) robust vitality they propagate and expend. In order to orchestrate a timely "explosion," Nietzsche attempts to exploit the significatory by-product of his self-overcomings. The public overflow of his private pursuit of self-perfection contributes a performative dimension to his teachings, supplementing his "saying" with a "showing." Indeed, he is counting on this performative dimension to found the community of readers who will join him in shepherding the aimless will through the duration of modernity.

This significatory function enables the political dimension of Nietzsche's self-overcoming, but it also places the meaning(s) of his performances beyond the sphere of his authorial control. Although he voluntarily elects to engage in aversive activity, this choice marks the limit of his volitional control over his self-experimentation; he neither chooses nor foresees its consequences. "To become what one is," he reminds us, "one must not have the faintest notion *what* one is" (EH II:9). By its very nature, then, his self-experimentation ultimately exceeds his own purview and control; he is neither privy to his own excesses, nor a reliable judge of their effects.

The dialogic reception and interpretation of his "explosion" need bear no resemblance to the meaning he monologically invests in it. He may attempt to anticipate his reception, by strategically adopting the dialogic perspective of his likely readers, but even this gambit will not protect him from gross misinterpretation and abuse. To transform himself into a sign is to place himself, and his precious teachings, in the hands of readers whom he neither trusts nor controls.

In Nietzsche's case this proved to be an extremely painful experiment, for it required him to overcome his abundant resentment of modernity, an age whose highest specimens fall pitifully short of the noble standards of bygone epochs. Like Socrates, whose interrogation of Athenian noblemen was designed to test the oracle's surprising pronouncement, he stubbornly resisted the conclusion that he might belong among the best his age has to offer. Indeed, the self-loathing displayed by Socrates and Nietzsche is apparently indicative of the aversive activities of all exemplary human beings who toil in twilight epochs.

Like any representative figure, however, Nietzsche turns this resistance to his own advantage. By dint of his own self-overcomings, he validates the ethical resources scattered throughout the microsphere and draws our attention to the *Versucherkunst* that produced him. Rather than simply describe the self-experimentation he recommends, he provides us with a map of its course and an embodied example of the success it can have— provided we learn to "see" what has heretofore been invisible to us. His occasional bursts of expendable affect serve to mark the path for anyone who can afford to follow. Indeed, if we are to appreciate Nietzsche as an exemplary human being, then we too must overcome our resentment (and despair) of an age so exhausted that we too might legitimately aspire to greatness.

6
Comedians of
the Ascetic Ideal

Around the hero everything turns into a tragedy; around the demi-god, into a satyr-play [*Satyrspiel*]; and around God—what? perhaps into "world"?—

—*Beyond Good and Evil*, 150

Unable to articulate a specific answer to the founding question of politics, Nietzsche resolves instead to attend to the survival of humankind, until that point at which the "philosophers of the future" create new values and found a new epoch. Toward this end, he undertakes a more modest, ancillary political task, which is consistent with his complicity in the decadence of modernity. It is his self-appointed task to safeguard the crippled human will throughout the twilight of the idols. He can certainly do no more than this, and even this task may prove too great for his diminished capacities.

The Ascetic Ideal

The political aims of Nietzsche's post-Zarathustran writings are obscured by his apparent ambivalence toward the ascetic ideal. On the one hand, he reveals that the dynastic reign of the ascetic ideal has culminated in a potentially apocalyptic "will to nothingness." If necessary, human beings will orchestrate their own self-annihilation, for even this goal is preferable to no goal at all (GM III:28). On the other hand, although he persuasively demonstrates that an alternative to the ascetic ideal would be desirable, and perhaps even redemptive, he fails to disclose any actual, viable alternatives that are presently available to us.

The "philosophers of the future" may someday succeed in framing a naturalistic, pro-affective alternative to the ascetic ideal, but Nietzsche himself will not. Seemingly reconciled to a continued reliance on the ascetic ideal, he registers his preference for a specific manifestation of it: "All honor to the ascetic ideal *insofar as it is honest*! so long as it believes in itself and does not play tricks on us!" (GM III:26). Despite its tone of apparent affirmation, however, this Apollinian statement of preference betrays a *pathos* of defeat and despair. *Nietzsche*, the self-proclaimed "last disciple of the philosopher Dionysus" (TI X:5), and an accomplished trickster in his own right, now demands constancy and fair play from his most formidable opponent? The manipulator of masks and purveyor of noble lies *par excellence* now honors the ascetic ideal only in its honest and self-conscious incarnations?

This humble plea may not put us in mind of the millennial Antichrist, who audaciously promises to "break history in two," but it faithfully conveys the profound sense of ambivalence with which Nietzsche approaches the ascetic ideal. Resigned to both the destructive force and the unchallenged hegemony of the ascetic ideal, he characteristically treats its reign as a necessary evil for the duration of modernity, and perhaps beyond.

In its most basic, essential form, the ascetic ideal enshrines the life of self-denial as the highest expression of human flourishing. Under the tragic aegis of the ascetic ideal, human beings seek to become "whole" and "complete" through complex operations of self-vivisection and self-laceration. Meaning is infused into one's otherwise meaningless existence through ever-escalating orgies of self-inflicted suffering. Although most human beings are unlikely to succeed in their quest for completeness, their immersion in ascetic disciplines will very likely distract them from their irremediable fragmentation. Unlike all other animals, human beings derive their threshold level of vitality (or, in Nietzsche's terms, their enabling feeling of power) indirectly and derivatively, as a consequence and by-product of the ascetic disciplines they impose upon themselves. Whereas other animals rely directly and pre-reflectively on their respective endowments of unconscious drives and impulses, the human animal is defined by the violent and irreversible introjection of its natural, instinctual heritage (GM II:16). This originary wound, which Nietzsche calls the "bad conscience," is the condition of all human life and achievement. In order to unleash the generative powers of this originary wound, human animals must fashion for themselves contexts of interpretation, which provide them with the baseline meaning they need in order to render sublime their existential suffering.

While it has become common to distinguish between "normal" and "extreme" practices of self-denial, reserving the term "ascetic" only for the latter, the ascetic ideal itself sanctions no such distinction. It is the silent, signature work of the ascetic ideal to co-opt ordinary, everyday practices of self-denial, so that human beings might "naturally" attain the threshold level of vitality that alone confers meaning onto their otherwise meaningless suffering. The ascetic ideal indifferently sanctions any and all practices of self-denial, from those that build character to those that destroy bodies. Familiar, conventional training regimens, such as those required of religious and athletic initiates, are neither more nor less ascetic than bizarre, subterranean rituals of self-mutilation—although particular cultures will invariably valorize the specific ascetic disciplines to which they assign a political preference.

In all of its forms and manifestations, the ascetic ideal thus sponsors the seemingly paradoxical contest of Life versus Life:

> [P]leasure is felt and *sought* in ill-constitutedness, decay, pain, mischance, ugliness, voluntary deprivation, self-mortification, self-flagellation, self-sacrifice. All this is in the highest degree paradoxical: we stand before a discord that *wants* to be discordant, that *enjoys* itself in this suffering and even grows more self-confident and triumphant the more its own presumption, its physiological capacity for life, *decreases*. (GM III:11)

As Nietzsche wisely indicates, however, this paradox is only apparent. The ascetic ideal actually serves the interests of Life itself, by seducing its weakest, sickest forms—those that attain their threshold level of vitality only in self-destruction—to a continued existence.

As we have seen, Nietzsche identifies the ascetic ideal as the dominant interpretation known to humankind of the existential suffering associated with the bad conscience. The ascension and authority of the ascetic ideal are therefore attributable to the onset of civilization, which, in exchange for the promise of peace and security, prohibits the spontaneous, outward expression of the unconscious drives and impulses. Indulging himself in a bit of speculative anthropology, he proposes that the ascetic ideal arose in response to a basic human craving for meaning:

> *This* is precisely what the ascetic ideal means: that something was *lacking*, that man was surrounded by a fearful void . . . The meaninglessness of suffering, *not* suffering itself, was the curse that lay over humankind so far—*and the ascetic ideal offered man meaning*! (GM III:28)

According to Nietzsche, moreover, the ascetic ideal constitutes the *only* response thus far to the suffering of the bad conscience (GM III:28). The reign of the ascetic ideal is therefore coextensive with civilization itself. To be human is to gain meaning, power, and vitality through disciplines of self-directed violence. Indeed, the governing taboo of civilization forbids human beings from flourishing via any non- or extra-ascetic means, a general proscription of which Freud would later propose the incest taboo as both representative and symbolic.

In providing meaning for the pain of the bad conscience, the ascetic ideal has presided over the protracted evolution of the human animal. Because death alone can still the existential suffering that attends the forcible introjection of animal drives, we might think of the bad conscience as the ineliminable opportunity cost of human civilization. Civilization demands suffering, and the ascetic ideal renders meaningful the existential suffering that human animals involuntarily inflict on themselves. While acknowledging that most human beings have found this existential suffering to be bearable only under the analgesic influence of metaphysical comforts, Nietzsche nevertheless insists that the bad conscience, under the aegis of the ascetic ideal, has impregnated the species with a future, transforming humankind from a "goal" into "a way, an episode, a bridge, a great promise" (GM II:16).

In light of Nietzsche's grim appraisal of the ascetic ideal, it is not surprising that many readers assume that he intends to offer or disclose an alternative ideal. Although he certainly ascertains the need for an alternative ideal, he nowhere exhibits the wherewithal to satisfy this need. He proclaims, for example, that *art* is "much more fundamentally opposed to the ascetic ideal than is science" (GM III:25), but he refuses to identify the artist as an opponent of the ascetic ideal; in a typically evasive fashion, he instead promises, falsely, to "return some day to this subject at greater length" (GM III:25). At the end of essay II of the *Genealogy*, he similarly invokes the image of a

> man of the future, who will redeem us not only from the hitherto reigning ideal but also from that which was bound to grow out of it, the great nausea, the will to nothingness, nihilism. (GM II:24)

But at this point he breaks off abruptly, deferring obscurely to "Zarathustra the godless" and resuming his obtrusive silence on the question of an alternative to the ascetic ideal. For many readers, this disappointing aposiopesis serves to punctuate his chronic failure to provide "serious" solutions to the grave political problems he addresses.

He elsewhere alludes, cryptically, to a "counter-ideal" promulgated by Zarathustra (EH XI),[1] but he neglects to identify for his patient readers the specific teaching(s) or speech(es) to which he refers. While it is certainly plausible to assume that he may have in mind here his gnomic teaching of eternal recurrence, this teaching is not currently available to us in the form of a "counter-ideal."[2] To *will* the eternal recurrence, after all, "*to crave nothing more fervently* than this ultimate eternal confirmation and seal" (GS 341), would seem to require a degree of vitality that is absolutely unknown to modernity. Zarathustra cannot distinguish "his" teaching of eternal recurrence from the various renditions of it that he rejects throughout his *Bildungsgang*, and Nietzsche himself is surprisingly un-familiar with (or uncharacteristically silent about) his own signature teaching of affirmation.

In light of his smug predictions for the reception of *Zarathustra*, more-over, any "counter-ideal" sheltered therein would seem to be framed not for us, but for the preterhuman audiences of the postmodern future:

> [H]aving understood six sentences from [*Zarathustra*]—that is, to have really experienced them—would raise one to a higher level of existence than "modern" men could attain. Given this feeling of distance, how could I wish to be read by those "moderns" whom I know! (EH III:1)

While it may still be the case that either Nietzsche or Zarathustra possesses an alternative to the ascetic ideal, any "counter-ideal" they might promul-gate would necessarily outstrip the diminished faculties of their late-modern readers. Indeed, by the time receptive audiences finally arrive on the scene, this supposed "counter-ideal" may be entirely otiose.

Hence Nietzsche's enduring ambivalence toward the ascetic ideal: while the installation of a "new" ideal would be desirable, it is also incompat-ible with civilization and the human species as we know them. He consequently delegates the installation of an alternative ideal to his myste-rious successors, while resigning himself to the maieutic task of bringing to term the troubled pregnancy of the bad conscience. He consequently undertakes to investigate—by way of self-experimentation—the unknown generative powers of the ascetic ideal. In order to mount a meaningful challenge to the hegemony of the ascetic ideal, that is, he must assume the difficult (and for him uncomfortably effeminate) role of the manly midwife.

Harming the Ascetic Ideal

Nietzsche's ambivalence toward the ascetic ideal reflects his (skeptical) appraisal of the limited political resources available to late modernity. Unable to depose the ascetic ideal, or to propose a viable successor ideal, he must attempt somehow to disrupt from within the "closed system" of the ascetic ideal. This endogenous disruption may in turn loosen the stran-glehold of the ascetic ideal, so that he and his "friends" might implement experimental strategies for surviving the twilight of the idols.

Toward the end of his investigation of the ascetic ideal in the *Genealogy*, Nietzsche finally entertains the question that his readers have long since formulated: "*where* is the opposing will that might express an *opposing ideal*?" (GM III:23). He quickly rules out science, the reigning idol of modernity. "Men of science" are not the free spirits he seeks, for their signature faith in truth bears witness to their underlying belief that truth alone can redeem the human condition (GM III:23). This belief in turn betrays the conviction that the human condition stands in need of redemption, a conviction symptomatic of decadence. For similar reasons, he also disqualifies the "unconditional honest atheism" that had become so fashionable in his day. A genuine alternative to the ascetic ideal must neither promise nor anticipate the redemption of the human condition.[3]

Having declined his most obvious and promising options, Nietzsche finally outlines *his* strategy for challenging the ascetic ideal. In an almost offhand remark, he declares that "the ascetic ideal has at present only *one* kind of real enemy capable of *harming* it: the comedians of this ideal [*die Komödianten dieses Ideals*]—for they arouse mistrust of it" (GM III:27). This, the only answer Nietzsche provides to the most important political question raised in the *Genealogy*, is so strange and unsatisfying, especially in light of the rhetorical crescendo that builds up to it, that few readers can take it seriously.[4] Nor does he deign to shed any additional light on these mysterious enemies of the ascetic ideal.[5] Having raised the tantalizing possibility of meaningful opposition to the ascetic ideal, he quickly changes the subject. He neither divulges the identity of these comedians nor explains how one might join them in harming the ascetic ideal. He lavishes the orotund prose of the *Genealogy* on such pressing political topics as diet, the chastity of philosophers, and German music, but he never again mentions these "enemies" of the ascetic ideal.

In a typical gesture of deferral, Nietzsche bequeaths to his readers the task of determining the identity and *modus operandi* of these mysterious "enemies" of the ascetic ideal. Relying once again on a strictly functional account of the notion he wishes to convey, he tells us only what these comedians *do*. All we know about them is that they "harm" the ascetic ideal by "arousing mistrust" of it. How they do so, and to what effect, remains unsaid, if not unknown. Nor is it clear why a burgeoning mistrust would prove harmful to the ascetic ideal, especially with no viable counter-ideal in sight. The unchallenged hegemony of the ascetic ideal thus rules out several promising interpretations of Nietzsche's cryptic reference to the "comedians of the ascetic ideal": it would do little good simply to ignore, ridicule, mock, slander, or demean the ascetic ideal, for there exist no alternative ideals to which rebels and critics might pledge their allegiance and petition for asylum. Any apostasy from the ascetic ideal is only apparent, only temporary, and the inevitable "return" of the repentant apostate only serves to reinforce the hegemony of the ascetic ideal.

Nietzsche may be uncharacteristically laconic on the question of opposing the ascetic ideal, but he nevertheless furnishes some important clues. No one better fits his description of these comedians than Nietzsche himself.[6] Although he nowhere identifies himself (or anyone else) as a comedian of the ascetic ideal, he regularly identifies himself as one of its opponents, claiming as his own the task he assigns to these mysterious comedians. He is furthermore uniquely suited to serve as a comedian of the ascetic ideal, both in terms of his knowledge of it and in terms of his historical situation. He may chafe at the notion that he must fulfill his destiny as a manly midwife, but his own account of the decadence of late modernity leaves him no greater political charge to fulfill. Finally, he could never know if he were actually a comedian of the ascetic ideal. Since these mysterious enemies are defined only by their function (irrespective of their avowed intentions), by their success in "arousing mistrust" of the ascetic ideal, only external witnesses can confirm the "harm" they have done. Only Nietzsche's readers can confirm that he is (or is not) in fact a comedian of the ascetic ideal, and their only criterion of judgment lies in the "mistrust" he has aroused in them.

Nietzsche's candid pronouncement of his own complicity in the besetting decadence of his epoch would seem to confirm his qualifications as a comedian of the ascetic ideal. Owing to the restricted confines of his historical situation, the only challenge he could hope to mount must be strictly immanent, exclusively internal to the economy of the ascetic ideal. While he does not explicitly identify the method of immanent critique as his preferred strategy for harming the ascetic ideal, he *does* indicate why this strategy might be effective.

On two separate occasions he describes the ascetic ideal as a *"faute de mieux"* (EH XI; GM III:28). He thus suggests that the success of the ascetic ideal is attributable not to any characteristics or properties essential to the ideal itself, but to the utter lack of alternative ideals and external challenges. As a *faute de mieux*, the ascetic ideal simply cannot tolerate competing estimations of the value of Life, and it owes its interpretive appeal solely to the monopoly it holds in the business of accounting for human suffering. It has sustained its hegemony not because its signature interpretation of suffering is *true*, but only because no rival ideals have yet emerged:

> The ascetic ideal has a *goal*—this goal is so universal that all the other interests of human existence seem, when compared with it, petty and narrow . . . it permits no other interpretation, no other goal; it rejects, denies, affirms, and sanctions solely from the point of view of *its* interpretation . . . [I]t believes that no power exists on earth that does not first have to receive a meaning, a right to exist, a value, as a tool of the ascetic ideal, as a way and means to *its* goal, to *one* goal. (GM III:23)

Because the ascetic ideal represents a "closed system of will, goal and interpretation" (GM III:23), all potential alternatives are quickly subsumed within, and co-opted by, the ascetic ideal. This means that the ascetic ideal can be harmed only by *itself*, in an inadvertent act of self-overcoming. If Nietzsche is to challenge the ascetic ideal, then he has no choice but to disrupt the economy of this "closed system" from within. He can harm the ascetic ideal only by contributing to its *self*-overcoming.

Although Nietzsche furnishes no alternative to the ascetic ideal, he does provide an example of the sort of endogenous disruption that might contribute to its eventual demise. As we have seen, he acknowledges as his ownmost task the self-overcoming of Christian morality (D P:4), a task that requires him to orchestrate the sublation of Christian morality from within. In order to contribute to the self-overcoming of Christian morality, he must force its native will to truth to confront *itself*. If he can somehow induce Christian morality to draw "its *most striking inference*, its inference *against* itself" (GM III:27), then Christian morality as we know it will perish by its own hand. It is within the context of his personal confrontation with Christian morality that Nietzsche operates, unwittingly, as a comedian of the ascetic ideal. He "harms" the ascetic ideal not by attacking it directly, but by arousing mistrust of its dominant, Christian interpretation.

Hijacking the Ascetic Ideal

The ascetic practices most familiar to us, those responsible for guiding our halting evolution from natural to human animals, have exhausted their usefulness for the continued development of humankind. They have furthermore engendered the "will to nothingness" that now threatens our very existence. In order to deflect the nihilistic impulse of our familiar complement of ascetic practices, Nietzsche attempts to institute an alternative set of ascetic practices, which, he believes, may enable him and his unknown "friends" to turn the *askēsis* demanded by civilization to their own advantage. Unable to despose the ascetic ideal or install an alternative, he attempts instead to hijack it for his own campaign to endow the successor age with a naturalistic, anti-Christian ideal.

While the ascetic ideal demands that all human beings practice self-denial, it does not require participation in any particular ascetic practices or disciplines. Nietzsche thus concludes from his genealogical investigations that no logical necessity binds the ascetic ideal to our current practices of self-denial and self-annihilation. Their linkage is the contingent, historically specific product of the dominant, Christian disposition of the ascetic ideal.

Hoping to exploit the historical contingency of the Christian disposition of the ascetic ideal, Nietzsche calls for a reversal of the process whereby the moral interpretation of the bad conscience gained ascendancy:

> Man has all too long had an "evil eye" for his natural inclinations, so that they have finally become inseparable from his "bad

conscience." An attempt at the reverse would *in itself* be possible—but who is strong enough for it?—that is, to wed the bad conscience to all the *unnatural* inclinations, all those aspirations to the beyond, to that which runs counter to sense, instinct, nature, animal, in short all ideals hitherto, which are one and all hostile to life and ideals that slander the world. (GM II:24)

The question he inserts into this otherwise promising passage conveys the enormity of the reversal he envisions: who would be "strong enough" to turn the ascetic ideal against its currently dominant disposition and impress the bad conscience into the service of the beleaguered affects?

While Nietzsche himself is not "strong enough" to effect this reversal on his own, he nevertheless believes that he and his unknown "friends" might collaborate in the strategic appropriation of the ascetic ideal. He imagines the appropriation of the ascetic ideal on the model of the original "slave revolt" that it is designed to reverse, and he anticipates for it a similarly protracted course of conflict. He prophesies that for the next two centuries at least, the fate of the reversal he initiates will remain uncertain (EH XIV:1). This wearying conflict will prove well worth its collateral casualties, however, for its successful resolution would eventually result in the installation of a naturalistic alternative to the ascetic ideal. Turning the formative power of *askēsis* to more constructive ends, the philosophers of the future would preside over the long-awaited completion of the human species. For the first time in their chequered history, human beings would stand security for their own future, subjecting to their design what had previously fallen to chance.

In order to play a modest preliminary role in realizing this redemptive vision of the future of humankind, Nietzsche aims to harness the corrosive power of the ascetic ideal for his campaign against Christian morality. Rather than overthrow or supplant the ascetic ideal, he attempts instead to foster mistrust of its reigning, Christian interpretation. He "harms" the ascetic ideal by multiplying its aspects, by providing an alternative to its dominant, Christian disposition. The endogenous shocks introduced by him into the economy of this closed system may temporarily disrupt and destabilize the dominant ascetic practices sanctioned by the institutions of Western culture. The ensuing slippage within the economy of the ascetic ideal may afford him an opportunity to promote his alternative interpretation of the ascetic ideal.

His goal for the remainder of modernity is to wed the bad conscience to the anti-affective "second" nature that humankind has acquired in the Christian period of its history. Because our "original" human nature is irretrievably lost to us, by virtue of our irreversible acculturation, any nature that we currently embody is an acquired, "second" nature. In essay II of the *Genealogy*, he demonstrates that institutionally reinforced ascetic practices can effectively reinscribe the code of human "nature," by engineering a "second" nature more amenable to the peculiar demands of particular, historically specific civilizations. Having set for itself the task of "breed[ing] an animal *with the right to make promises*" (GM II:1), Nature creates the machine of culture, which, through the gradual institutionalization of mnemotechnics, establishes the techniques through which humankind develops. Owing to the plasticity of the human soul, what was once culture has now become "second" nature.

Unable to legislate the completion of this transition from natural to human animal, Nietzsche undertakes instead to investigate the generative and recuperative properties resident within our largely unknown "second" nature. Hoping to turn our Christianized acculturation against itself, he experiments with ascetic disciplines that may safeguard the will and thereby enable humankind to survive the twilight of the idols. The immediate goal of his self-experimentation is to implement a set of ascetic practices that will redistribute the strain placed on the affects by the ascetic ideal, thus sparing them the mortal toll of any single, sustained ascetic discipline. He consequently attempts to divert the destructive focus of the ascetic ideal from our "original," affective nature to our acquired, anti-affective "second" nature.

Gambling that the *askēsis* required by civilization can be satisfied by an assault on the "second" nature that humankind has acquired, Nietzsche harnesses the erotic power of ascetic practices to tempt some individuals away from the anti-affective animus of Christian morality. For himself and his unknown comrades, he advocates what we might call—anticipating the full force of the oxymoron—an "ascetic naturalism." Hoping to relieve the affects of the mortal strain exerted against them by the Christian-moral interpretation of the bad conscience, he inaugurates a set of ascetic disciplines that target those anti-affective impulses that have become "second" nature within us. His "insane" task, he explains, is

> To translate man back into nature; to become master over the many vain and overly enthusiastic interpretations and connotations that have so far been scrawled and painted over that eternal basic text [*Grundtext*] of *homo natura*. (BGE 230)

By means of his naturalistic alternatives to the dominant ascetic strategies of Western civilization, he intends to scour "the eternal basic text of *homo natura*," gradually dissolving the moral accretions that have been "scrawled and painted" over it. He boastfully describes this experiment as his "attempt to assassinate two millennia of antinature and desecration of man" (EH IV:4).

The "tragic age" that Nietzsche foresees will be distinguished by the thoroughgoing naturalism of its sustaining values and ideals; metaphysical comforts will be dispensed only to those invalids whose existential suffering cannot otherwise be relieved. In preparation for this coming age, he must inaugurate—or so he believes—a campaign to eliminate the anti-natural vestiges of Christian morality. The goal of this campaign is to deliver to the "philosophers of the future" a fully naturalized model of the human soul, complete with the generative powers and faculties produced by two millennia of Christian acculturation.

Strictly speaking, however, the logic of Nietzsche's "ascetic naturalism" describes a position of anti-anti-naturalism; the installation of an originary, non-reactive naturalism lies beyond the compass of his depleted resources. He must consequently prosecute his assault on Christian morality by waging an antinatural attack on the "second" nature humankind has acquired in the process of submitting to Christian disciplines of *askēsis*. As we have seen, Nietzsche himself is occasionally able to direct his own resentment of modernity against itself, thereby turning his antinatural affects against his acquired, "second" nature.

This practice of internal disruption derives its promise and plausibility from the totalizing impulse of the ascetic ideal. In order to sustain itself as a closed system and co-opt any emerging alternatives, the ascetic ideal must expend a great deal of energy in the maintenance and regulation of its monopoly. Because this diffuse energy can—and must—be harnessed by agents who serve the ascetic ideal, it might also be appropriated by agents who oppose the ascetic ideal. While disciplining agents to serve its monolithic ends, the ascetic ideal also invests these agents with residual discretionary powers, which can, under certain circumstances, simultaneously be turned *against* the ascetic ideal itself. Owing to the lavish wealth of energy squandered by the ascetic ideal in the maintenance of its sprawling empire, agents who serve the ascetic ideal might also function as comedians of the ascetic ideal, provided that they can withstand the self-referential reverberations of their double agency. Indeed, these "comedians" would oppose the ascetic ideal, even as they continue to serve its ends.

The implementation of ascetic disciplines, especially those that place ever-escalating demands on the structural integrity of the soul, thus creates in some *übermenschlich* agents a feedback loop of heretofore unknown powers and faculties. In order to undergo the prescribed *askēsis*, agents must first be invested with sufficient power and vitality to wield effectively the ascetic instruments entrusted to them. In most cases, the ascetic demands placed on agents more or less cancel out any residual powers created in them, leaving the self-disciplined agents with no net gain in freedoms or faculties. In some extraordinary cases, however, ascetic disciplines will have a fortifying, fructifying effect on agents, inadvertently endowing them with unanticipated freedoms and affording them greater political latitude.

Hence Nietzsche's enduring interest in the paradox of the saint: in order to *tame* the will (as opposed to acknowledging one's weakness of will as a pre-existing condition), one must already possess a superhuman will, which disciplines of "taming" actually strengthen and fortify. As opposed to lesser ascetics, the saint discovers that his monkish life of solitude and self-denial has in fact succeeded in inflaming his prepotent will. Rather than simply quiet his noisome affects and castrate his tumescent will, his *askēsis* serves to arouse powers and faculties previously unknown to him. Nietzsche's own "autobiography" furnishes a related example of the feedback loop inadvertently created in extraordinary agents by ascetic disciplines. His own period of "convalescence" was governed by ascetic practices that not only enabled him to survive his bout with romantic pessimism, but also afforded him the novel perspective of a sickly, declining form of life. His "wisdom," he later allows, lies in his ability to reverse perspectives at will (EH I:1), which ability he unwittingly gained as a by-product of the ascetic disciplines that secured his convalescence.

Knowledge: A Form of Asceticism

Nietzsche's investigation into the history of morality is not merely academic, for he aims thereby to discover those ascetic practices that are most likely to be effective in deflecting the "will to nothingness." He consequently attempts to catalogue the full range of ascetic disciplines known to humankind, for he believes that, depending on the agents in question, all ascetic techniques are potentially both coercive and empowering.

While it is true that all ascetic practices declare war on the affective *Grundtext* of human "nature," it is also true that, in doing so, they invariably furnish (some) agents with a novel, heretofore undisclosed "second" nature. Nietzsche treats this acquired "second" nature as comprising, in extraordinary cases, a feedback loop invested with residual, and potentially productive, powers of self-denial. Under the aegis of the ascetic ideal (and often under the threat of death), human beings have learned to exploit the plasticity of the human soul. Self-denial is still the only game in town, but several millennia of ascetic experimentation have transformed the rules of this game and raised its stakes. The self that currently presents itself for *askēsis* is far more complex and variegated than ever before.

Nietzsche's campaign to "harm" the ascetic ideal thus sanctions his experimentation with a vast array of ascetic disciplines and practices. The philosopher in late modernity must appropriate the ascetic heritage of Western civilization, turning it to the advantage of humankind as a whole. Seeking to persuade his unknown friends of the possibilities that reside for them in an ascetic heritage that they cannot escape in any event,

Nietzsche contends that

> The most spiritual men, as the *strongest*, find their happiness
> where others would find their destruction: in the labyrinth, in
> hardness against themselves and others, in experimentation
> [*Versuch*]; their joy is self-conquest; asceticism becomes in them
> nature, need and instinct. Difficult tasks are a privilege to them;
> to play with burdens which crush others, a *recreation* [*Erholung*].
> *Knowledge—a form of asceticism.* (AC 57, emphasis added)

But how does one transform asceticism into a *recreation*? Nietzsche's
recourse to self-experimentation furnishes *his* answer, which may or may
not become our own. "Knowledge as a form of asceticism" is not simply
the subject matter of his post-Zarathustran method of investigation, but
its performative structure as well. His unique appropriation of *genealogy*,
for example, enables him to experiment with novel conceptions of agency,
untested methods of inquiry, and previously undetected connections
between seemingly unrelated phenomena.[7] In order to acquire genealogical knowledge, however, he must implement a specific set of ascetic
disciplines, which exact, among other casualties, the supposed validity of
his spurious claims to epistemic privilege. Indeed, the *Genealogy* both is
and is about an ascetic strategy for gaining knowledge, and it consequently tempts (some of) his readers to conduct similar experiments of
their own. As practiced and performed by Nietzsche, genealogy becomes
a *Versuch*, an experiment *and* a temptation, which entices (some of) his
readers "to play with burdens which crush others" (AC 57). His self-
experimentation in the pursuit of knowledge thus awakens the dormant
erōs of (some of) his readers.

To his fellow Dionysian travelers, Nietzsche recommends genealogy as
an ascetic discipline that both targets those anti-affective impulses that
have become "second" nature to us and inoculates against the nihilism
that attends the exhaustion of modernity. For those readers whose *erōs*
Nietzsche awakens, the aim or topic of his genealogies may ultimately be
irrelevant; it is his self-imposed *askēsis* that piques their interest in him.
His resistance to his own decay thus affiliates him with the exemplary
individuals who alone warrant the future of humankind. While his experiments with genealogy will neither reverse nor arrest the advance of
decadence in late modernity, they may lend unity and structure to the
ethical life of the Nietzschean "we."

Nietzsche's recommendation of asceticism as a "recreation" reflects his
enduring fascination with the political significance of *play*. Referring
explicitly to himself, he proclaims, "I do not know of any other way of
associating with great tasks than *play*: as a sign of greatness, this is an
essential presupposition" (EH II:10). He similarly attributes to Napoleon

a "naturalness where great tasks are something one plays with, one *may* play with" (TI IX:48). While it has become popular to figure Nietzsche as a champion of innocence, nature, dance, song, spontaneity, and play, the ludic elements of his thought must be carefully situated within the context of his larger philosophical enterprise. The free play and spontaneity available to the philosopher issue not from the suspension of ascetic disciplines and practices, but from their cultivation and perfection. To experiment on oneself requires an unmistakable violence, to which ascetic instruments are uniquely suited. Nietzsche consequently praises "the discipline of suffering, of *great* suffering," for "only *this* discipline has created all enhancements of humankind thus far" (BGE 225). As this passage indicates, only a select few, their battle-tested souls fortified by excruciating discipline and self-experimentation, may realistically come to view asceticism as a recreation; the rest of us can only play at playing.

As we have seen, Nietzsche tends to describe *askēsis* as producing in us a "second" nature to replace our obsolete, "original" nature. While he steadfastly insists, *contra* Rousseau, that our "first" nature is forever lost to us, we might wonder why he retains the residually romantic imagery of "Nature" at all. Indeed, as his own predilection for "sloughing" dead skins would seem to confirm (H II:2; GS P:4), he apparently conceives of Nature as irrepressibly regenerative, as unquenchably plenteous in its wealth and extravagance. He thus assumes that humankind will achieve its perfection within the economy of Nature, even if the "complete" human beings of the future bear little resemblance to their primitive forbears.

If we are to remain faithful to the experimental spirit of Nietzsche's philosophy, however, then we must identify and resist the prejudices that contour (and delimit) his own political thinking. While Nature has proven its resiliency time and again in this century, confounding all attempts by philosophers and scientists to vanquish it as a ground or condition of political life, the perfection of humankind may nevertheless lie *beyond* the plenum of Nature, in a cyborg artifice or machinic similacrum of human "nature."[8] Indeed, it is entirely possible, especially against the shifting background of contemporary science and technology, that Nietzsche's vision of the *Übermensch* will be realized only in the emergence of a post-natural being whose terrifying incarnation we have not yet begun to imagine.

Therapies of Survival: Educating the Body

Although Nietzsche often describes the philosopher's self-experimentation as wild and unprincipled, his more sober reflections convey a sense of the great care and strict discipline required to turn one's soul inside out. The goal of self-experimentation in late modernity, as in any decadent epoch, is to contribute to the development of therapies of survival.

Like Wittgenstein, Nietzsche ascribes to philosophy a salutary, if limited, therapeutic function. The general goal of self-experimentation is to develop a specific regimen of self-overcoming that better enables one to negotiate the practical exigencies peculiar to one's age. Nietzsche's own regimen of self-overcoming is designed to deliver him neither to autonomy nor authenticity, but to a strategically advantaged situation within his epoch, such that he might expend his residual vitality in the service of his aversion to the decadence of modernity. In light of the strict discipline required to develop the "ascetic naturalism" he envisions, he recommends self-overcoming only to those "free spirits" who can both afford and withstand the *askēsis* involved in self-experimentation. These experiments are furthermore designed to produce only rare and exotic selves. There is no room for the "letting go" and *laisser aller* prized by the *demos*; Nietzsche has no interest in reproducing bloodless permutations of the last man.

As an example of the disciplined self-experimentation he has in mind, Nietzsche extols the martial wisdom of Julius Caesar, who cultivated in himself those "inexorable and fearful instincts that provoke the maximum of authority and discipline against themselves" (TI IX:38). Caesar's greatness lies not in the outward, macropolitical expressions of his legislations, but in his lawgiving itself, in which his unique regimen of self-overcoming is manifestly reflected. While orthodox historians locate Caesar's genius in the magisterial vitality that he involuntarily propagates, Nietzsche directs our attention to Caesar's unmatched capacity to manage and direct the vitality with which destiny endows him. He consequently treats the military and political exploits for which Caesar is famous as the expressions or by-products of a more basic regimen of self-overcoming.

Nietzsche similarly applauds Goethe for developing a regimen of self-overcoming that enabled him to master the inherent tensions and contradictions of his age. He describes Goethe as a

> [M]agnificent attempt to overcome the eighteenth century by a return to Nature, by an *ascent* to the naturalness of the Renaissance—a kind of self-overcoming on the part of that century . . . What he wanted was *totality*; he fought the mutual extraneousness of reason, senses, feeling and will. . . (TI IX:49)

By "creating himself," Goethe attained an immanent critical standpoint within the age that shaped him, and he conveyed his critique of the eighteenth century by means of the embodied reproach he disciplined himself to enact. By turning his destiny to his full advantage, Goethe elicits Nietzsche's highest praise:

> Goethe conceived a human being who would be strong, highly educated, skillful in all bodily matters, self-controlled, reverent

toward himself, and who might dare to afford the whole range
and wealth of being natural. . . (TI IX:49)

Whereas Goethe was spared the advanced decay of the nineteenth century,
Nietzsche has no choice but to embody the diminished vitality of an age
he describes as "merely an intensified, *brutalized* eighteenth century" (TI
IX:50). He therefore must fashion for himself a regimen of self-overcoming
that is appropriate to the dwindling vitality of his epoch. Like Caesar and
Goethe before him, he aims not to increase the residual vitality at his
disposal, but to manage its expression efficiently and strategically. He
consequently transforms himself into a specific kind of decadent, one who
expresses his dwindling vitality by means of an aversion to decadence.
This alternate expression of decadence, he gambles, may be sufficient to
safeguard the will and guarantee its survival.

Toward this end, he develops a regimen of self-overcoming designed
to produce in himself a modified "second" nature. While he cannot realistically hope to equip himself with an entirely new system of instincts,
the modest "counter-instincts" he cultivates may succeed in mitigating
slightly the decadence he involuntarily enacts. His volitional resources are
limited, but so are his (revised) goals.

In attempting to modify the functional specifications of his own destiny,
he aims to implement an insight that he attributes to the Greeks:

> It is decisive for the lot of a people and of humanity that culture
> should begin in the right place—not in the "soul" (as was the
> fateful superstition of the priests and half-priests): the right place
> is the body, the gesture, the diet, physiology; the rest follows
> from that. Therefore the Greeks remain the first cultural event
> in history: they knew, they *did*, what was needed; and
> Christianity, which despised the body, has been the greatest
> misfortune of humanity so far. (TI IX:47)

Like the Greeks, then, Nietzsche begins his therapy of survival "in the
right place," by educating his body. Unlike the Greeks, however, who
enjoyed the luxury of an overflowing will, he must carefully manage a
dwindling store of vitality. We should therefore not expect his regimen
of self-overcoming to fashion anything resembling the noble warriors of
Greek antiquity, for late modernity simply cannot afford to stage such
lavish productions.

In order to see how seriously Nietzsche takes the education of the body,
one need only look to his "autobiography." *Ecce Homo* describes in detail
the regimen of self-overcoming that delivered him to his "destiny." Here
he speaks not of his momentous and lasting achievements, but of "all

these small things which are generally considered matters of complete indifference" (EH II:10). When expressly dispensing the basic tenets of "his morality," he speaks not of the *Übermensch*, the Antichrist, active forgetting, or virile warriors, but of his insights into *diet* (EH II:1). When accounting for "everything that deserves to be taken seriously in life," he turns not to the questions that exercise kings, judges, and priests, but to the more fundamental "questions of nourishment, abode, spiritual diet, treatment of the sick, cleanliness and weather" (EH XIV:8). Through his seemingly idle experiments with nutrition, location, climate, and recreation, he gradually became what he is: a modern who takes the measure of modernity, a decadent who opposes decadence, a truthful critic of truth, a manly midwife, and a pious Antichrist.

Ecce Homo thus conveys a sense of the subtle, nuanced transformations that Nietzsche undertakes, and it provides a more realistic picture of the self-experimentation he recommends to the highest specimens of a dying epoch. Whereas Zarathustra longs to wield his cruel hammer and release the *Übermensch* imprisoned in the stubborn granite of humanity (Z II:2), Nietzsche employs a much lighter touch, and a tuning-fork (TI P), in sculpting a destiny for himself. Rather than clarify important teachings, revise core insights or recant abandoned dogmas, he corrects a single note in the score of his lugubrious, and largely forgotten, *Hymn to Life*: "Last note of the A-clarinet, c flat, not c: misprint" (EH IX:1).

Of course, the magnitude of any feat of self-overcoming corresponds to the residual vitality at one's disposal. Nietzsche attends to "all the small things" only because he cannot afford to tackle anything greater. Like Wagner, "who crowds into the smallest space an infinity of sense and sweetness," Nietzsche achieves his greatest success as a *miniaturist* (CW 7). Unable to legislate on the grand scale to which he naturally aspires, he presides masterfully over the minute details of his own project of self-overcoming. Here he turns his destiny to his own advantage, artfully perfecting the limited domain to which his decadence confines him. He not only attains an unequalled mastery of the philosophical aphorism, abandoning the grand, systematic ambitions of his youth, but also permits his artist's gaze to settle, finally, on the subtle shades and delicate nuances of quotidian life. Pundits and potentates may ignore his angry little books, but Turinese costermongers honor him with their sweetest grapes (EH III:2).

Which experimental selves should the decadent philosopher attempt to embody? While all techniques of the self are equally heteronomous, some will prove more advantageous (and more dangerous) in the pursuit of particular ends. Nietzsche, for example, is intent on discovering those ascetic disciplines that will prove most resistant to the advent of the "will to nothingness." He consequently privileges those ascetic disciplines that promise to retard the deterioration of the affects. Since he does not know a priori which specific ascetic practices will be least threatening to a crippled will, he resorts to self-experimentation. He consequently probes the resiliency of decadence, implementing and embodying "next" selves that accommodate an increasingly greater range and depth of affective expenditure. He "guesses what remedies avail against what is harmful," a gambit that proves that he "has turned out well" (EH I:2). If successful in his guesses, he may seduce his fellow travelers to their "next" selves and perhaps help them to resist their own decadence. If unsuccessful in his guesses, or if slow to revise them, he may inadvertently hasten the exhaustion of late modernity.

In fashioning his therapy of survival, Nietzsche combats danger with danger. He can offer no assurance that self-experimentation—either as a general strategy or in his own specific experiments—actually succeeds in retarding decadence. It may be, as he suggests in his more pessimistic moments, that the project of resisting the decadence of modernity is simply futile. Or it may be, as he suggests in his more exuberant moments, that philosophers can successfully wage war with their age and thus resist those strains of decadence to which they are most vulnerable. All he "knows" from his genealogy of morals is that the available range of selves has been artificially and dangerously circumscribed in late modernity, and that the predilection for self-destructive techniques of the self threatens the very survival of the will. He thus hopes to contribute to a proliferation of rare and exotic selves, whose identities he cannot begin to predict.

Nietzsche's advocacy of self-experimentation, though deliberately outrageous, is neither purely rhetorical nor merely idle. In his own attempt to achieve the "timelessness" that he believed would expand the horizon of human perfectibility, he subjected himself to dangerous forms of self-experimentation. He regularly turned the scalpel on himself, flaying protective tissues of prejudice and probing the darkest recesses of his labyrinthine soul.[9] Hoping to develop a regimen of self-overcoming that would enable him and his "friends" to resist more effectively the decadence of late modernity, he endured solitude, loneliness, physiological torment and exhaustion, wonder diets, miracle cures, panacetic drugs, and even the onset of madness. As is his wont, he presents a heroic face throughout, advertising his experiments as symptoms of his own "*great* health, that superfluity which grants to the free spirit the dangerous privilege of living *experimentally* [*auf den Versuch hin leben*] and of being allowed to offer itself to adventure" (H I:P4).

More emphatically than any other aspect of his life and work, however, this penchant for self-experimentation conveys his despair at the inexorable advance of decay in late modernity. In this respect, his experiments represent a desperate gamble, for his therapy of survival may actually contribute to the production of frightening monstrosities, and even to his own demise. Strategies of self-directed violence always run the risk of inflicting wounds that are not only significative, but also mortal. Nietzsche's own experiment with protracted solitude, for example, nearly killed him before securing his convalescence (GS P), and it may ultimately have hastened his departure from sanity. In the end, the urgency of his experimental spirit was rivalled only by that of his fears for the future.

7
Nietzsche's Political Legacy

I am no man, I am dynamite . . . It is only beginning with me that the
earth knows *great politics*.

(EH XIV:1)

The only valid tribute to thought such as Nietzsche's is precisely to use
it, to make it groan and protest. And, if the commentators say I am
being unfaithful to Nietzsche, that is of absolutely no interest.

—Michel Foucault, "Prison Talk"

Nietzsche's political legacy is notoriously difficult to reckon, in large part
because his thinking so readily invites misinterpretation and misappro-
priation. "*Non legor, non legar,*" he boasts in his autobiography,
perversely citing his lack of worthy readers as evidence of his untimely
wisdom (EH III:1). For all of his complaints about the numbing inade-
quacies of his readers, however, he did virtually everything in his power
to encourage confusion and misunderstanding. Shifting masks, multiple
personae, polytropaic paroxysms, nested ironies and self-referential paro-
dies, wayward textual strategies, hastily conceived thought experiments,
Zarathustran exotericisms, hagiographic autobiographies, insincere attempts
at self-criticism—all of these signature rhetorical ploys have contributed
to the bewilderment of his readers. That he is not read, or not read well,
may be the inevitable fruition of a self-fulfilling prophecy.

The Standard Reading of Nietzsche

Nietzsche's strategy of indirection has backfired egregiously and often.
Rather than discourage unworthy readers from attempting to divine his
Promethean wisdom, his rhetorical gyrations have in fact issued a blanket
invitation to cranks and scholars alike. Encountering no insurmountable

textual obstacles to their own interpretations of his elusive teachings, Nietzsche's readers regularly conscript him as the philosophical progenitor of their respective political schemes. As evidence of the runaway ramifications of his political legacy, his influence and inspiration are now claimed by virtually every possible constituency—including many sects, movements, schools, and cults that he expressly repudiated in his writings.

Hitler's *Mein Kampf* is littered with ersatz Nietzscheanisms, which Nazi ideologues dutifully cobbled together to serve as the philosophical platform for their insane, misanthropic vision of political dystopia. Nietzsche's defenders rightly point out that these anti-Semitic, pro-genocidal "teachings" were mercilessly wrenched from their subtle philosophical contexts, that he was heartlessly betrayed to the National Socialists by his self-appointed executrix, the opportunistic Elisabeth. Despite his obvious and well-documented animadversions to the brand of political thuggery exemplified by National Socialism, however, nothing he says rules out definitively the Nazi interpretation of his teachings. He deliberately orchestrated the proliferation of a multiplicity of diverse readings, and the resulting farrago of interpretations constitutes his true political legacy.

Although roundly rejected as an interpretive abomination, the Nazi appropriation of Nietzsche's political thinking has nevertheless exerted an indirect influence on the articulation of its extant legacy. Owing in large part to the "family resemblance" obtaining between some of his teachings and certain tenets of Nazi ideology, even sympathetic readers have refused to take seriously his political thinking on its own terms. He is occasionally lauded as a perspicacious critic of liberalism, Christianity, or modernity itself; as a keen judge of the political resources and achievements of Greek antiquity; as a vocal champion of autonomy, self-reliance and authenticity; as a prescient opponent of the likely evolution of German nationalism; as an astute diagnostician of cultural malaise; as a vigilant sentry posted on the advancing frontier of postmodernity; and so on. But he is rarely considered, on the strength of his teachings, an important political thinker in his own right.

Indeed, a standard reading has emerged of Nietzsche as a *failed radical voluntarist*, whose shrill call for the redemption of modernity, at the hands of the enigmatic *Übermensch*, is simply incompatible with his trenchant critique of modernity. By fatuously entrusting the future of humankind to a titanic act of *übermenschlich* will, or so the story goes, Nietzsche betrays his own greatest insights into the complexities of political life in modernity. In doing so, he prematurely abandons the residual political resources of late modernity, which, many critics insist, shelter more promising possibilities of regeneration than the desperate hopes he invests in the coming of the redemptive *Übermensch*. In the end, his political thinking is compromised by a grave mismeasure of his own epoch, a misunderstanding so pervasive and systemic that it renders his political thinking irrelevant to the lives of modern agents.[1]

This standard reading of Nietzsche as a failed radical voluntarist owes its authority in large part to Martin Heidegger's influential interpretation. Heidegger describes Nietzsche as the "last metaphysican of the West," whose ingenious attempt to overcome the metaphysical tradition of Western philosophy ultimately founders, like all such attempts, on the shoals of subjectivism. Rather than signal his emigration beyond metaphysics (which Heidegger views as coextensive with nihilism), Nietzsche's doctrine of will to power constitutes the final stage in the development of metaphysical thinking:

> Because thinking in terms of values is grounded in the metaphysics of the will to power, Nietzsche's interpretation of nihilism as the event of the devaluing of the highest values and the revaluing of all values is a metaphysical interpretation, and that in the sense of the metaphysics of the will to power.[2]

According to Heidegger, Nietzsche proposes an irreducibly subjectivistic solution—a "revaluation of all values"—to the problem of nihilism. He consequently remains a residually metaphysical thinker, albeit the "last" of this misbegotten breed: "even Nietzsche's own experience of nihilism, i.e., that it is the devaluing of the highest values, is after all a nihilistic one."[3] Nietzsche's residual subjectivism is crystallized, Heidegger believes, in his teaching of eternal recurrence, which entrusts to the will the Promethean task of "eternalizing the moment." This desperate recourse to radical voluntarism may not succeed in overturning the metaphysical tradition, but it does succeed in constituting the "final" unfolding of this tradition, as it distills the whole of subjectivism into a single, transformative explosion of the *übermenschlich* will.

Although Heidegger prefers to situate Nietzsche's failed voluntarism in the context of his ill-fated attempt to overcome the tradition of metaphysical thinking, this interpretation is readily translated into distinctly political terms: Nietzsche's otherwise promising confrontation with modernity is subverted by his stubborn insistence on a voluntaristic solution to the besetting problems of nihilism and decadence. This standard reading thus takes the form articulated in the following general outline:

1. Nietzsche advances a withering critique of the signature institutions of modernity: liberalism, Enlightenment, democracy, Christianity, and so on.
2. His critique exposes the abject failure of these signature institutions to fashion for themselves the rational justifications that allegedly distinguish them from the "primitive," unjustifiable institutions of premodern political regimes.

3. Reacting to the failure of these signature institutions to ground and defend themselves rationally, Nietzsche desperately capitulates to the "other" of reason, declaring all claims of reason to be nothing more (nor less) than disguised expressions of will to power.
4. Because political life in modernity cannot justify itself by appeal to rational terms and principles, he appeals instead to will to power as the sole adjudicating standard of "nobility," "mastery," "health," "genius," and all other superlative political values.
5. As his critique of modernity demonstrates, however, the age itself is simply too decadent, too depleted in its native volitional resources, to sustain a "noble," aristocratic political regime.
6. Blinded by his romantic, nostalgic allegiances to the manly political regimes of Greek and Roman antiquity, Nietzsche declares modernity to be irrecuperably decadent and sterile. He prematurely abandons the imperfect projects and institutions by means of which the epoch has defined itself.[4]
7. Having judged modernity to be incapable of restoring and regenerating its signature projects and institutions, Nietzsche locates the salvation of modernity in the transformative volitional resources of those shadowy redemptive figures who someday will come: the "free spirits," the "philosophers of the future," the *Übermensch*, and, finally, Dionysus himself.
8. Owing to Nietzsche's premature rejection of the regenerative powers resident within modernity, and to the irrational hopes he invests in a mysterious, redemptive act of *übermenschlich* will, his confrontation with modernity transgresses the recognizable boundaries of sane political thinking—as confirmed, some would say, by his clinically diagnosed slide into madness.

Variations on the general theme of Nietzsche's failed voluntarism are found in virtually all influential studies of his political thinking, including those proffered by Arendt, Kaufmann, Strong, MacIntyre, Yack, Schutte, Warren, Vattimo, Habermas, Detwiler, Ansell-Pearson, and Berkowitz. In all of these studies, Nietzsche is initially (if warily) applauded as an astute critic of political life in modernity, only to be dismissed in the end as a naive voluntarist. Rather than accurately assay the residual restorative powers of modernity (especially those contained within reason itself), he prematurely disowns the epoch as a whole. As a consequence of the failure of his radical voluntarism, Nietzsche's political thinking may be provocative, ingenious, insightful, and entertaining, but it is largely irrelevant to contemporary political life. Despite his engaging vitality, he has nothing to say of lasting constructive value to agents laboring in the twilight epoch of modernity.[5] His standing in the canon of Western political thought remains that of a hideous scarecrow, whose horrifying, irrational excesses frighten us into renewing our tepid commitments to the democratic reforms and liberal ideals of modernity—despite our nagging doubts about their continued value and efficacy.

A strong case can be made for this standard reading of Nietzsche as a failed radical voluntarist, and the scholars mentioned above have collectively presented such a case. But is this the most promising line of interpretation to pursue? While this standard reading of Nietzsche is certainly plausible on a textual basis, its primary attraction lies, I believe, in the definitive judgment it renders against the National Socialists' appropriation of his political thinking. If Nietzsche is a failed voluntarist (and thus irrelevant to modern political life), then the Nazi ideology that grew out of this voluntarism is similarly bankrupt. In order to discredit the philosophical pretensions of National Socialism (and all kindred political monstrosities), the standard reading of Nietzsche discredits the source of these pretensions, which it locates in his irrational appeal to the transformative properties of the *übermenschlich* will.[6]

The contribution of this standard reading to a condemnation of Nazi ideology is certainly commendable, but it is not so helpful in arriving at a clear understanding of Nietzsche's political thinking. I have attempted in this study to challenge the standard reading of Nietzsche's political thinking, to show that he works carefully within the context of his own critique of modernity, and to illuminate the relatively unexplored moral content of his political teachings. While his irrational voluntarism constitutes one branch of his tangled political legacy, it is neither the most prominent ramification nor the most fruitful to cultivate.

Nietzsche and Contemporary Liberalism

Nietzsche was an outspoken, unrelenting critic of liberal political ideals, which he interpreted as symptomatic of the irreversible decay of the modern epoch. For obvious reasons, then, most liberal theorists have refused to embrace his political legacy. As we have seen, his perfectionism does not fare very well in John Rawls's survey of potential sources for (liberal) principles of justice.

Nietzsche and MacIntyre

Another critic of liberalism, Alasdair MacIntyre, actually proposes Nietzsche's political thinking as representative of the signature errors and failures of liberalism. Although Nietzsche may appear to be a critic of the Enlightenment project, his "criticisms" in fact reflect the natural, self-referential development of liberal individualism. Hence, MacIntyre insists, the irreducible irrationality of Nietzsche's political thinking:

The rational and rationally justified autonomous moral subject of the eighteenth century is a fiction, an illusion; so, Nietzsche resolves, let will replace reason and let us make ourselves into autonomous moral subjects by some gigantic and heroic act of the will. . . .[7]

MacIntyre thus cites Nietzsche's irrational excesses as evidence of the shipwreck of liberal political theory:

[T]he Nietzschean stance turns out not to be a mode of escape from or an alternative to the conceptual scheme of liberal individualist modernity, but rather one more representative moment in its internal unfolding.[8]

Interpreting the doctrine of will to power as the logical outcome of the project of Enlightenment, MacIntyre presents Nietzsche as a negative exemplar of modernity, whose misguided quest to produce the *Übermensch* exemplifies the bankruptcy of liberal individualism:

[E]*ither* one must follow through the aspirations and the collapse of the different versions of the Enlightenment project until there remains only the Nietzschean diagnosis and the Nietzschean problematic *or* one must hold that the Enlightenment project was not only mistaken, but should never have been commenced in the first place.[9]

MacIntyre thus exploits the supposedly dead ends and blind alleys of Nietzsche's political thinking to call for a reconsideration of the Aristotelian moral tradition, whose premature rejection, he believes, constitutes the signal error of modernity:

[T]he defensibility of the Nietzschean position turns *in the end* on the answer to the question: was it right in the first place to reject Aristotle? For if Aristotle's position in ethics and politics— or something very like it—could be sustained, the whole Nietzschean enterprise would be pointless.[10]

Despite his manifest allegiances to Aristotle, MacIntyre nevertheless subscribes to a surprisingly Nietzschean account of the political resources and options available to late modernity. The discontinuities and incommensurabilities that characterize moral discourse in late modernity are largely antithetical to a retrieval or recuperation of the Aristotelian moral tradition. Considerable time is needed to heal the wounds inflicted by the runaway excesses of liberal individualism, and MacIntyre bids us to begin this slow process of moral convalescence by founding, and cultivating, local ethical communities.

These micro-communities will not succeed in restoring the moribund Aristotelian tradition, but they may ensure that "both morality and civility might survive the coming ages of barbarism and darkness."[11] Invoking a remarkably Nietzschean image of the plight of moral agents in late modernity, MacIntyre expresses guarded optimism that ethical life may yet withstand the advance of decadence:

> What matters at this stage is the construction of local forms of community within which civility and the intellectual and moral life can be sustained through the new dark ages which are already upon us. And if the tradition of the virtues was able to survive the horrors of the last dark ages, we are not entirely without grounds for hope . . . We are waiting not for a Godot, but for another—doubtless very different—St. Benedict.[12]

Nietzsche and Habermas

MacIntyre's criticisms of Nietzsche are echoed in the work of Jürgen Habermas, who nevertheless deploys them in the service of his own spirited defense of the modern Enlightenment project. According to Habermas, MacIntyre is right about Nietzsche, but wrong about the Enlightenment project whose Nietzschean bankruptcy he declares:

> Nietzsche enthrones taste . . . as the organ of a knowledge beyond true and false, beyond good and evil. But he cannot legitimate the criteria of aesthetic judgment that he holds on to because he transposes aesthetic experience into the archaic, because he does not recognize as a moment of reason the critical capacity for assessing value that was sharpened through dealing with modern art—a moment that is still at least procedurally connected with objectifying knowledge and moral insight in the processes of providing argumentative grounds.[13]

Nietzsche's irrational appeals to the will to power constitute the logical, self-referential consequences not of reason *per se*, but of what Habermas calls "subject-centered reason." As an articulation of subject-centered reason, the dominant philosophical discourse of modernity has indisputably reached a point of crisis and implosion, but this particular discourse is neither singular nor privileged within the political life of modern agents. According to Habermas, in fact, Nietzsche himself has contributed greatly to our growing appreciation of the crisis of subject-centered reason. Rather than abandon subject-centered reason in favor of a revised, more promising concept of reason, however, Nietzsche concludes his critique of rationality by enshrining the "other" of reason, the will to power:

> The aesthetic domain, as the gateway to the Dionysian, is hypo-statized instead into the other of reason. The disclosures of power theory get caught up in the dilemma of a self-enclosed critique of reason that has become total . . . [Nietzsche] could muster no clarity about what it means to pursue a critique of ideology that attacks its own foundations.[14]

According to Habermas, then, Nietzsche's own critique of modernity manifests contradictions and justificatory lacunae that are structurally similar to those he detects in subject-centered reason:

> Like all who leap out of the dialectic of enlightenment, Nietzsche undertakes a conspicuous leveling. Modernity loses its singular status; it constitutes only a last epoch in the far-reaching history of a rationalization initiated by the dissolution of archaic life and the collapse of myth.[15]

Although Nietzsche's critique is both valid and valuable, it is insufficient on its own terms to sanction his subsequent (and precipitous) "leap out of the dialectic of enlightenment." Had he responded to this crisis by returning to the "counterdiscourse" of modernity, his contribution to the Enlightenment might not have been strictly destructive.

Having prematurely rejected reason, as well as the "counterdiscourse" potentially available to him, Nietzsche has no choice but to consign the fate of modernity to those mysterious lawgivers and commanders who will follow:

> On the one hand, historical enlightenment only strengthens the now palpable diremptions in the achievements of modernity; reason as manifested in the form of a religion of culture no longer develops any synthetic forces that could renew the unifying power of traditional religion. On the other hand, the path of restoration is barred to modernity. The religious-metaphysical world views of ancient civilizations are themselves already a product of enlightenment; they are *too rational*, therefore, to be able to provide opposition to the radicalized enlightenment of modernity.[16]

To Habermas, Nietzsche's lurid enactment of the shipwreck of subject-centered reason demonstrates not so much the eclipse of rationality itself (as many of Nietzsche's French scions have apparently concluded), as the need to articulate a more adequate concept of reason. Habermas consequently attempts to revive the "counterdiscourse" of modernity, wherein subject-centered reason has been intermittently confronted with the sorts of criticisms that Nietzsche and MacIntyre rehearse. A careful attention to this counterdiscourse, and especially to the critical clashes that have determined the course of its chequered career, reveals to Habermas a "road not taken," i.e., the possibility of a concept of reason that is immune to the now-familiar objections to subject-centered reason.

Drawing on his excavations thus far of the counterdiscourse of modernity, Habermas proposes the concept of "communicative action," which, he believes, might enable us to construct a model of reason grounded in mutual recognition and reciprocity. Communicative action posits as its ideal the rational discourse that obtains within a non-strategic, distortion-free communication situation, between parties who freely agree to appeal to, and abide by, reciprocally binding validity claims. Within the intersubjective paradigm of communicative action, reason dispenses a restorative dose of enlightenment, which is precisely the prescription Habermas recommends for the ills diagnosed by Nietzsche and MacIntyre.

Habermas reserves no part for Nietzsche in either the retrieval of the counterdiscourse of modernity or the ongoing articulation of the model of communicative action. Nietzsche's role in the renewed dialectic of Enlightenment is exclusively negative, as a warning to other philosophers who would prematurely abandon the claims of rationality. While Habermas may ultimately be justified in rejecting Nietzsche's political thinking, I hope to have shown in this study that he is mistaken to exclude Nietzsche from his attempts to revive the dialectic of Enlightenment. The popular interpretation of Nietzsche as a "prophet of extremity," who fetishizes the "other" of reason, trades upon a caricature of his post-Zarathustran thinking. As I have attempted to demonstrate, Nietzsche actually continues his critique of subject-centered reason while experimenting with alternative concepts. In fact, Habermas's deflationary approach to Nietzsche's political thinking is remarkably similar in form and execution to the "leveling" operation that he accuses Nietzsche of undertaking with respect to modernity as a whole.[17] As in the case of MacIntyre's grandiose polemic, many of the ethical and political resources Habermas seeks to recover can perhaps be found in the lair of his sworn enemy, Nietzsche.

Although Nietzsche unequivocally declares bankrupt the grand, sweeping dream of the Enlightenment, his genealogical method nevertheless celebrates the subversive, unmasking power of local applications of reason. Drawing on a familiar image of Enlightenment, he praises the demystifying power of his *Genealogy*: "In the end, in the midst of perfectly gruesome detonations, a *new* truth becomes visible every time among thick clouds" (EH XI). He subsequently advertises himself as the lone champion of truth, proudly claiming to be "the first to *discover* the truth" and accounting for his "calamitous" destiny by representing himself as "truth enter[ing] into a fight with the lies of millennia" (EH XIV:1). In light of his complex political aims, a muted celebration of his own will to truth is perfectly understandable. If he is to contribute to the *self*-overcoming of Christian morality, then it *must* be the case that he too labors in the service of the will to truth, that he too takes his flame "from the fire ignited by a faith millennia old, the Christian faith, which was also Plato's, that God is truth, that truth is *divine*" (GS 344, cited in GM III:24).

Nietzsche and Rorty

Richard Rorty has defended in recent years a "postmodernist bourgeois liberalism," whose Nietzschean debts he readily acknowledges.[18] Undeterred (and unimpressed) by Nietzsche's scathing critique of liberal ideals, Rorty undertakes a selective appropriation of the basic elements of his political thinking. The key to reconciling Nietzsche's overtly illiberal thought with the guiding ideals of liberalism lies in restricting his moral perfectionism to the private sphere. This reconciliation is possible, Rorty explains, because Nietzsche's cranky attacks on liberalism are not germane to his enduring philosophical insights:

> Nietzsche often speaks as though he had a social mission, as if he had views relevant to public action—distinctly antiliberal views. But, as also in the case of Heidegger, this antiliberalism seems adventitious and idiosyncratic—for the kind of self-creation of which Nietzsche and Heidegger are models seems to have nothing in particular to do with questions of social policy.[19]

Explicitly building on the narrative model of self-creation that Alexander Nehamas attributes to Nietzsche,[20] Rorty enlists Nietzsche to galvanize the ethical life of contemporary liberal democratic societies. Enamored of Nietzsche's anti-essentialism and perspectivism but repulsed by his recidivistic appeal to the metaphysics of the will to power, Rorty articulates a purified, postmodern interpretation of Nietzschean self-creation. To create oneself anew, Rorty explains, is simply a matter of fashioning for oneself an enabling narrative, in which one exercises and displays one's own "final vocabulary," a designation he proposes for the evolving constellation of terms, concepts, and expressions whereby one conveys one's ownmost hopes, fears, and aspirations. The goal of narrative self-creation, which Rorty calls "autonomy," is achieved when one successfully deploys a final vocabulary that one calls one's own. Rorty's postmodernist bourgeois liberalism would not only encourage such self-creation in its citizenry, but also foster a tolerance for the self-creation of others. Borrowing a Zarathustran image for his sketch of the "liberal ironists" who inhabit his political utopia, Rorty maintains that "[a]ll any ironist can measure success against is the past—not by living up to it, but by re-describing it in his terms, thereby becoming able to say 'Thus I willed it.'"[21]

While Nietzsche's political thinking is undeniably inimical to the flourishing of liberal ideals, it poses a genuine threat to liberal democracy only if allowed to contour political discourse in the public sphere. The liberal ironists who populate Rorty's utopia may incorporate Nietzsche's moral perfectionism into their own private disciplines of self-creation, seeking to arrive at a final vocabulary that expresses their ownmost achievement of autonomy, but they publicly pledge allegiance only to the liberal ideals that protect and sustain their private pursuits of self-perfection. The fruits of their private labors of self-creation may eventually be imported into the public sphere, but *only* insofar as they uphold the signature ideals of liberal democracy.

Rorty thus enshrines Nietzsche as a private hero, who, if refused access to the public sphere, indirectly furnishes the dynamism and vitality of a thriving democracy. In order to convey the essence of his postmodernist bourgeois liberalism, Rorty proposes the following "compromise":

> *Privatize* the Nietzschean—Sartrean—Foucauldian attempt at authenticity and purity, in order to prevent yourself from slipping into a political attitude which will lead you to think that there is some social goal more important than avoiding cruelty.[22]

In this limited respect, Rorty's appropriation of Nietzsche as the unacknowledged progenitor of liberal democracy is not unlike Cavell's defense of Nietzsche's role in the moral education of democratic citizens.

While Rorty's appropriation of Nietzsche's moral perfectionism is ingenious, we might wonder about the political value of an ideal of "autonomy" whose expression and enactment can realistically be limited to the private sphere. Nietzsche unequivocally insists that "healthy" self-creation is never strictly private. Any attempt to contain the public reverberations of moral perfectionism will succeed only in artificially restricting the range of possible "next" selves to be created. "Healthy" self-creation always involves a Dionysian element of excess or superfluity, which would obliterate Rorty's guiding distinction between public and private:

> The genius, in work and deed, is necessarily a squanderer: that he squanders himself, that is his greatness. The instinct of self-preservation is suspended, as it were; the overpowering pressure of outflowing forces forbids him any such care or caution. (TI IX:44)

In order to maintain his guiding distinction, Rorty must repress (or otherwise contain) those elements of excess that Nietzsche claims are essential to self-creation. Although Rorty sincerely invites the citizens of his utopia to create themselves anew, he also requires that whatever "next" selves they create will be compatible with the (conservative) liberal pluralism he envisions.

One possible "solution" to the problem of excess lies, of course, in the advancing decadence of modernity. If the pursuit and achievement of self-perfection *can* be restricted to the confines of the private sphere, then Rorty's postmodernist bourgeois liberalism may constitute a feasible model for political life in late modernity.[23] If Rorty *has* accurately surveyed the compass of moral perfectionism in late modernity, however, then perhaps his postmodernist bourgeois liberalism should be collected under the rubric Allan Bloom proposes for Rawls's theory of justice: *A First Philosophy for the Last Man*.[24]

Nietzsche and Feminism

On the basis of the textual evidence alone, we would be hard pressed to propose a less likely champion of feminist politics than Nietzsche. His occasional remarks on the status of women, or the problem of *das Weib an sich*, are rivalled in their misogyny only by the retrograde musings of his *Erzieher*, Arthur Schopenhauer.[25] Although feminist scholars have recently devoted a great deal of productive energy to the strategic (and selective) appropriation of Nietzsche's political thinking,[26] his greatest contribution to feminist politics remains both indirect and unintended. His political legacy for contemporary feminism descends most vitally from his critique of objectivity, which some feminist scholars have recently adapted for incorporation into the epistemological frameworks of their own political projects.

Nietzsche's perspectivism, an epistemic thesis conveyed via a host of masculinist and residually misogynist images, might seem an unlikely precursor of feminist epistemologies. But in fact Nietzsche articulates an epistemic position that both acknowledges and accommodates the radically situated experiences that are prized by feminist thinkers. In the following passage, which contains his most detailed and sustained discussion of the position now known as "perspectivism," he both exposes the snares of traditional epistemology and points us in a more promising direction:

> [L]et us be on guard against the dangerous old conceptual fiction that posited a "pure, will-less, painless, timeless knowing subject";
> let us guard against the snares of such contradictory concepts as "pure reason," "absolute spirituality," "knowledge in itself":

these always demand that we should think of an eye that is completely unthinkable, an eye turned in no particular direction, in which the active and interpreting forces, through which alone seeing becomes seeing *something*, are supposed to be lacking . . . There is *only* a perspectival seeing [*perspektivisches Sehen*], *only* a perspectival "knowing"; and the *more* affects we allow to speak [*zu Worte kommen*] about one thing, the *more* eyes, different eyes, we can use to observe one thing, the more complete will our "concept" of this thing, our "objectivity," be. (GM III:12)

In this brief passage, Nietzsche records several observations with which feminist theorists have recently expressed agreement. First of all, he warns his readers to beware of the traditional interpretation of Objectivity as *disinterested contemplation*. The goal of disinterested contemplation presupposes "conceptual fictions" and "contradictory concepts," and it furthermore requires us to posit a disembodied, disinterested knowing subject, "an eye turned in no particular direction." His perspectivism thus attempts to account for those affective ingredients and determinants of knowledge that traditionally have been ignored or discounted by orthodox epistemologists. His reconstituted notion of objectivity (consistently noted by his use of quotation marks) suggests that knowledge is a function of the embodied expression of our affective investment in the world. His perspectivism thus presupposes an account of knowing subjects as radically situated in the world and in their bodies.

Second, if we interpret these "eyes" as perspectives, whose "interpretive forces" are sustained by a suffusion of affect, then we see that, for Nietzsche, perspectives are not disembodied points of view that hover disinterestedly over the world. Indeed, his perspectivism is strategically designed to recuperate the metaphorics of vision that have dominated (and perverted) representational epistemology. In order to appropriate the metaphorics of vision for his reconstituted notion of objectivity, he deploys the twin sensory images of "eyes" and "voices":

[T]he *more* affects we allow to speak about one thing, the *more* eyes, different eyes, we can use to observe one thing, the more complete will our "concept" of this thing, our "objectivity," be. (GM III:12)

Eyes and affects, knowing and feeling, seeing and speaking, conception and perception, situation and expression: the pursuit of Nietzschean objectivity requires us to deconstruct these binary oppositions and integrate the supposedly antagonistic terms within each. His reconstituted notion of objectivity encourages a maximal expression of affective investment in the world—a chorus of radically situated "voices"—and thus stands 180 degrees removed from the traditional epistemological goal of disinterested, disaffected contemplation. In fact, he concludes his warning against disinterested contemplation by graphically likening the pursuit of Objectivity to an act of self-inflicted castration: "to suspend each and every affect, supposing we were capable of this—what would that mean but to *castrate* the intellect?" (GM III:12).

"There is *only* a perspectival knowing" thus means that knowledge is possible only if one's affective engagement with the world is both recognized and expressed. If it is not, then one may lay claim at best to a desiccated, bloodless simulacrum of knowledge. Nietzsche's recuperation of the metaphorics of vision thus enables us to understand perspectives as *bodies*: suffused with affect, inextricably situated in the world, and inscribed with the pain and torment inflicted by normalizing mores and institutions. He consequently reconstitutes the notion of objectivity to derive from an aggregation of radically situated perspectives (or bodies)— none of which affords us an epistemically pure glimpse of the world. The task of the philosopher who aspires to Nietzschean objectivity is to compile an exhaustive aggregation of perspectives, to assemble an unprecedented chorus of affective voices.

Third, Nietzsche recommends his perspectivism not for its epistemic purity, but for the strategic advantage that accrues to his reconstituted notion of objectivity. His discussion of "perspectivism" appears within the context of his analysis of the ascetic ideal, with which he associates the traditional understanding of Objectivity as disinterested contemplation. He frequently contends that the pursuit of Objectivity involves a concomitant assault on the affects, which in turn leads, paradoxically, to a diminution of our knowledge, to the subordination of situated knowledges to lifeless simulacra of knowledge. The strategic advantage of *his* objectivity lies in "the ability to *control* one's Pro and Con and to dispose of them, so that one knows how to employ a *variety* of perspectives and affective interpretations in the service of knowledge" (GM III:12).

Fourth, Nietzsche willingly accepts the self-referential implications of his endorsement of situated knowledges. He readily acknowledges that his own perspectivism too is situated, that it reflects the peculiar political interests of its author. "Perspectivism" is itself perspectival in nature, for it is the product of the partial perspective and embodied affect peculiar to Herr Nietzsche. Rather than stake an illicit claim to epistemic purity, he quite openly voices the hostility and resentment that inform his own political campaign against the ascetic practices of traditional epistemology. It is no coincidence that his most illuminating articulation of his perspectivism appears in the *Genealogy*, a book in which he both announces and displays his own vested political interests in compiling a genealogy of morals.

Nietzsche's perspectivism thus provides a promising epistemological model for feminist theorists. But let us be clear about the political costs of embracing his perspectivism: if we accept this reconstituted notion of objectivity, and seek an aggregation of radically situated perspectives, then we must abandon the quest for a privileged, epistemically pure, God's-eye perspective on the world. We need not disavow our cultural, genealogical or political preferences for certain perspectives, but we must be careful to situate these preferences within a discernible political agenda. The privilege of a particular perspective will derive entirely from its situation within the political agenda it expresses, and not from its internal coherence or privileged access to the real world.

Several feminist theorists have recently acknowledged their debts to Nietzsche's "perspectivism," which they have borrowed in order to articulate the theory of knowledge that underlies their political projects and agendas. Declaring a provisional truce with a potentially vicious opponent, these theorists join Nietzsche in rejecting the traditional epistemological ideal of Objectivity. Feminist theorists have long maintained that the pursuit of Objectivity would require agents to accede to a disembodied, trans-perspectival, patriarchal standpoint—a chimerical gambit that Donna Haraway calls "the God trick."[27] As Susan Bordo argues, this "view from nowhere" acquires the privilege and cachet of a "view from everywhere," and it effectively devaluates the experiences of those agents whose knowledges of the world are most obviously and ineluctably situated.[28] These theorists thus conclude that the ideal of disinterested, detached Objectivity is pursued at the expense and exclusion of the situated knowledges of women, especially women of color. Traditional (patriarchal) epistemology consequently delivers only a simulacrum of objectivity, for its emphasis on disinterested detachment precisely discounts the partiality that defines a radically situated perspective.

At the same time, however, some feminist theorists are understandably reluctant to abandon the *notion* of objectively valid knowledge as the goal of philosophical inquiry. According to Sandra Harding, some such critical standard is crucial to the very project of feminist epistemology:

> What would be the point of a theory of knowledge that did not
> make prescriptions for how to go about getting knowledge or
> of a prescription for getting knowledge that did not arise from
> a theory about how knowledge can be and has been produced?[29]

A reconstituted notion of objectivity would provide a standard whereby theorists might claim, for example, that one scientific theory is better or more complete or more promising than another. In this light, we might think of one goal of feminist epistemology as the reconstitution of the notion of objectivity, such that feminist theorists might continue the critical enterprise of science without subscribing to its most pernicious concepts.

The legacy of Nietzsche's "perspectivism" is perhaps most vitally preserved within the experimental epistemologies of several radical feminist theorists. Following Nietzsche, for example, Donna Haraway contends that the objectivity of a perspective is a function of its *partiality*:

> The moral is simple: only partial perspective promises objective vision . . . Feminist objectivity is about limited location and situated knowledge, not about transcendence and splitting of subject and object. In this way we might become answerable for what we learn how to see.[30]

The partiality that Haraway prizes is achieved not through the disinterested detachment of subjects from the world, but through the radical situation of subjects in the world. Her suggested reconceptualization of "feminist objectivity" thus devolves from her more fundamental reconceptualization of the world we seek to know in terms of the world in which we live.

Haraway's brand of feminism conveys a postmodern sensibility in large part because she has abandoned the quest for an epistemically pure, foundationally innocent standpoint. Indeed, a primary aim of her writing is to disabuse feminists of the perceived need for an untainted, originary standpoint from which they might launch their various political campaigns:

> The science question in feminism is about objectivity as positioned rationality. Its images are not the products of escape and transcendence of limits, i.e., the view from above, but the joining of partial views and halting voices into a collective subject position that promises a vision of the means of ongoing finite embodiment, of living within limits and contradictions, i.e., of views from somewhere.[31]

Partiality thus stands as the sole determinant of objectivity, and there exists no verifiable epistemic relation between objectivity and standpoints informed by positions of exclusion, oppression or victimization:

> A commitment to mobile positioning and to passionate detachment is dependent on the impossibility of innocent "identity" politics and epistemologies as strategies for seeing from the standpoints of the subjugated in order to see well.[32]

Postmodern feminists register a preference for the standpoints of excluded, subjugated women not because such standpoints are epistemically pure, but because "they seem to promise more adequate, sustained, objective, transforming accounts of the world."[33]

This preference is clearly political in nature, and Haraway makes no pretense of aspiring to epistemic purity or foundational innocence. For Haraway, any epistemic privilege necessarily implies a political (i.e., situated) preference. Her postmodern orientation elides the boundaries traditionally drawn between politics and epistemology, and thus renders otiose the ideal of epistemic purity. All perspectives are partial, all standpoints situated—including those of feminist theorists. It is absolutely crucial to Haraway's postmodern feminist project that we acknowledge her claims *about* situated knowledge as *themselves* situated within the political agenda she sets for postmodern feminism; feminist theorists must therefore accept and accommodate the self-referential implications of their own epistemic claims.

The political agenda of postmodern feminism thus assigns to (some) subjugated standpoints a political preference or priority. Haraway, for example, believes that some subjugated standpoints may be more immediately revealing, especially since they have been discounted and excluded for so long. They may prove especially useful in coming to understand the political and psychological mechanisms whereby the patriarchy discounts the radically situated knowledges of others while claiming for its own (situated) knowledge an illicit epistemic privilege:

> The standpoints of the subjugated . . . are savvy to modes of denial through repression, forgetting, and disappearing acts— ways of being nowhere while claiming to see comprehensively. The subjugated have a decent chance to be on to the god-trick and all its dazzling—and, therefore, blinding—illuminations.[34]

But these subjugated standpoints do not afford feminist theorists an epistemically privileged view of the world, independent of the political agendas they have established. Reprising elements of Nietzsche's psychological profile of the "slave" type, Haraway warns against the

> serious danger of romanticizing and/or appropriating the vision of the less powerful while claiming to see from their positions. To see from below is neither easily learned nor unproblematic, even if "we" "naturally" inhabit the great underground terrain of subjugated knowledges. The positionings of the subjugated are not exempt from critical re-examination, decoding, deconstruction, and interpretation; that is, from both semiological and hermeneutic modes of critical enquiry. The standpoints of the subjugated are not "innocent" positions.[35]

A subjugated standpoint may shed new light on the ways of an oppressor, but it in no way renders superfluous or redundant the standpoint of the oppressor. Because neither standpoint fully comprises the other, the aggregation of the two would move both parties (or a third party) closer to a more objective understanding of the world. If some feminists have political reasons for disavowing this project of aggregation, or for adopting it selectively, then they must pursue their political agenda at the expense of the greater objectivity that they might otherwise have gained.

Continuing this Nietzschean line of investigation, Bat-Ami Bar On exposes the dangers involved in conceiving of "mastery" as emanating from a single, static center.[36] Attempting to translate the guiding insights of Nietzsche's "perspectivism" into distinctly political terms, Bar On points out that in the complex societies of advanced industrial capitalism, virtually all agents simultaneously stand in relations of "mastery" to some and "enslavement" to others. As an alternative to the "single-center" theory of power preferred by traditional epistemologists, Bar On proposes a "theorized dispersion of power among multiple centers."[37] In a similarly Nietzschean vein, bell hooks warns that the romanticization of "marginality" may actually dispossess oppressed agents of a fruitful "place of resistance."[38] Here hooks follows Nietzsche in reminding feminist theorists not to discount prematurely the potentially restorative powers that conditions of oppression can, under certain circumstances, engender.

Haraway completes the political appropriation of Nietzsche's epistemic legacy by exposing the dystopic by-products of a "dream" that continues to guide the political struggles of some feminists:

> The permanent partiality of feminist points of view has consequences for our expectations of forms of political organization and participation. We do not need a totality in order to work well. The feminist dream of a common language, like all dreams for a perfectly true language, of perfectly faithful naming of experience, is a totalizing and imperialist one.[39]

This "dream" of foundational innocence is not only epistemically bankrupt, but also politically disastrous, for it imposes upon feminist politics conditions of justification that are impossible to meet. Haraway's campaign to expose and debunk this "dream" effectively absolves feminists of any perceived responsibility for grounding or justifying a political agenda by appeal to epistemic criteria. Haraway regards both epistemology and politics as serious endeavors, but she does not require of the latter that it acquire its justificatory and motive force from the former—especially if the former retains any residue of its familiar patriarchal cast. The "privilege" of any postmodern feminist agenda must and will be purely political; the desire or need for a further, epistemic privilege will only frustrate feminist political activity.

As an antidote to the dream of foundational innocence, Haraway proposes various imaginative exercises designed to liberate feminists from the perceived need for an originary, epistemically pure standpoint. As an enabling narrative for postmodern feminists, Haraway submits the myth of the cyborg, a composite, hybrid creature that enacts the irresolvable tensions and dualities that characterize late modernity.[40] The cyborg represents the embodiment of purely prospective agency, an unhistorical mutant to which the past—along with the allure of innocence, origin, and redemption—is irretrievably lost. If feminists can imagine themselves in their political activity as cyborgs—which, in reality, women have always been—then they can perhaps exorcize the immobilizing specter of *das Weib an sich*, which continues to haunt their political practices.

Here too Haraway follows Nietzsche. The prototype cyborg is none other than Zarathustra, the consummate micropolitical agent of late modernity. Indeed, we might profitably read the *Bildungsgang* of Zarathustra as something like a cyborg myth: operating in the shadow of the dead God, consigned by his crepuscular destiny to a belief in crumbling idols that he can neither respect nor reject, Zarathustra must somehow neutralize his romantic dreams of return and redemption. He eventually "becomes what he is" by turning that which oppresses him— his destiny and fatality—to his own strategic advantage. He is ineluctably both free spirit and ascetic priest, and he implements both strands of this dual heritage to found a micro-community of "higher men" (Z IV:2–9). This community is unstable and ephemeral, lacking altogether in theoretical justifications, institutional reinforcements, and foundational myths. This community of higher men is exclusively prospective in its orientation; it has no laws, no traditions, no mores, no history, and no goal above and beyond the survival of European nihilism.

Zarathustra founds this cyborg community, supplying it with a minimal micropolitical infrastructure in the form of an inaugural "Ass Festival" (Z IV:17–18), but he eventually withdraws from it. He comes to realize that his dual heritage renders him both life-giving and life-destroying. Although he has consecrated this micro-community in the twilight of the idols, he has also encouraged his new companions to invest their redemptive hopes in him. Sensing that he has surreptitiously enslaved them and usurped the station of the dead God—having become someone for the sake of whom "living on earth is worthwhile" (Z IV:19)—he banishes the higher men and dissolves the micro-community he founded.

The final scene of *Zarathustra*, framed in cyclical imagery that suggests a closed system, captures the purely prospective agency of the cyborg. Restless in his sheltering solitude but chastened by the prospect of reprising the pathogenesis that doomed his previous political endeavors, Zarathustra rises nonetheless to greet the dawn. Bereft of hopes for ultimate success, armed solely with the will to survive the decadence of late modernity,

Zarathustra departs his cave once again to found yet another, equally ephemeral, cyborg community.

Nietzsche and Foucault

The legacy of Nietzsche's political confrontation with late modernity endures most vitally in the work of Michel Foucault (1926–1984). Foucault largely accepts Nietzsche's general diagnosis of late modernity, as a distintegrating epoch fraught with contradictions and disarray, and he arrives at a similar inventory of the political resources and options available to agents in late modernity. While he resists the biologistic terms and categories that convey Nietzsche's critique of modernity, Foucault nevertheless agrees that the project of critique can continue only if philosophers acknowledge their participation and complicity in the cultural malaise they intend to investigate. As a response to the uncertainty and contingency that cloud philosophical investigation in the twilight of the idols, Foucault adopts Nietzsche's experimental methods and adapts them to his own unique fields of inquiry.

Archaeology

Foucault is perhaps most famous for the experimental method he called *archaeology*, which he developed in order to explore the peculiar epistemic conditions of late modernity. The guiding aim of the archaeologist is twofold: 1) to identify historical periods of epistemic convergence across a cluster of sciences and disciplines; and 2) to chart the transformation, and eventual disintegration, of epistemic coherence within the discursive practices of science. He thus intends his archaeological investigations to reveal the epistemic principles governing a period of discursive convergence. Foucault introduced the term *episteme* to designate the epistemic coherence of various discursive practices within a single historical period. The sciences and disciplines clustered within an episteme all share a common epistemic framework and specialized vocabulary; they consequently exhibit general agreement on the basic conditions and criteria of truth, knowledge, verification, and certainty.

The subject matter investigated by the archaeologist is the discourse of the human sciences. By "discourse" Foucault means not only the shared, common language of scientific disciplines, but also the background structures and practices that determine the form and content of this language. The discourse of the human sciences thus comprises the specialized language spoken by scientific authorities, as well as the extra-linguistic conditions that determine what can be said, and by whom, in the production and distribution of scientific knowledge. Archaeology ascribes primary agency not to the experts who claim to conduct scientific inquiry, but to the "anonymous field of practices" embedded within the discourse itself. The discourse thus produces its representative "experts," as well as the knowledge they carefully disseminate. Unwittingly serving the hidden interests of the discursive practices in which they involuntarily participate, subjects contribute to the production and dissemination of knowledge, which they claim to discover through "objective," scientific inquiry.

Like Nietzsche, Foucault attempts to exploit the unique conditions of his historical situation, treating the advanced decay of modernity as an uncharted field for philosophical investigation. An archaeology of knowledge is possible only when an episteme begins to disintegrate, as the clustered sciences and disciplines become conscious of the nature—and limitations—of the common epistemic framework they share. Indeed, discursive practices become visible to the archaeologist only when they manifest their internal instabilities, as evidenced by the mounting failures of their defining epistemic projects. As an episteme disintegrates, its signature constellation of conditions and criteria for knowledge becomes both manifest (to the archaeologist) and epistemically bankrupt.

A representative deployment of Foucault's archaeological method is found in *The Order of Things*.[41] Foucault is primarily concerned in *The Order of Things* to document the "profound upheaval" that occurred at the end of the eighteenth century, when the episteme of the Classical Age began to disintegrate.[42] The project of representation, which had served to unify the Classical episteme, proved itself incapable of accounting for the act and the agent of representing. "Man," the supposed focus of inquiry in the human sciences, had eluded the frame of representation. Despite the systemic failure of the project of representation, and the disintegration of its corresponding episteme, "man" nevertheless remains the (faulted) object of scientific inquiry in the nineteenth and twentieth centuries. The Age of Man, Foucault proposes, is defined by a series of ingenious (and failed) schemes to derive from human finitude itself the conditions of scientific knowledge. Reflecting the fragmentation of their avowed subject matter, the human sciences now labor in the absence of the sort of epistemic convergence that presided over their birth and development. The very possibility of truth and knowledge is now in question, as the human sciences scramble to construct theories and propositions in the space vacated by their proper object of investigation.

Rather than bemoan the disappearance of "man," or attempt to restore epistemic coherence to the human sciences, Foucault presents the irrecuperable fragmentation of "man" as legislating new directions for scientific inquiry. *The Order of Things* proposes human finitude not as a new certainty that might solve the epistemic riddles of the human sciences, but as a new possibility in its own right, within which fruitful experimental thinking might take place.[43] Like Nietzsche, Foucault intends his investigations to limn the unacknowledged (and unanticipated) successes sheltered within the failures of modernity. The disintegration of the episteme may very well illuminate heretofore neglected ethical and political resources.

Subjectivation

Foucault designed his archaeologies to yield purely descriptive results. He neither claimed nor expected to derive from them a critical appraisal of the discourse or episteme under investigation. While archaeology afforded him the critical distance he sought from the discursive practices he wished to investigate, it did not enable him to address the concrete social problems that concerned him. The most significant development in his political thinking thus occurred in the late 1960s, when he diverted his primary focus from discursive practices to the power relations that inform and sustain them.

By virtue of their involuntary participation in discursive practices, human beings are transformed into specific types of subjects, uniquely enabled and disabled to serve particular regimes of power.[44] The defining characteristic of power is its capacity for "infinite displacement" within a complex network of discursive practices. All discourse is ultimately concerned with power, albeit in complicated, disguised ways. Because power can be effective only when it remains partially hidden, it always shelters itself within a discourse about something else. Power is both ubiquitous and capillary in its manifestations, and it announces its presence only as a diversion from its more central activities.

In order to supplement his archaeological expeditions with a critical, political dimension, Foucault developed the method of historical investigation known as "genealogy," which he self-consciously borrowed from Nietzsche. The genealogical method enabled Foucault not only to investigate hidden power relations, but also to deliver a critique of concrete social practices. Although he never abandoned his archaeological method, he eventually came to rely on genealogy to expose the subtle transformations that signal the consolidating movement of power toward domination.

By tracing the historical descent of authoritative discursive practices, the Foucauldian genealogist is able to chart the shifting relationships between power and knowledge within the historical transformation of these practices. The genealogist can glimpse power only as it adjusts and reconfigures itself within the social and political relations it strategically inhabits, as it silently transforms institutions and discursive practices. Foucault was especially concerned to investigate the exclusionary power of discursive practices, including those reponsible for the institutionalized definitions of madness, criminality, and sexual deviancy.

Foucault's subsequent turn to ethics comprises an extension of the development of his genealogical method.[45] His contribution to ethics involved neither the articulation of a new moral theory, nor the advocacy of an alternative to the signature "techniques of the self" that govern late modernity. He was concerned rather to investigate the conditions under which particular "docile" subjects are formed, and to expose the hidden power interests that are served by these subjects. He consequently centered his ethical investigations on the process he called *subjectivation*, whereby human beings are gradually transformed into subjects invested with unique powers and limitations. Of specific concern to him, especially in his final writings, were the techniques of subjectivation deployed by "bio-power," which organizes the resources of modern societies under the pretense of attending to the care of the species and the health of individual human beings.[46]

In his late writings on ethics, Foucault began to carve out for the subject a modest domain of agency and causal efficacy. His genealogies of the modern sexual subject revealed that the process of subjectivation is not strictly coercive and disabling. Power relations also manifest themselves in productive discursive practices, including those that distribute goods and information, satisfy limited desires, manage resources, and secure the material conditions of social harmony. Modern subjects are rendered docile through a battery of normalizing disciplines, but they can also turn the productive power invested in them against regimes of power that threaten to accede to domination.

Foucault's ethical investigations thus revealed that regimes of power can realize their ends only if human beings are transformed into productive subjects, invested with a limited capacity for self-legislation. The subjects depicted in his later genealogies are not merely the unwitting products of clandestine discursive practices, for they are able to resist the totalization of power within its most ambitious and monolithic regimes. To expose the mobilization of power within mechanisms of transformation is to render it temporarily less effective and less dangerous. Power can neither be eradicated nor contained, but its inexorable tendency toward domination can often be neutralized within local regimes.

Toward a Politics of Resistance

Nietzsche's experimentation with unexplored configurations of agency is taken up by Foucault in the later, "ethical" period of his career. Although Foucault located in the dominant regimes of bio-power a masked impulse toward domination, he also acknowledged their productive, empowering roles in the formation of the modern subject. At the end of his career, he attempted a partial recuperation of the agency of the subject, outlining the conditions under which subjects might constitute themselves in opposition to dangerous techniques of subjectivation. Under certain conditions, modern subjects can—and do—resist the totalization of power within specific structures and local regimes.[47]

Foucault's writings from the "ethical" period of his career thus approximate most closely the experimental politics of resistance outlined by Nietzsche. Especially in his investigations into *The History of Sexuality*, Foucault seriously entertains Nietzsche's "affirmative" thesis that (some) modern subjects may turn ascetic disciplines to their own advantage. Techniques of subjectivation are always both repressive *and* empowering, investing subjects with residual faculties that may be deployed in the resistance of domination. Acknowledging that the constitution of the subject produces, as an unintended by-product, a feedback loop of potentially generative powers, Foucault gestures toward an experimental investigation of the untested modes of agency available—though perhaps unknown—to modern subjects.[48] His efforts to resist *domination*, by which he means the totalizing consolidation of power within specific regimes of bio-power, thus emerge as analogous to Nietzsche's attempts to deflect the advent of the "will to nothingness." For both thinkers, the immediate goal of political resistance is to safeguard the continued development of human subjectivity, such that it might someday stand security for its own future.

Unlike Nietzsche, Foucault declined the mantle of the political lawgiver. Wary of his own complicities in the regimes of power he sought to illuminate, he refused to posit alternative ethical systems or "techniques of the self," which might in turn serve as sites for the consolidation of power into structures of domination. He consciously limited himself to an investigation of the historical conditions that sustain the array of subject constitutions available to us. Here Foucault deviated most obviously from Nietzsche as a political thinker. In suspending his subversive genealogical practices to declare war on Christian morality, Foucault might say, Nietzsche unwittingly contributes to the formation of regimes of power that are potentially more dangerous than those manifested within the discourse of Christian morality. Foucault's stubborn refusal to situate himself on the "political checkerboard"[49] was thus intended to minimize his own deleterious influence on the exploration of the novel configurations of agency he discovered. While it is doubtful that his strategy for neutralizing his own negative influences was, or could have been, entirely successful, his desire to avoid the fate of Nietzsche is certainly understandable.

Like Nietzsche, Foucault never completed the ambitious genealogical agenda he set for himself. The guarded optimism conveyed by his final writings has been taken up by successor genealogists, and the articulation of a Foucauldian political position remains, for some, an ongoing project.[50]

Notes

Introduction

1. Mark Warren draws a useful distinction between Nietzsche's political philosophy and his "philosophy of power," in *Nietzsche and Political Thought* (Cambridge, MA: MIT Press, 1988), pp. 1–8, 207–223. According to Warren, Nietzsche's political philosophy does not merit further consideration because it belies the promise of his "philosophy of agency" and his "critique of Western culture." Although I reject Warren's dismissive characterization of Nietzsche's politics as a "neoaristocratic conservatism" (p. 211), as well as his endorsement of Nietzsche's "philosophy of power" as a "framework for a critically postmodern political philosophy" (p. 207), his distinction helpfully illuminates the potential discontinuities that obtain between Nietzsche's antifoundationalist philosophical insights and his less revolutionary political sentiments.

1 Political Perfectionism

1. Nietzsche's interest in "breeding" human types, as opposed to producing a "successor" species, would seem to militate against the thesis of Tracy Strong's pioneering study, *Friedrich Nietzsche and the Politics of Transfiguration* (Berkeley: University of California Press, 1974). Strong attributes to Nietzsche a "politics of transfiguration," which undertakes "the development of beings who simply do not live as human-all-too-human" (p. 13), which in turn "require[s] a change in the very stuff of humanity" (p. 260). I am both sympathetic and indebted to Strong's general line of interpretation, but I find his emphasis on "the politics of transfiguration" to be misleadingly freighted with images of transcendence and radical discontinuity. If, as Nietzsche suggests in this passage, "man is an *end*," then a "politics of transfiguration" would constitute an inappropriate, overzealous, and nihilistic response to the problem of modernity. As I hope to show in this study, Nietzsche's primary political goal is the perfection or completion of humankind, not its transfiguration.

2. My reading of Nietzsche's perfectionism is indebted to Stanley Cavell's seminal essay, "Aversive Thinking: Emersonian Representations in Heidegger and Nietzsche," in *Conditions Handsome and Unhandsome: The Constitution of Emersonian Perfectionism* (Chicago: University of Chicago Press, 1990), pp. 33–63. Cavell restricts his attention almost exclusively to the early essay *Schopenhauer as Educator*, but his account of Nietzsche's perfectionism is relevant for an examination of the post-Zarathustran writings as well.

3. Nietzsche explicitly recommends the conditions under which Schopenhauer emerged (SE 7), but if we endorse his later observation that his *Untimely Meditations* "speak only of [him]" (EH V:3), then the conditions he describes are (also) responsible for his own development as a genius.

4. Nietzsche futher explains that "This *instinct for freedom* forcibly made latent—we have seen it already—this instinct for freedom pushed back and repressed, incarcerated within and finally able to discharge and vent itself only on itself: that, and that alone, is what the *bad conscience* is in its beginnings" (GM II:17).

5. Bruce Detwiler suggests that "Nietzsche distinguishes between what he calls the 'good conscience' characteristic of the noble type and the 'bad conscience' that characterizes the slavish type," in *Nietzsche and the Politics of Aristocratic Radicalism* (Chicago: University of Chicago Press, 1990), p. 124. Detwiler's suggestion is especially helpful in explaining why Nietzsche believes that certain individuals are (or have been) spared the existential suffering that attends the introversion of the natural impulses. Whereas civilization demands of *everyone* the inward discharge of the "instincts," only those who are disadvantaged by the reigning social order are debilitated by the existential suffering of the bad conscience. On this interpretation, the "good conscience" would be the privilege of those whose social standing affords them the opportunity to compensate somehow for the introversion of their animal impulses.

6. My distinction between the "existential suffering" of the bad conscience and the "surplus suffering" of guilt draws on Arthur C. Danto's distinction between "extensional suffering and intensional suffering, where the latter consists of an interpretation of the former," in "Some Remarks on *The Genealogy of Morals*," in *Reading Nietzsche*, ed. Robert C. Solomon and Kathleen M. Higgins (New York: Oxford University Press, 1988), p. 21.

7. I am indebted for this particular formulation of the point to Cavell, pp. 58–59.

8. Alasdair MacIntyre, for example, decrees that "the *Übermensch* . . . belong[s] in the pages of a philosophical bestiary rather than in serious discussion." *After Virtue* (Notre Dame, IN: Notre Dame University Press, 1984), p. 22.

9. For a superbly rich account of the development of Zarathustra (and his teachings) throughout the course of his travels, see Laurence Lampert, *Nietzsche's Teaching* (New Haven: Yale University Press, 1986). I take up the question of Zarathustra's reliability in my essay, "Solving the Problem of Socrates:

Nietzsche's *Zarathustra* as Political Irony," *Political Theory*, vol. 16, no. 2, May 1988, pp. 257–280.

10. Several scholars distinguish profitably between the *Übermensch* and "higher humanity." See, for example, Richard Schacht, *Nietzsche* (London: Routledge, 1983), p. 339; and Ofelia Schutte, *Beyond Nihilism: Nietzsche Without Masks* (Chicago: University of Chicago Press, 1984), p. 122. Wolfgang Müller-Lauter similarly maintains that the *Übermensch* represents the "apotheosis" of "higher humanity," in *Nietzsche: Seine Philosophie der Gegensätze und die Gegensätze seiner Philosophie* (Berlin: de Gruyter, 1971), p. 127; cf. Schacht, p. 482.

11. In a letter dated 20 October 1888, Nietzsche tells Malwida von Meysenbug that the *Übermensch* is a type of human being who is "a hundred times more similar" to the type instantiated by Cesare Borgia than to the type instantiated by Christ. *Friedrich Nietzsche, Sämtliche Briefe: Kritische Studienausgabe*, ed. G. Colli and M. Montinari (Berlin: de Gruyter/Deutscher Taschenbuch Verlag, 1986), vol. 8, #1135, p. 458.

12. Explaining his "destiny," Nietzsche allows that he fears further misunderstandings of his teachings: "I have a terrible fear that one day I will be pronounced *holy*: you will guess why I publish this book before; it shall prevent people from doing mischief with me" (EH XIV:1). The "before" refers here to the publication of *The Antichrist(ian)*, which Nietzsche intended to withhold until the reception of *Ecce Homo* had sufficiently reduced the likelihood of censorship and confiscation.

13. For a measured critique of the interpretation of the *Übermensch* as constituting an "ideal type," see Bernd Magnus, "Perfectibility and Attitude in Nietzsche's *Übermensch*," *The Review of Metaphysics*, vol. 36, March 1983, pp. 633–659.

14. Nietzsche again defines the *Übermensch* in relational terms when he identifies "the type of man" that "Zarathustra wants" as "a relatively superhuman [*übermenschlicher*] type" (EH XIV:5).

15. My interpretation of the founding labors of the *Übermensch* is indebted to David Owen's discussion of "agonism," and its capacity for contributing to the cultivation of *virtù*, in *Nietzsche, Politics and Modernity* (London: Sage, 1995), esp. pp. 132–154; and to William Connolly's Nietzsche-inspired account of "agonistic democracy" in *Identity/Difference* (Ithaca: Cornell University Press, 1991), pp. 184–197.

16. MacIntyre, for example, describes the *Übermensch* as "the man who transcends, finds his good nowhere in the social world to date, but only in that in himself which dictates his own new law and his own new table of the virtues . . . [T]he great man cannot enter into relationships mediated by appeal to shared standards or virtues or goods; he is his own only authority and his relationships to others have to be exercises of that authority" (pp. 257–258).

17. According to J.P. Stern, for example, Nietzsche "seems unaware that he is giving us nothing to distinguish the fanaticism that goes with bad faith from

his own belief in the unconditioned value of self-realization and self-becoming—that is, from his own belief in the Superman . . . No man came closer to the full realization of self-created 'values' than A. Hitler." *A Study of Nietzsche* (Cambridge: Cambridge University Press, 1979), p. 117.

18. Alexander Nehamas astutely observes that "the characters Nietzsche admires . . . are overwhelmingly literary and artistic." *Nietzsche: Life as Literature* (Cambridge, MA: Harvard University Press, 1985), p. 227.

19. Emerson's commitment to the exemplary standing of "representative men" is evidenced throughout his essays and lectures. For a summary account, see his introductory essay on the "Uses of Great Men," in *The Collected Works of Ralph Waldo Emerson*, vol. IV: *Representative Men: Seven Lectures*, ed. Wallace E. Williams and Douglas Emory Wilson (Cambridge, MA: Harvard University Press, 1987), pp. 1–20.

20. My reckoning of Nietzsche's psychological debts to Emerson is indebted to Graham Parkes, *Composing the Soul: Reaches of Nietzsche's Psychology* (Chicago: University of Chicago Press, 1994), esp. ch. 4.

21. Gianni Vattimo argues that the *Übermensch* can emerge only in a (future) world that has already been made *übermenschlich*—a task which outstrips the volitional capacities of late modernity. The trajectory of Nietzsche's political thinking may consequently describe a vicious circle: the *Übermensch* is its own precondition. *The Adventure of Difference: Philosophy after Nietzsche and Heidegger*, trans. Cyprian Blamires and Thomas Harrison (Baltimore: Johns Hopkins University Press, 1993), pp. 33–36; 55–58.

22. Robert Pippin attributes to Zarathustra the realization that the *Übermensch* represents "a radically temporal, contingent 'ideal'; it answers *only* the specific, practical incoherence of the ideals of late bourgeios culture." "Irony and Affirmation in Nietzsche's *Thus Spoke Zarathustra*," in *Nietzsche's New Seas*, ed. Michael Allen Gillespie and Tracy B. Strong (Chicago: University of Chicago Press, 1988), p. 52.

23. MacIntyre persuasively maintains that "The concept of the Nietzschean 'great man' is also a pseudo-concept . . . It represents individualism's final attempt to escape from its own consequences." *After Virtue*, p. 259.

2 The Uses and Disadvantages of Morality for Life

1. John Rawls, *A Theory of Justice* (Cambridge, MA: Harvard University Press, 1971), p. 325.

2. Ibid.

3. Ibid.

4. Nietzsche finds a "natural" basis for the pyramidal structure he prefers for hierarchically organized societies, in the "powerful pyramidal rock" he spies near the lake at Silvaplana, at the time that the thought of eternal recurrence descends upon him (EH III:1).

5. Letter to Franz Overbeck on 24 March 1887. Friedrich Nietzsche, *Sämtliche Briefe: Kritische Studienausgabe*, ed. G Colli and M. Montinari (Berlin: de Gruyter/Deutscher Taschenbuch Verlag, 1986), vol. 8, #820, p. 48.

6. Nietzsche thus adds a third caste to the two-tiered system he proposed in H I:439.

7. Nietzsche distinguishes himself from the "whole European and American species of *libres penseurs*," who "still believe in the 'ideal'." Declaring himself "the first *immoralist*," he thus implies that immoralists no longer want "to 'improve' humankind, in their own image" (EH V:2).

8. Nietzsche maintains that "the claim for independence, for free development, for *laisser aller* is pressed most hotly by the very people for whom no reins would be too strict. This is true *in politics*, this is true in art" (TI IX:41).

9. As early as his *Untimely Meditation* on Schopenhauer, Nietzsche proposed that the task of culture is to correct for the profligacy of Nature: "Nature propels the philosopher into humankind like an arrow; it takes no aim but hopes the arrow will stick somewhere. But countless times it misses and is depressed at the fact . . . The artist and the philosopher are evidence against the purposiveness of nature as regards the means it employs, though they are also first-rate evidence as to the wisdom of its purpose" (SE 7).

10. Allowing that Manu "found it necessary to be *terrible* [*furchtbar*]" in the struggle against "the unbred man, the mish-mash man, the chandala," Nietzsche recounts some of the more grisly edicts of Manu's law (TI VII:3).

11. While Nietzsche's endorsement of slavery may be irrecuperably offensive to contemporary liberal sensibilities, we should bear in mind the plethora of forms—many of them documented by Nietzsche himself—that slavery has assumed over the millennia. Surely the most efficient forms of slavery are those psychological forms embraced by the slaves themselves, such that their slavery becomes the precondition for their perceived happiness or freedom. Although Nietzsche's perfectionism expressly dismisses the political claim of demotic interests, it could nevertheless inspire a "Grand Inquisitor" regime that rewards its "slaves" with material comforts and spiritual anesthesia. In his notes, he speculates that "European democracy must become ultimately" a "new and sublime development of slavery." A political regime that could "make use of" democracy to further the enhancement of humankind would represent "a kind of goal, redemption and justification for the democratic movement" (WP 954).

12. Mill argues that even those who do not benefit personally and directly from "individuality" should nevertheless endorse its promotion, for they derive an indirect benefit from the "individuality" of others. *On Liberty*, ed. Elizabeth Rapaport, (Indianapolis: Hackett, 1978), ch. 3: "Of Individuality," esp. pp. 61–68.

13. Nietzsche does argue that "The philosopher and the artist . . . strike home at only a few, while they ought to strike home at everybody" (SE 7), but his remarks on education later in that essay indicate that he does not intend a democratic justification of culture.

14. Nietzsche's shift in orientation to the political microsphere deflects many of the criticisms leveled against his political thinking. Keith Ansell-Pearson, for example, argues that "[Nietzsche] too demands a politics of transfiguration in which modern individuals are to elevate themselves through a process of 'going-down' and 'going-across' to higher tasks and to higher responsibilities (the *Übermensch*). But the conditions—namely, a tragic culture—which would serve to cultivate such individuals are absent in modern liberal societies." *Nietzsche contra Rousseau* (Cambridge: Cambridge University Press, 1991), p. 224. If Nietzsche *were* invested in some such "politics of transfiguration," then it might be true that "modern liberal societies" lack the resources "to cultivate such individuals." But Nietzsche does not rely on the macropolitical resources of modern liberal societies to produce the exemplary human beings he has in mind. He is well aware that the macropolitical ambitions of his youth are simply incompatible with his historical situation.

15. For a sympathetic treatment of Nietzsche's attempt to legislate an "aristocracy of soul," see Leslie Paul Thiele, *Friedrich Nietzsche and the Politics of the Soul* (Princeton: Princeton University Press, 1990), esp. chs. 3–4.

3 Perfectionism in the Twilight of the Idols

1. These unpublished lectures are reproduced in vol. 1 of the *Kritische Studienausgabe*, pp. 643–752.

2. For an excellent study of Nietzsche's attempt to articulate "physiological" diagnoses of the decadence of late modernity, see Daniel Ahern, *Nietzsche as Cultural Physician* (University Park, PA: Pennsylvania State University Press, 1995), esp. ch. 1.

3. In a note from 1888, which echoes several others from that year, Nietzsche writes, "Basic insight regarding the nature of decadence: *its supposed causes are its consequences*" (WP 41; cf. 42–45). He maintains that "it is an error to consider 'social distress' or 'physiological degeneration' or, worse, corruption, as the *cause* of nihilism" (WP 1).

4. I borrow this phrase from Bernard Yack's provocative study, *The Longing for Total Revolution* (Princeton: Princeton University Press, 1986). As Yack "supposes," he perhaps "relies too heavily" on the pre-Zarathustran writings in proposing this "longing" as representative of Nietzsche's political thinking as a whole (p. 313). While the persistence of this longing is difficult to dispute, Yack does not acknowledge the transformations and complexity introduced into Nietzsche's political thinking by the critique of modernity advanced in his post-Zarathustran writings.

5. For example, Nietzsche expresses his "hope" for the advent of "men of the future who in the present tie the knot and constraint that forces the will of millennia upon *new* tracks" (BGE 203).

6. For a stimulating interpretation of Nietzsche's "desperate" turn (from aesthetics) to politics at the end of his sane life, see Tracy Strong, "Nietzsche's Political Aesthetics," in *Nietzsche's New Seas*, ed. Michael Allen Gillespie and Tracy Strong (Chicago: University of Chicago Press, 1988), pp. 153–174.

7. Responding to Rawls's decision to bar Nietzsche's perfectionism from the original position, Cavell remarks, "[I]f Nietzsche is to be dismissed as a thinker pertinent to the founding of the democratic life, then so, it should seem, is Emerson, since Nietzsche's meditation on Schopenhauer is, to an as yet undisclosed extent, a transcription and elaboration of Emersonian passages. Emerson's dismissal here would pain me more than I can say, and if that is indeed the implication of *A Theory of Justice*, I want the book, because of my admiration for it, to be wrong in drawing this implication from itself." Stanley Cavell, "Aversive Thinking: Emersonian Representations in Heidegger and Nietzsche," in *Conditions Handsome and Unhandsome: The Constitution of Emersonian Prefection* (Chicago: University of Chicago Press, 1990), p. 49.

8. Ibid., p. 53.

9. Ibid., p. 56.

10. Cavell acknowledges a similar objection, commenting that "This is important, but it does not seem to me enough to say" (ibid., p. 102).

11. Cf. Pindar, *Pythian Odes*, II, 72. Nietzsche fondly recommended Pindar's imperative to Lou Salomé just before their final estrangement. He closes his letter of 10 June 1882 with the sentence: "Pindar sagt einmal, 'werde der, der du bist!'" *Sämtliche Briefe: Kritische Studienausgabe*, ed. G. Colli and M. Montinari (Berlin: de Gruyter/Deutscher Taschenbuch Verlag, 1986), vol. 6, #239, p. 203.

12. John Rawls, *A Theory of Justice* (Cambridge, MA: Harvard University Press, 1971), pp. 442–446.

13. Cavell, pp. 49–53.

14. See Cavell, p. 59.

15. For a fine account of Nietzsche's deployment of the image of the household, or *oikos*, and of its Platonic origins, see Graham Parkes, *Composing the Soul: Reaches of Nietzsche's Psychology* (Chicago: University of Chicago Press, 1994), pp. 42–52, 215–225.

16. Socrates proposes his noble lie, via the "myth of the metals," in book III of the *Republic*, at 414b–417b.

4 Regimens of Self-Overcoming

1. This point is forcefully stated by Stanley Cavell, "Aversive Thinking: Emersonian Representations in Heidegger and Nietzsche," in *Conditions Handsome and Unhandsome: The Constitution of Emersonian Perfectionism* (Chicago: University of Chicago Press, 1990) pp. 46–57.

2. The theme of the philosopher's "soulcraft" is treated sympathetically and at length by Leslie Paul Thiele, *Friedrich Nietzsche and the Politics of the Soul* (Princeton: Princeton University Press, 1990), esp. ch. 4.

3. See Cavell, pp. 112–113.

4. See Cavell, pp. 47–48.

5. In a passage ideally suited to establish the distinction I have suggested, Nietzsche observes no terminological distinction between macrosphere and microsphere: "The self-overcoming [*Selbstüberwindung*] of morality, out of truthfulness; the self-overcoming [*Selbstüberwindung*] of the moralist, into his opposite—into me—that is what the name of Zarathustra means in my mouth" (EH XIV:3). Were Nietzsche inclined toward the distinction I have suggested, he presumably would have replaced the former instance of *Selbstüberwindung* with *Selbstaufhebung*.

6. Wolfgang Müller-Lauter argues that this "aggregate" model of self-overcoming stands in tension with Nietzsche's praise of those individuals who command a single, monolithic perspective. As a consequence of this tension, Müller-Lauter concludes, Nietzsche alternately describes the *Übermensch* in terms of the superhuman command of a single perspective, to the exclusion of all others, and in terms of a superhuman accommodation of a multiplicity of perspectives. *Nietzsche: Seine Philosophie der Gegensätze und die Gegensätze seiner Philosophie* (Berlin: de Gruyter, 1971), pp. 116–134.

7. For an excellent treatment of Nietzsche's reliance on political metaphors for the cultivation of the soul, and of the Platonic provenance of these metaphors, see Graham Parkes, *Composing the Soul: Reaches of Nietzsche's Psychology* (Chicago: University of Chicago Press, 1994), pp. 346–362.

8. For an even-handed chronicle of Nietzsche's use and abuse of Rousseau, see Keith Ansell-Pearson's excellent study, *Nietzsche contra Rousseau* (Cambridge: Cambridge University Press, 1991), esp. ch. 1.

9. David Owen delivers an excellent reading of the "agonism" that emerges from this early essay in *Nietzsche, Politics and Modernity* (London: Sage, 1995), pp. 139–169.

10. Richard Rorty apparently derives his account of Nietzschean self-creation from his anti-essentialism and historicism. *Because* no authentic self exists to be be discovered through cognitive processes, he reasons, the self is *therefore* a construct. *Contingency, Irony and Solidarity* (New York: Cambridge University Press, 1989), ch. 2. Rorty's reasoning is valid, of course, only in the event that his guiding disjunction—discovery vs. creation—is both exclusive and warranted.

11. I develop this point further in my essay, "Disembodied Perspectives," *Nietzsche-Studien*, vol. 21, 1992, pp. 281–289.

12. Nietzsche's revision of the motto he adopts from Pindar perhaps reflects this growing emphasis on self-discovery. "Become who you are" (GS 270) is replaced by "Become what one is" (EH; see also GS 335).

13. Persuasively maintaining that Nietzsche never decides between the discovery of truth and its invention (p. 234), Nehamas works productively in the interstitial spaces between volition and cognition in Nietzsche's thought.

14. Several commentators have located Nietzsche's "solution" to the problem of consciousness in his recommendation of a process known as "active forgetting." According to Bernard Yack, for example, "Self-conscious forgetting is the remedy that Nietzsche, the self-appointed doctor of sick cultures, prescribes." *The Longing for Total Revolution* (Princeton: Princeton University Press, 1986), p. 335. While Nietzsche explicitly describes forgetting as "an active and in the strictest sense positive faculty of repression" (GM II:1), and while he praises in Mirabeau the "excess of the power . . . to forget" (GM I:10), I see little evidence that Nietzsche prescribes "active forgetting" (or anything else) to a dying culture. If Nietzsche's contemporaries were capable of "active forgetting," then would they not, like Mirabeau, already be engaged in it—even if unbeknownst to themselves? In light of the formidable epistemological problems involved in exhorting a dying culture "to remember to forget," it comes as little surprise that Yack subsequently judges Nietzsche's "prescription" for modernity to yield "paradox" and "self-contradiction."

15. See, for example, Nehamas, pp. 184–190.

16. Nietzsche suggests this image of himself as a "cave" in his letter to Reinhard von Seydlitz on 12 February 1888. *Sämtliche Briefe*, vol. 8, #989, p. 248.

17. My attention here to Nietzsche's polycentric model of the soul is indebted to Parkes, esp. ch. 9.

5 The Philosopher's *Versucherkunst*

1. My investigations of the rich *Versuch* motif in Nietzsche's post-Zarathustran thought have been informed and contoured by the following studies: Eric Blondel, *Nietzsche: The Body and Culture*, trans. Séan Hand (Stanford: Stanford University Press, 1991), ch. 6; Jacob Golomb, *Nietzsche's Enticing Psychology of Power* (Ames: Iowa State University Press, 1989); Laurence Lampert, *Nietzsche and Modern Times* (New Haven: Yale University Press, 1993), pp. 330–334; and Henning Ottman, *Philosophie und Politik bei Nietzsche* (Berlin: de Gruyter, 1987), section V: "Versuch über Nietzsches 'Versuche,'" pp. 346–388.

2. In his pathbreaking study, Walter Kaufmann calls attention to the perfectionism that lies at the heart of Nietzsche's moral philosophy. *Nietzsche: Philosopher, Psychologist, Antichrist*, 4th edn (Princeton: Princeton University Press, 1974), pp. 242–256. In accordance with his own campaign to rehabilitate Nietzsche's philosophy, however, Kaufmann insists that Nietzschean self-perfection is an exclusively private enterprise.

3. The provocation unwittingly initiated by the *Erzieher* is discussed at length by Emerson in his "Divinity School Address," in *Selected Writings of Ralph Waldo Emerson*, ed. William H. Gilman (New York: Penguin, 1983), pp. 241–257.

4. For an eloquent reckoning of Nietzsche's inheritance from Emerson of the notions of "intuition" and "provocation," see Tracy Strong, "Nietzsche's

Political Aesthetics," in *Nietzsche's New Seas*, ed. Michael Allen Gillespie and Tracy Strong (Chicago: University of Chicago Press, 1988), pp. 158–159.

5. For a compelling account of Nietzsche's affinities to Plato, particularly with respect to *erōs*, see Graham Parkes, *Composing the Soul: Reaches of Nietzsche's Psychology* (Chicago: University of Chicago Press, 1994), ch. 6.

6. *Kritische Studienausgabe*, vol. 13, 14 [120], p. 299.

7. In an important insight, Strong notes that the philosopher creates himself not only as an artwork, but also as a "source of this-worldly authority" (p. 158). According to Strong, however, Nietzsche despairs toward the end of his life that the nomothetic properties of art are simply inadequate to the task of creating a "source of this-worldly authority" suitable to the peculiar conditions of late modernity. Abandoning aesthetics, Nietzsche "comes in desperation to politics" (p. 168). Although Nietzsche, according to Strong, "is not a thinker of domination . . . at the end he can only try to prevent a politics of domination by proposing one of his own" (p. 171).

8. Bruce Detwiler offers an instructive account of the political role of the "artist-philosopher" in *Nietzsche and the Politics of Aristocratic Radicalism* (Chicago: University of Chicago Press, 1990), ch. 6. Detwiler's account suffers, however, from its strict association of the "artist-philosopher" with the "new order" that Nietzsche ostensibly envisions for the future. Detwiler consequently misplaces Nietzsche's own efforts as an "artist-philosopher," as well as the communities he creates in response to the decadence of late modernity.

9. Nietzsche speaks of himself in a similar way: "when I described Dionysian music I described what *I* had heard—that instinctively I had to transpose and transfigure everything into the new spirit that I carried in me" (EH IV: 4).

10. On the indirect and ironic products of Socrates' political teachings, see Leo Strauss, *The City and Man* (Chicago: University of Chicago Press, 1964), pp. 73–87 and 122–127; and Allan Bloom's "Interpretive Essay," in *The Republic of Plato*, 2nd edn, trans. Allan Bloom (New York: Basic Books, 1991), pp. 408–412.

11. On the self-creation of the philosopher, see Leslie Paul Thiele, *Friedrich Nietzsche and the Politics of the Soul* (Princeton: Princeton University Press, 1990), p. 131.

12. Nietzsche later adds that "Before tragedy, what is warlike in our soul celebrates its Saturnalia; whoever is used to suffering, whoever seeks out suffering, the heroic man praises his own being through tragedy—to him alone the tragedian presents this drink of sweetest cruelty" (TI IX:24).

13. Drawing perhaps on his own limited experiences, he offers the following "definition" of heterosexual love: "Has my definition of love been heard? It is the only one worthy of a philosopher. Love—in its means, war; at bottom, the deadly hatred of the sexes" (EH III:5).

14. *Sämtliche Werke*, vol. 13, 14 [120], pp. 299–300. My attention to this passage is indebted to Martha C. Nussbaum's essay, "The Transfigurations of Intoxication: Nietzsche, Schopenhauer, and Dionysus," *Arion*, vol. 1, no. 2, 1991, pp. 75–111.

15. In a cynical corollary to this thesis, Nietzsche maintains, "The cure for love is still in most cases that ancient radical medicine: love in return" (D 415).

16. For an important political elaboration of Nietzsche's appeal to "aesthetic communities," see Salim Kemal, "Nietzsche's *Genealogy*: Of Beauty and Community," *Journal of the British Society for Phenomenology*, vol. 21, no. 3, October 1990, pp. 234–249.

17. This question perhaps illuminates the limitations of Georges Bataille's attempt to follow Nietzsche, to "push the possibilities of his teaching to the limit," in Georges Bataille, *On Nietzsche*, trans. Bruce Boone (New York: Paragon House, 1992), p. xxiv. Bataille characteristically locates Nietzsche's excesses in his *writing*—hence the importance for Bataille of his own writing—but the nature of these excesses themselves, independent of their representative inscriptions, eludes Bataille's grasp.

18. Nietzsche's depiction of the "music-practicing Socrates" trades on a reference to an early scene in Plato's *Phaedo* (60c–d). In this scene, however, Socrates quite clearly understands his attempt to versify several of Aesop's fables as a tribute to Apollo (61a–b), who is ultimately responsible for ordaining Socrates the wisest of men. That Socrates has the time and leisure to "practice music" is attributable, moreover, to the festival of the Delia, which is itself a tribute to Apollo (58a–c). Finally, Asclepius, the physician to whom the "music-practicing" Socrates attempts to make advance payment (118a), is the son of Apollo. A more appropriate candidate for a "music-practicing" Socrates would be the Socrates who wears the wreath of Dionysus at the conclusion of Plato's *Symposium*.

19. Walter Kaufmann apparently agrees, for he presents Nietzsche as scoring a definitive triumph over his *ressentiment*: "In *Ecce Homo* Nietzsche embodies . . . this triumph over *ressentiment*. Instead of bearing a grudge toward the world that treated him so cruelly, instead of succumbing to the rancor of sickness, he relates the story of his life and work in a spirit of gratitude—and goes out of his way to pay his respects to Paul Rée and Lou Salomé, with whom he had fallen out." *On the Genealogy of Morals/Ecce Homo*, trans. Walter Kaufmann (New York: Vintage Books, 1989), pp. 206–207.

20. Nietzsche actually defines resentment as a concoction of affects. He lists "anger, pathological vulnerability, impotent lust for revenge, thirst for revenge" as "the affects of *ressentiment*" (EH I:6).

21. This thesis is persuasively advanced in Stanley Rosen's provocative essay, "Nietzsche's Revolution," in *The Ancients and the Moderns* (New Haven: Yale University Press, 1989), pp. 191–198.

22. Robert Solomon inventories the potentially productive properties of resentment in his essay, "One Hundred Years of Resentment: Nietzsche's *Genealogy*

of Morals," in *Nietzsche, Genealogy, Morality: Essays on Nietzsche's "On the Genealogy of Morals,"* ed. Richard Schacht (Berkeley, CA: The University of California Press, 1994), pp. 95–126. See also Henry Staten, *Nietzsche's Voice* (Ithaca: Cornell University Press, 1990), ch. 2.

23. Nietzsche attributes his "cleverness," for example, to his economic hygiene: "I have never reflected on questions that were none—I have not squandered [*verschwendet*] myself" (EH II:1).

24. Hence the inadequacy of the influential distinction between "active" and "reactive" forces, as drawn by Gilles Deleuze in *Nietzsche and Philosophy,* trans. Hugh Tomlinson (New York: Columbia University Press, 1983), pp. 39–72. Nietzsche's guiding distinction here is not between action and reaction, but between genuine [*eigentliche*] reaction and imaginary [*imaginäre*] reaction (GM I:10). What Deleuze calls "active forces" do not stand in opposition to "reactive forces" but actually emerge from them, as unanticipated permutations and by-products.

25. See Staten, p. 38.

26. By 1887, Nietzsche was aware of, and took great delight in, his growing influence within the political microsphere. In a letter to Overbeck on 24 March 1887, Nietzsche reports "a comic fact, of which I am becoming ever more conscious. I have gradually come to exert an 'influence,' very subterranean, as it understands itself. I enjoy an amazing and almost mysterious reputation among all radical parties (Socialists, Nihilists, anti-Semites, Orthodox Christians, Wagnerites). The extreme purity of the atmosphere in which I have placed myself is enticing [*verführt*]." *Sämtliche Briefe*, vol. 8, #820, p. 48.

6   Comedians of the Ascetic Ideal

1. In all fairness, we should note that Nietzsche's text is somewhat ambiguous: he could mean that *Zarathustra* somehow presents the "counterideal," perhaps in spite of Zarathustra himself. For a fruitful exploration of this possibility, see Laurence Lampert, *Nietzsche's Teaching* (New Haven: Yale University Press, 1986), pp. 255–263.

2. Maudemarie Clark arrives at this conclusion through a process of elimination: "I can find only two serious candidates for the counterideal Zarathustra teaches: the *Übermensch* and the ideal of affirming eternal recurrence . . . I argue that the *Übermensch* ideal is still too closely tied to the ascetic ideal, and that, in the course of Z, affirming eternal recurrence replaces it as the true alternative to the ascetic ideal." *Nietzsche on Truth and Philosophy* (New York: Cambridge University Press, 1990), p. 253. Of course, Clark's deduction is valid only in the event that 1) she has successfully isolated the only two "serious candidates for the counterideal Zarathustra teaches"; and 2) Zarathustra/ *Zarathustra* actually promulgates to "us" the advertised counterideal.

3. Tracy Strong has long maintained that Nietzsche's preoccupation with a politics of "transfiguration" or "redemption" compromises the relevance for modern readers of his political thinking. Most recently, Strong has claimed

that "at the end of Nietzsche's life . . . [he] comes to despair of the possibility of ever accomplishing such a transfiguration" ("Nietzsche's Political
Aesthetics," in *Nietzsche's New Seas*, ed. Michael Allen Gillespie and Tracy
Strong (Chicago: University of Chicago Press, 1988), pp. 13–14). As I hope
to have shown in this study, by the end of Nietzsche's sane life, he had long
since acknowledged the nihilistic ramifications of his youthful longings for a
redemption of modernity. Strong thus chronicles the despair of a Nietzsche
whom Nietzsche himself had long since subjected to a withering regimen of
self-criticism.

4. A notable exception here is Alexander Nehamas, who associates Nietzsche's
    "comedy" with the complex rhetorical task of resisting (while not renewing)
    the destructive impulse of the ascetic ideal. *Nietzsche: Life as Literature*
    (Cambridge, MA: Harvard University Press, 1985), pp. 130–137.

5. Nietzsche's sole prior reference to these comedians hardly inspires our confi-
    dence in their redemptive powers. In the previous section, he wonders "how
    many *comedians* of the Christian-moral ideal would have to be exported
    from Europe today before its air would begin to smell fresh again" (GM
    III:26).

6. As Nehamas instructively points out, Nietzsche is uniquely suited to carry
    out the complex task involved in "harming" the ascetic ideal: "[To be such
    a comedian] involves the effort to reveal the inner contradictions and decep-
    tions of asceticism, to denounce it, and yet not produce a view that itself
    unwittingly repeats the same contradictions and deceptions, for to repeat
    these is to fail to arouse mistrust in the ascetic ideal; on the contrary, it is
    to offer a demonstration that it is inescapable" (pp. 133–34).

7. The experimental spirit of Nietzschean genealogy is conveyed by the essay
    competition Nietzsche proposes, in which scholars would explore the connec-
    tions between morality and etymology, physiology, psychology, and medicine
    (GM I:17, *Anmerkung*).

8. For a provocative, post-natural extension of Nietzsche's experimentalism, see
    Gilles Deleuze and Félix Guattari, *Anti-Oedipus: Capitalism and
    Schizophrenia*, trans. Robert Hurley, Mark Seem, and Helen R. Lane
    (Minneapolis: University of Minnesota Press, 1983); and *What is Philosophy?*,
    trans. Hugh Tomlinson and Graham Burchell (New York: Columbia
    University Press, 1994), especially their conclusion, "From Chaos to the
    Brain."

9. On the intersection of Nietzsche's self-experimentation and his evolving
    psychological model, see Parkes's epilogue, "A Dangerous Life," in
    Composing the Soul: Reaches of Nietzsche's Psychology (Chicago: University
    of Chicago Press, 1994), pp. 363–381.

7 Nietzsche's Political Legacy

1. A representative statement of this position is found in Mark Warren,
    Nietzsche and Political Thought (Cambridge, MA: MIT Press, 1988). Warren

writes, "The key to understanding Nietzsche's actual political positions is not in his philosophy of power as such, but rather in his misunderstanding of essential features of modern society. This caused him to misconstrue the limits of social and political organization, as well as to distort the causes of modern nihilism" (p. 237).

2. Martin Heidegger, *The Question Concerning Technology and Other Essays*, trans. and ed. William Lovitt (New York: Harper & Row, 1977), p. 95.

3. Ibid., p. 105.

4. For a trenchant critique of Nietzsche's alleged mismeasure of modernity, see Warren. Objecting to the "politics of domination" sheltered within Nietzsche's "neoaristocratic conservatism" (p. 211), Warren maintains that "Nietzsche did not give his own philosophy a plausible political identity" (p. 246). Notwithstanding his commendable "philosophy of agency" and "critique of Western culture," Warren claims, "[Nietzsche] failed to elaborate the broad range of political possibilities that are suggested by his philosophy" (p. 246). Hoping to salvage Nietzsche's philosophy from his retrograde political prejudices, Warren allows that "the politics of [Nietzsche's] philosophy [is] still to be determined" (p. 210). Attempting his own elaboration of the "broad range of possibility," Warren sketches a "political vision" featuring the "values" of "individuation, communal intersubjectivity, egalitarianism, and pluralism" (p. 247).

5. Bernard Yack thus concludes, for example, that "Nietzsche too must make a leap into the absurd, for the problem he seeks to resolve cannot be resolved without self-contradiction." *The Longing for Total Revolution* (Princeton: Princeton University Press, 1986), p. 355.

6. This point is forcefully made by Robert Eden: "So much intelligence has been invested in saving Nietzsche from the Nazi vulgarization that it is demoralizing to realize that Nietzsche intended a veritable jungle growth of such partial or mis-understandings to spring from the fertile soil of his writings." *Political Leadership and Nihilism* (Tampa: University Presses of Florida, 1983), p. 226.

7. Alasdair MacIntyre, *After Virtue* (Notre Dame, IN: Notre Dame University Press, 1984), p. 114.

8. Ibid., p. 259.

9. Ibid., p. 118.

10. Ibid., p. 117.

11. Ibid., p. 263.

12. Ibid.

13. Jürgen Habermas, *The Philosophical Discourse of Modernity: Twelve Lectures*, trans. Frederick G. Lawrence (Cambridge, MA: MIT Press, 1987), p. 96.

14. Ibid., p. 96.

15. Ibid., p. 87.

16. Ibid., p. 86.

17. Ibid., p. 87.

18. Rorty originally outlined this position in his 1983 essay, "Postmodernist Bourgeois Liberalism," in *Objectivity, Relativism, and Truth: Philosophical Papers, Volume 1* (Cambridge: Cambridge University Press, 1991), pp. 197–202. He later refines and expands this position, now known as "liberal ironism," in *Contingency, Irony and Solidarity* (New York: Cambridge University Press, 1989), esp. ch. 4.

19. Rorty, *Contingency*, p. 99.

20. Ibid., pp. 98–99.

21. Ibid., p. 97.

22. Ibid., p. 65.

23. In keeping with the tenets of his "liberal ironism," Rorty apparently would rather forgo the potential benefits of a self-perfection that exceeds the bounds of the private sphere than endure the inevitable harm it would cause. "Cruelty is the worst thing we do," he maintains (*Contingency*, p. xv), and any incursion into the public sphere of an individual's private pursuit of self-perfection is potentially cruel.

24. Allan Bloom, "Justice: John Rawls versus the Tradition of Political Philosophy," in *Giants and Dwarves: Essays 1960–1990* (New York: Simon & Schuster, 1990), p. 345.

25. For a representative sample of recent feminist appraisals of Nietzsche's thought, see *Nietzsche, Feminism and Political Theory*, ed. Paul Patton (London: Routledge, 1993). See especially the excellent essays by Rosalyn Diprose, "Nietzsche and the Pathos of Distance"; Keith Ansell-Pearson, "Nietzsche, Woman and Political Theory"; Elizabeth Grosz, "Nietzsche and the Stomach for Knowledge"; and Frances Oppel, "'Speaking of Immemorial Waters': Irigaray with Nietzsche."

26. See, for example, Kelly Oliver's exemplary study, *Womanizing Nietzsche: Philosophy's Relation to the "Feminine"* (New York: Routledge, 1994).

27. Donna J. Haraway, *Simians, Cyborgs and Women* (London: Free Association Books, 1991), p. 189.

28. Susan Bordo, "Feminism, Postmodernism, and Gender-Scepticism," in *Feminism/Postmodernism*, ed. Linda Nicholson (New York: Routledge, 1990), pp. 133–156.

29. Sandra Harding, "Rethinking Standpoint Epistemology: What is 'Strong Objectivity'?," in *Feminist Epistemologies*, ed. Linda Alcoff and Elizabeth Potter (New York: Routledge, 1993), p. 72.

30. Haraway, p. 190.

31. Ibid., p. 196.

32. Ibid., p. 192.

33. Ibid., p. 191.

34. Ibid.

35. Ibid.

36. Bat-Ami Bar On, "Marginality and Epistemic Privilege," in *Feminist Epistemologies*, ed. L. Alcoff and E. Potter (New York: Routledge, 1993), pp. 83–100.

37. Ibid., p. 94.

38. bell hooks, "Choosing the Margin as a Space of Radical Openness," in *Yearning: Race, Gender, and Cultural Politics* (Boston, MA: South End Press, 1990), pp. 150–151.

39. Haraway, p. 173.

40. Haraway, ch. 8, "A Cyborg Manifesto."

41. Michel Foucault, *The Order of Things: An Archaeology of the Human Sciences* (New York: Random House/Vintage Books, 1973).

42. My interpretation of *The Order of Things* is greatly indebted to the compelling reading advanced by Charles Scott in *The Question of Ethics: Nietzsche, Foucault, Heidegger* (Bloomington: Indiana University Press, 1990), ch. 3, sections 3–4.

43. For a discerning survey of the productive ethical implications arising from the "death of Man," see Scott, pp. 79–93.

44. In *Discipline and Punish: The Birth of the Prison*, trans. Alan Sheridan (New York: Random House/Vintage Books, 1979), Foucault documents the role of the prison in (unwittingly) producing particular types of subjects and in policing the flows of knowledge and power. See especially Foucault's discussion of torture, pp. 32–69.

45. My reckoning of the "periodization" of Foucault's scholarly activity draws upon Alan Schrift's excellent discussion in *Nietzsche's French Legacy: A Genealogy of Modernity* (New York: Routledge, 1995), pp. 34–58.

46. Michel Foucault, *The History of Sexuality*, vol. 1: *An Introduction*, trans. Robert Hurley (New York: Random House/Vintage Books, 1990), pt. 5: "Right of Death and Power Over Life."

47. Michel Foucault, *The History of Sexuality*, vol. 3: *The Care of the Self*, trans. Robert Hurley (New York: Random House/Vintage Books, 1988).

48. For a sympathetic reconstruction of Foucault's "transgressive middle course in relation to power and resistance," see Jon Simons, *Foucault & the Political* (London: Routledge, 1994), ch. 7.

49. Michel Foucault, "Politics, Polemics, and Problematizations: an Interview," in *The Foucault Reader*, ed. Paul Rabinow (New York: Pantheon Books, 1984), pp. 383–386.

50. For a provocative defense of the "democratic sensibility" that emerges from a consideration of Nietzsche through the lens of his Foucauldian legacy, see William Connolly, "Beyond Good and Evil: The Ethical Sensibility of Michel Foucault," *Political Theory*, vol. 21, no. 3, pp. 365–89.

Index

agape 82–3
agon 57, 69–70
Ahern, D. 148
amor fati 7, 72
Ansell-Pearson, K. 122, 148, 150
Apollo 95, 101
Arendt, H. 122
Aristophanes 11
Aristotle 57, 124–5
art 84–7
ascetic ideal: and art 87; and ascetic
 naturalism 109–11; and bad
 conscience 16, 102–04; as closed
 system 104-05; comedians of
 105–07; as *faute de mieux* 106–07;
 and knowledge 111–13; and self-
 experimentation 116–18

bad conscience 15–16, 18, 73,
 101–03, 107–09
Bar On, B. 136
Bataille, G. 153
beauty 85–7
Berkowitz, P. 122
Berlin, I. 55
Bizet 9
Blondel, Eric 151
Bloom, A. 130, 152
Bordo, S. 133
Borgia, C. 22–3, 25

Caesar 2, 9, 23, 39, 75, 114
Cavell, S. 52–5, 129, 144, 149
Clark, M. 154
Connolly, W. 145, 159
consciousness 14–15, 73

Danto, A. 144
Deleuze, G. 154–5
democracy 1, 38–9, 41, 53–4, 123,
 128
Detwiler, B. 122, 144, 152
Dionysus 17, 72, 74, 88, 94–8, 101,
 122, 126

Eden, R. 156
education: and aesthetics 50–2; of the
 body 113–18; and danger 89–90;
 institutions of 44–5
egoism 56–60
Emerson, R.W. 25, 52–6, 63–4, 78
enlightenment 125–8
Epicurus 2
Eros 40, 65, 82–3, 86–93
eternal recurrence 103–04
ethical life 10–11, 23–5, 30, 33–4,
 47, 63

feminism: epistemology 131–4; and
 Nietzsche 130–3
Feuerbach 18
Foucault, M.: archaeology 138–40;
 and Nietzsche 138–42; politics of
 resistance 141–2; subjectivation
 140–1
Frederick II 23
Freud, S. 102

Gast, P. 32
Goethe, J.W. 9, 23, 85, 114
Golomb, J. 151
Grand Inquisitor 55, 147
guilt 16, 18–19

Habermas, J. 122, 125–8
Haraway, D. 133–8
Harding, S. 133
Hegel, G.W.F. 4, 54, 66–7
Heidegger, M. 121–2
Hitler, A. 120
Homer 2, 69, 77
hooks, b. 136
Hymn to Life 116

immoralism 4–5, 35

Jesus 10, 90

Kaufmann, W. 122, 151, 153
Kemal, S. 153

Lampert, L. 144, 151, 154
lawgiver 11–13; 17, 37, 74–5, 142
law of Life 66–7
liberalism: contemporary 123;
    Nietzsche's critique of 1–5
love: *see Eros*

Machiavelli 55
MacIntyre, A. 122–5, 127, 144–5
madman 13
madness 50, 91–2, 118
Magnus, B. 145
Manu 2, 34–9, 75
martyrdom 87–91
Marx, G. 33
McCarthy, C. 78
Michelangelo 9
Mill, J.S. 37–8, 55, 147
modernity: and decadence 1–7, 31,
    42–7, 75–6, 93, 106, 125, 137;
    late 25, 31, 39, 49–51, 61, 98,
    117, 122–3; Nietzsche's critique of
    43–7
morality: of breeding 34–9; Christian
    9, 18–20, 56, 67, 83–4, 107,
    100–10, 128, 142; Nietzsche's
    critique of 28–30; noble 29, 32, 39,
    58–9; pluralism 28–31, 33–4; of
    taming 19–20 35–7, 41; slave 29,
    45, 59, 135
Müller-Lauter, W. 145, 150

Napoleon 9, 19–20, 23, 39, 75,
    112–13
National Socialism 120, 122–3
nature 8, 13–16, 19, 34–6, 42, 83, 103
Nehamas, A. 146, 150, 155
neighbor 59
nihilism 1–4, 13, 16, 93, 137
noble lie 60
Nussbaum, M. 153

Oliver, K. 157
Ottman, H. 151
Owen, D. 145, 150
Owl of Minerva 4

Parkes, G. 146, 149–52, 155
pathos of distance 39–42, 44, 47, 49,
    76, 86, 93
perfectionism: and exemplary human
    beings 7–11; moral 52–6; political
    6–11
perspectivism 130–3
philosopher: of the future 17, 39, 98,
    100; as genius 81–4; as lawgiver
    61–5; as therapist 113–16
Pilate 23
Pindar 54
Pippin, R. 146
Plato 2, 11, 54, 58, 91, 94–9
play 112–13
politics: aristocracy 34–42, 80;
    founding question of 2–7, 12, 26;
    macrosphere 48–50; microsphere
    47–50; Nietzsche's contributions to
    1–3, 119–23
potlatch 59
Prometheus 9

Rawls, J. 28–9, 52–5, 123, 130
realism 9, 21–2, 35
Rée, P. 32
resentment: as expendable affect 89,
    95–8; and late modernity 51;
    Nietzsche's own 97–9
revaluation of all values 21
Rorty, R. 55, 128–30, 150
Rosen, S. 153
Rousseau, J.J. 69, 113

Salomé, L. 32
St. Paul 2, 90
Sartre, J.-P. 55
Schopenhauer, A. 8, 47, 55, 62, 64,
    80–1, 88, 130
self-overcoming: Nietzsche's own
    75–7, 94; as self-creation 70–1,
    85–6; as self-discovery 71–2; and
    self-experimentation 72–5, 99,
    113–14, 116; two senses of 65–70
Schacht, R. 145
Schrift, A. 158
Schutte, O. 122, 145
Scott, C. 158
shame 64–5
Silenus 7, 93
Simons, J. 158
slavery 36–8, 59
Socrates 2, 11, 33, 35, 47, 59–60, 69,
    75, 86, 90, 95, 99
solipsism 57–8
Solomon, R. 153–4
soul 58–9, 69, 76–7, 80–4, 89–90,
    111–12
Staten, H. 154
Stern, J.P. 145–6
Strauss, L. 152
Strong, T. 122, 143, 148, 151–2,
    154–5

Thiele, L.P. 148–9, 152
Thucydides 2, 9
tragedy 27, 44, 86, 95

Übermensch: as economic type 23–4,
    62; as ethical exemplar 23–6, 116;
    and higher humanity 20–1; and late
    modernity 26, 51–2, 94; and
    realism 21–3; as redemptive ideal
    120–2, 124

Vattimo, G. 122, 146
Versuch 78–81, 99, 117

Wagner, R. 32, 44, 50, 88
Warren, M. 122, 143, 155–6
will 16–17, 86–7, 117
will to nothingness 3–4, 6, 16–17, 20,
    90, 93, 111, 117, 142
Wittgenstein, L. 55, 114

Yack, B. 122, 148, 151, 156

Zarathustra 10, 17, 20–2, 25–6, 30,
    32, 46, 51, 56, 59, 76, 79, 81, 85,
    98, 103–4, 116, 137–8